Cone 5–6 Glazes

Second Edition

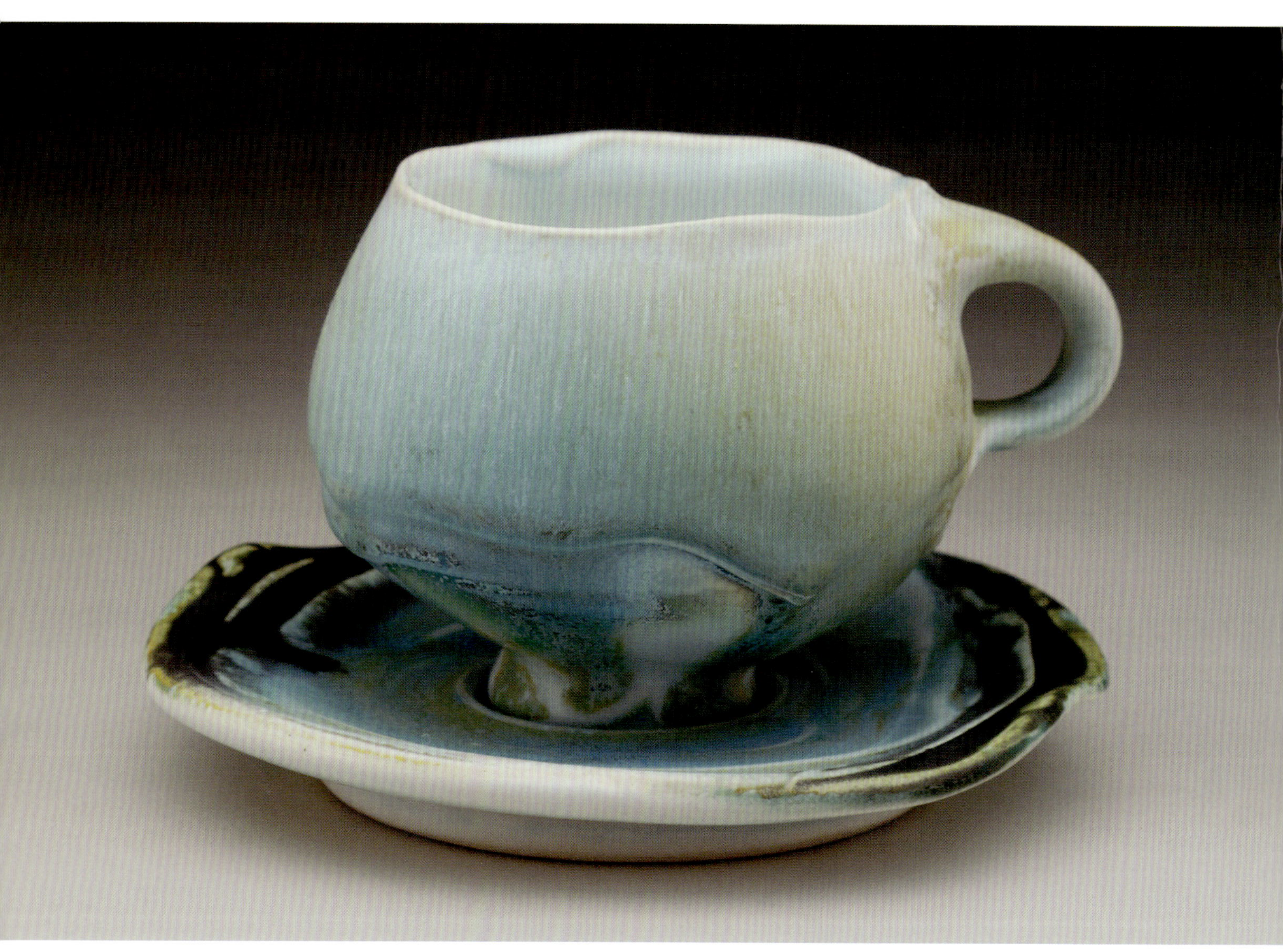

Ceramic
Arts
Handbook
Series

Cone 5–6 Glazes
Second Edition

Edited by Bill Jones
The American Ceramic Society
600 N. Cleveland Ave., Suite 210
Westerville, Ohio 43082
www.CeramicArtsDaily.org

The American Ceramic Society
600 N. Cleveland Ave., Suite 210
Westerville, OH 43082

ISBN: 978-1-57498-342-5 (Paperback)

ISBN: 978-1-57498-577-1 (PDF)

Publisher: Charles Spahr, Executive Director, The American Ceramic Society

Art Book Program Manager: Bill Jones

Editor: Bill Jones

eBook Manager: Steve Hecker

Graphic Production: Erin Pfeifer

Series Design: Melissa Bury

Cover Image: Detail of plate by Jayne Shatz

Frontispiece: Mug and saucer by Steven Hill

Table of Contents

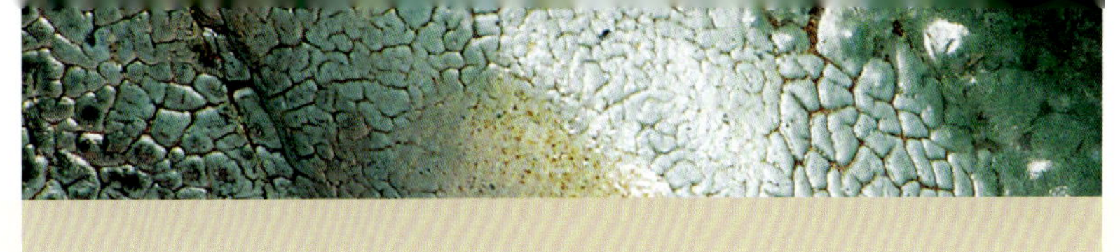

5 Recipes

Preface

For those involved in ceramic art, cone 5–6 is the most common firing range in use today. This has been driven by several factors—the increasing popularity of firing stoneware and porcelain, the desire of traditional high-fire potters to conserve energy at lower temperatures, and the potters working at low-fire looking for the durability that the mid-range offers over earthenware.

As the popularity of mid-range firing increased over the years, the number of potters testing glazes for their own work increased. Many potters who have gained knowledge freely given by others have in turn shared their results. On page 126, Anthony Bellesorte exemplifies this by stating "Because the following recipes work for me, I would like to share them. But I also know how difficult it is to duplicate glaze results. I've tried many glaze recipes that were highly recommended, but was unable to achieve satisfactory results because of differences in raw materials, kiln, water, whatever each potter introduces as an individual set of variables to any glaze equation. Still, these recipes may work as well for you as they do for me."

This book is comprised of materials previously published in *Ceramics Monthly* and *Pottery Making Illustrated* over the past 30 or so years; some have been reprinted in various books or online; and others have been passed around among hundreds of potters at craft centers and schools. Where previously published materials included recipes only as a part of a story or technique, just the recipes and pertinent information have been included.

For anyone who has ever mixed glazes from recipes can attest, results can be anything from surprise to disappointment due to all the variables. First of all, glaze materials are mined, not manufactured so the chemical makeup of materials change over time. For example, feldspars from one part of a mine can vary from another part, or some materials may disappear altogether when a mine closes. For the most part, all recipes remain as originally published, and all ingredients are listed in the Resources with notes concerning substitutions. Additionally, all recipes in this book require testing to allow for the variables introduced by not only materials, but also clay bodies, firing temperatures, cooling rates, mixing styles, even your water supply.

I would like to thank the many potters and ceramic artists who have shared their hard-earned glaze results with readers over the years. Your efforts will continue to be appreciated even by those who have not even begun their clay adventure yet.

Bill Jones

Safety

When mixing glazes, safety should be your main concern. Every supplier is required to keep Material Safety Data Sheets (MSDS) on hand for every material used in a glaze. These contain safe handling procedures and any toxicity warnings. Wearing a HEPA-rated and professionally fitted respirator, safety glasses, and dedicating clothing for the studio will lessen your risks to hazardous exposure. Store materials in plastic containers or approved bins out of reach of children. Heed all warnings for the proper handling of the materials.

1

The Basics
GETTING STARTED

by Jonathan Kaplan

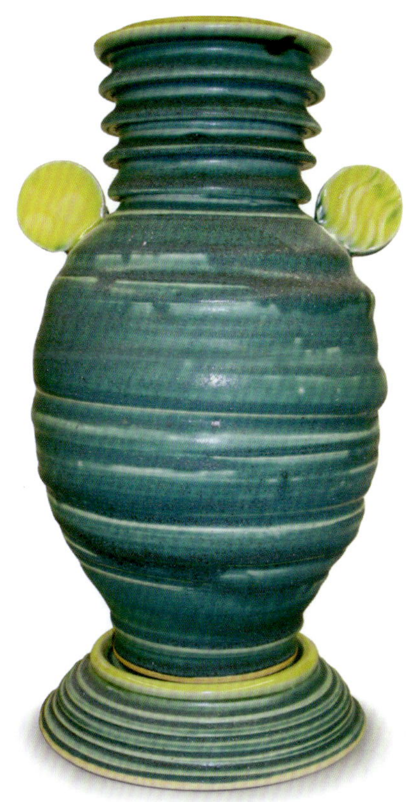

Vase with Circular Attributes and Stand, 15 inches in height, with Edgy Green glaze. This glaze contains barium, which helps in the formation of small suspended crystals giving it a satin matt finish.

Color and texture in cone 6 glazes are the result of three variables: First, selecting proper glazes; second, learning how to layer and combine different glazes by pouring, dipping and spraying; and third, using a controlled cooling cycle to further enhance the color and texture. This slow cooling not only creates a visual dialog in thick and thin areas of glaze application, but also helps with the crystallization of certain materials, which adds depth and interest to the glaze.

Glaze Selection

With so many cone 6 glazes, how do you know which glazes will work for you? It's impossible to look at a written glaze formula and know how it will look when it's fired and cooled. However, there are some things to look for that may provide some insight as to the surface texture. I like to use glazes that have a strong presence of calcium, provided by whiting and wollastonite in the formula. Dolomite, which is a combination in equal parts of both calcium and magnesium is also very helpful. These materials, when included in any glaze along with other ceramic materials, form small, suspended crystals in the glaze when cooled in a controlled manner.

Glaze Application

I spray or dip glazes over each other. My experience is that no single glaze can provide a visually interesting surface in an electric kiln, although there certainly may be exceptions. My layering technique allows the many differing glaze materials to combine and melt in unique ways providing a visually interesting surface with depth. All of this is caused by the interactions of multiple materials applied over each other. Applying glazes over textures in the clay allows the melted glaze to pool. A thicker concentration of glaze materials in these areas yields different areas of color.

When mixing and testing glazes for future use on your pottery, it is useful to try different methods of combining glazes. For example, if you mix up a few small test batches of different glazes, try dipping one glaze over the other on the top rim of your test tile. Then reverse the order. For instance, if you dip glaze A over glaze B, then do another tile with glaze B dipped over glaze A.

Firing

Most glazes have a range of several cones. I fire my cone 6 glazes to cone 7 using a programmable controller with the following heating and cooling cycle, which I have found provides a better melt and allows a good mingling of the many layers of glaze.

FIRING SCHEDULE	
1st segment	50°F/hour to 220°F
2nd segment	250°F/hour to 2167°F
3rd segment	150°F/hour to 1500°F

It's necessary to experiment and test your glazes to determine their range. Using kiln wash on the shelves or stilts under your ware is a necessity!

You can program a "hold" into the end of the second segment if you have a single zone kiln and wish to try to even out the firing from top to bottom. With the introduction of multiple zone controls on many of the new kilns, a soak at the end is not really necessary. If you don't have a computer-controlled kiln, use the infinite switches to "fire down" the kiln. With the addition of a pyrometer and a decent thermocouple, you can achieve a reasonable controlled cooling cycle.

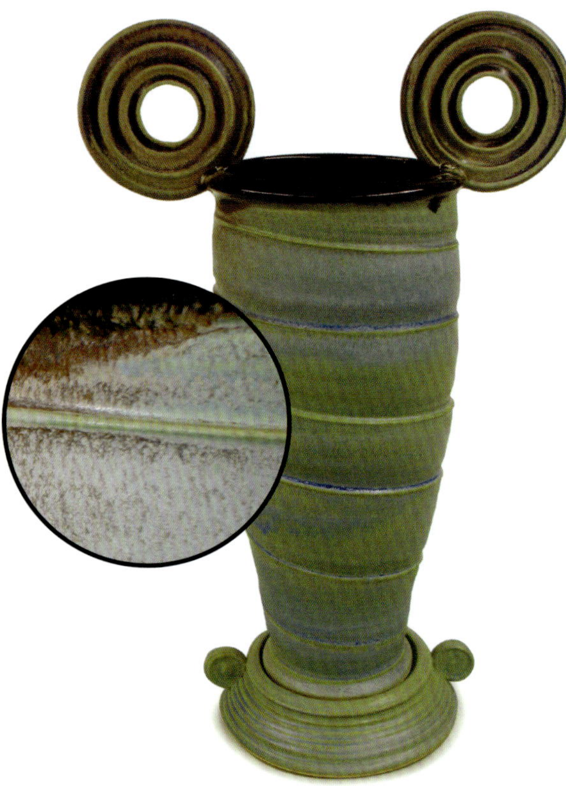

Disk Vase, 18 inches in height, with Blue/Green/Purple variation of VC Glaze with PV Black Liner Glaze sprayed over. The detail shows the cooling crystals that developed during a controlled slow cooling.

Record Keeping

Keep accurate records so you can repeat pleasing results. In an electric kiln this is easy, especially if it is equipped with a programmable controller. There is no substitute for experimenting. It takes time and persistence to achieve the surfaces that are pleasing to you. No one glaze or method will work. It is a combination of glazes and applications, followed by the proper firing with a controlled cooling cycle.

PV BASE
Cone 6

Gerstley Borate	30 %
Whiting	10
PV Clay	15
Custer Feldspar	35
Silica	10
	100 %

Black Liner Glaze

Add: Mason 6600	6 %

An excellent gloss base. Spray or dip over Blue/Green/Purple. This glaze is very receptive to commercial stains. Again, with encapsulated stains, an opacifier is not necessary. If a more opaque surface is desired, add between 6–10% opacifier such as zircopax.

VC GLAZE
Cone 6

Whiting	6.9 %
Gerstley Borate	11.6
Titanium Dioxide	6.9
Nepheline Syenite	46.8
Kaolin	13.9
Silica	13.9
	100.0 %

Blue/Green/Purple Variation

Add: Cobalt Oxide	1.1 %

An excellent base glaze over which to spray or dip other glazes.

EDGY GREEN
Cone 6

Barium Carbonate	15.6 %
Gerstley Borate	10.4
Wollastonite	15.6
Nepheline Syenite	39.7
Kaolin	10.4
Silica	8.3
	100.0 %
Add: Black Copper Oxide	3.1 %

The Basics

GLAZE TESTING

by Jonathan Kaplan

Testing glazes has both educational and practical advantages. A methodical and well-organized regimen can provide you with a great deal of very useful information. You can learn how glazes work alone and in combination with other glazes, engobes and other decorative processes. If a glaze shows potential for problems, you can make adjustments to it or choose to try another glaze. You can learn about the materials, their properties and how they function in a glaze. Here's a simple system that's easy, repeatable and understandable, requiring only a small investment of time and some very basic equipment.

Test Tiles

Test tiles are the heart of the system since a test glaze sits on the tile and provides information on its fired properties. Tiles can be thrown, extruded or made from slabs of your clay body. If you're testing glazes on different clay bodies, make sure you mark the tiles with a code for that particular body. Test tiles can show a host of additional information if they're prepared correctly.

Angle—bending a section or creating an angled tile provides information about the fluidity of a glaze.

Texture—a textured pattern shows how glazes break "thick and thin" over a surface.

Color—applying white and black engobes on green tile shows how a fired glaze breaks over the raised colored clay.

Hole—a hole in the tile provides a way to display it on a board or secure it to the glaze bucket with a twist tie, wire or string.

In about 2 hours you can easily produce a few hundred test tiles.

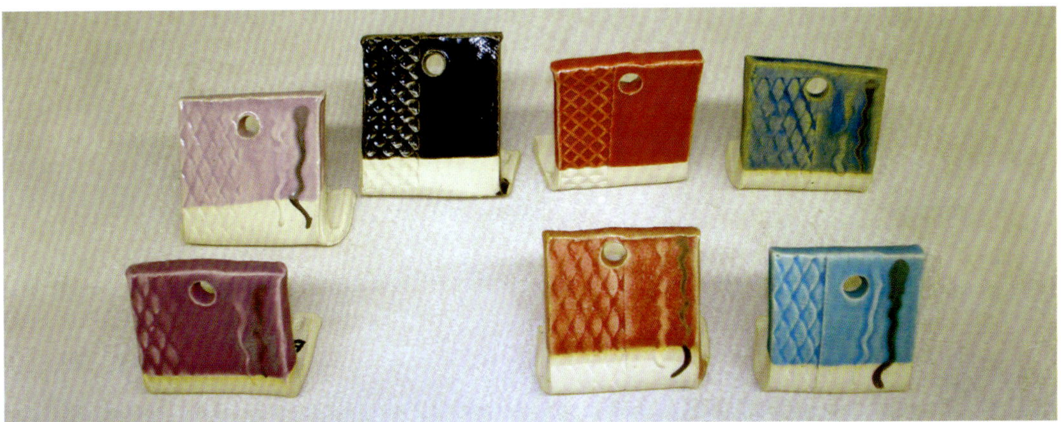

An organized system for testing glazes is simple to implement and can provide a valuable record you'll be able to access for years.

Record Keeping

Keep your identification system simple and you'll be able to refer to your notes years after a test. At the base of each tile, use black underglaze to write the date in MMDDYY format, for example, 021307 for February 13, 2007, then add the test number for that day. (Note: Don't write on the bottom of the tile as it can leave a ghost image from the underglaze on the kiln shelf.) Enter these numbers in a glaze notebook next to each test. There's no reason to include any other information on the test tile other than the date and test number as all the other information pertaining to the glaze is in your notebook.

You can also use computer glaze programs as a database for your glazes. There are many excellent applications for PCs and Macs, such as Insight, Hyperglaze, Matrix and Glaze Master (see "Resources"). If using a computer, be sure to always have a hard copy or electronic backup of your work. While I use glaze calculation software to calculate my batch sizes and help with correcting any problems, most entries in my notebook are by longhand.

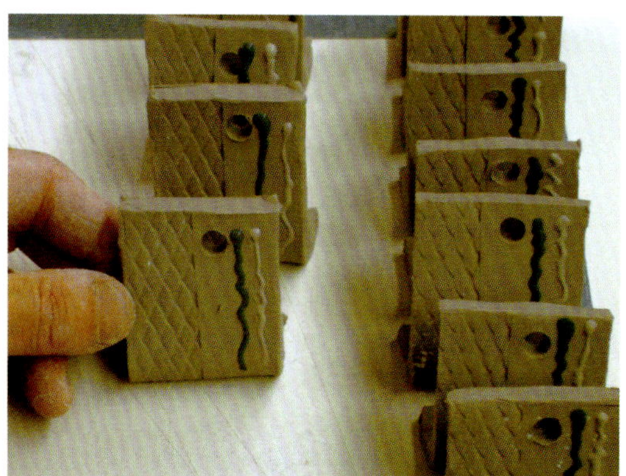

A self-supporting angled tile with texture, as well as black-and-white slip, provides information on several properties of a glaze.

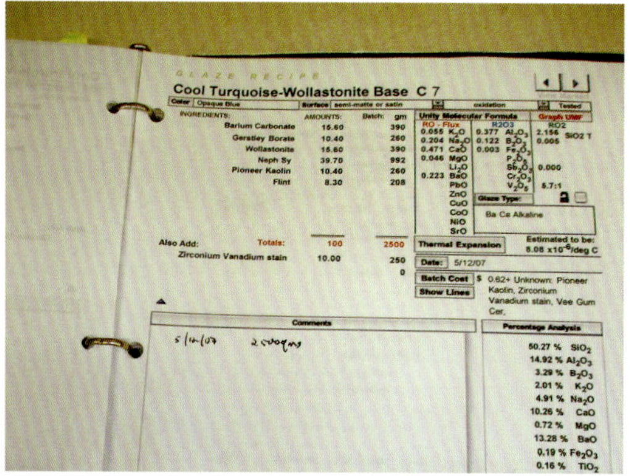

Keep all notes in a three-ring binder. If using a glaze software program, be sure to print out a hard copy for a permanent record.

Testing Method

- *Step 1. Select two glazes.* For simple glaze testing, work with only two glazes at one time. This allows you to develop a fairly organized way of working with glazes directed toward what you need to accomplish without getting so overloaded with information that you lose track.
- *Step 2. Convert the recipes.* The batch recipe should add up to 100. If it doesn't, divide the total of the original glaze into the amount of each ingredient. Do not include any colorants or additives in your calculations, just the basic recipe.
- *Step 3. Calculate the batch.* When testing, mix 2000 grams of dry materials to make a gallon of glaze. This is done by simply multiplying each number in the batch formula by 20.
- *Step 4. Weigh the ingredients.* Use a gram scale to measure out the ingredients for the batch glaze. After weighing each ingredient, double check weight on the scale, then place it in a large resealable storage bag. As you add each ingredient, check it off the list in the notebook. Since this is base glaze, do not add any colorants or additives.
- *Step 5. Dry mix the glaze.* Seal the bag and mix the ingredients by dumping the materials back and forth to ensure good dispersion. Label the bag with a permanent marker with the name of the glaze, date and cone number.
- *Step 6. Select test materials.* I've found that if I write down all the tests I wish to do prior to any mixing, the testing sequence goes much faster and is better organized. Select metallic colorants (for example, iron oxide, cobalt oxide, copper carbonate) or any pigments (commercial stains) to test. Many books have lists of coloring oxides percentages sorted by temperature and atmosphere that you can use as a reference point.

- *Step 7. Mix a test.* You'll need 100 grams of dry mix for a test which means you'll get 20 tests from a batch. When mixed with 100–125ml of water (3.4–4.2 oz.), a 100 gram test batch yields approximately 1 cup of liquid glaze. Weigh out 100 grams of dry mix, then add the additional test material to it. By carefully adding the required amount of coloring material, you can be precise with any addition.
- *Step 8. Blending.* Use an old kitchen drink mixer or blender to mix test batches. (Caution: These mixers must no longer be used for food.) Allow the materials to slake for a few minutes, then blend for a few seconds.
- *Step 9. Sieve the glaze.* Taking a small 100 mesh test sieve and a small clear plastic cup, pour the mixed material through the sieve. Use a bent toothbrush to help the wet material through the sieve. Mark the cup with the date and test number. Tip: You can bend the handle of an old toothbrush by holding it over a heat gun or hair dryer until it's pliable.
- *Step 10. Glaze a tile.* Take a test tile and wipe the surface with a damp sponge to remove any dust. Dip the tile into the glaze and hold it there while slowly counting to 10. The "10 count" allows a sufficient quantity of wet glaze to adhere to the surface. Remove the tile slowly from the cup, allow it to dry then label it with the date and test number. Save the test glaze for a few days in case you need to retest or adjust the mix.

Tip: You can bend the handle of an old toothbrush by holding it over a heat gun or hair dryer until it's pliable.

Two Times Better

If you test two base glazes at one time, you can easily add coloring oxides or stains to each base without much extra effort. In addition, you can now put one glaze over another to see how they interact with each other. First, create a series of tiles with glaze #1 over glaze #2, then a set with glaze #2 over glaze #1. You only need to dip a small section of the top of each tile to provide enough glaze to interact with what is below it and not run off the tile.

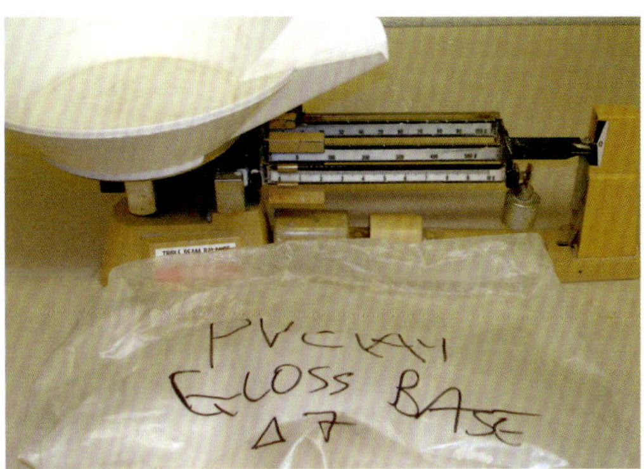

Weigh out materials for a test base glaze into a large resealable plastic bag. Label the bag.

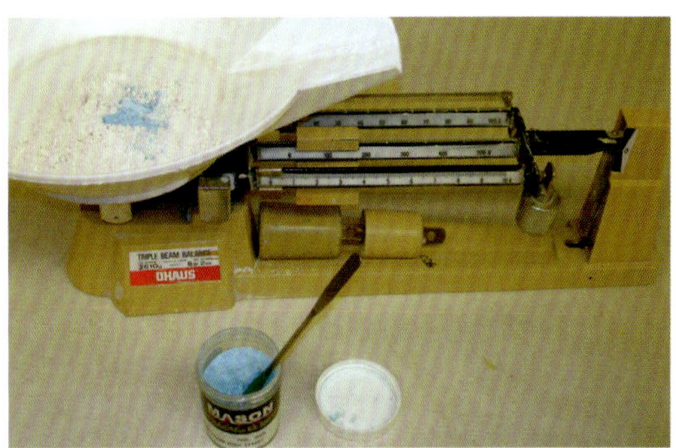

After measuring out a 100 gram test batch, carefully add colorants.

GRANNY'S SHORTS

Cone 4–7

Whiting	14
Gerstley Borate	42
Custer Feldspar	49
Plastic Vitrox Clay (PV Clay)	21
Silica	14
	140

Step 1: Divide each amount by 140 to convert to a 100 batch

Whiting	14/140	= 10
Gerstley Borate	42/140	= 30
Custer Feldspar	49/140	= 35
PV Clay	21/140	= 15
Silica	14/140	= 10
		100

Step 2: For a 2000 gram batch, multiply each line item by 20.

Whiting	10×20	= 200
Gerstley Borate	30×20	= 600
Custer Feldspar	35×20	= 700
PV Clay	15×20	= 300
Silica	10×20	= 200
		2000

The Basics

VOLUMETRIC GLAZES

by Sumi von Dassow

People new to glazing may be unsure whether they really want to mix up their own glazes, but they would like to experiment. Since the cost of an accurate gram scale can be an obstacle, an economical way to get started is with a volumetric recipe. Such a recipe requires the ingredients to be measured in cups (or teaspoons, tablespoons or buckets). While less exact than weighing ingredients to the tenth of a gram, this type of recipe can yield fine results and lends itself to experimentation.

A good place to start might be with the very basic recipe of 2 parts colemanite to 1 part Minspar 200 feldspar to 1 part silica. This becomes a clear glaze at cone 5–6, but because of the high level of boron in the colemanite, it's rather milky. It's easy to add various coloring oxides or opacifiers in teaspoons and tablespoons to achieve a wide range of colors from this simple recipe.

Other experiments might be to substitute various feldspars for the Kona F-4, or to try simple additions of other common glaze ingredients. Keeping a supply of test tiles handy—or even pieces of broken bisque-ware—means that any time you get the urge to mix up a quick experimental glaze, you'll have something to try it on.

Learning about glazes this way undoubtedly produces some strange results, as well as some successful surprises. As long as you keep good records,

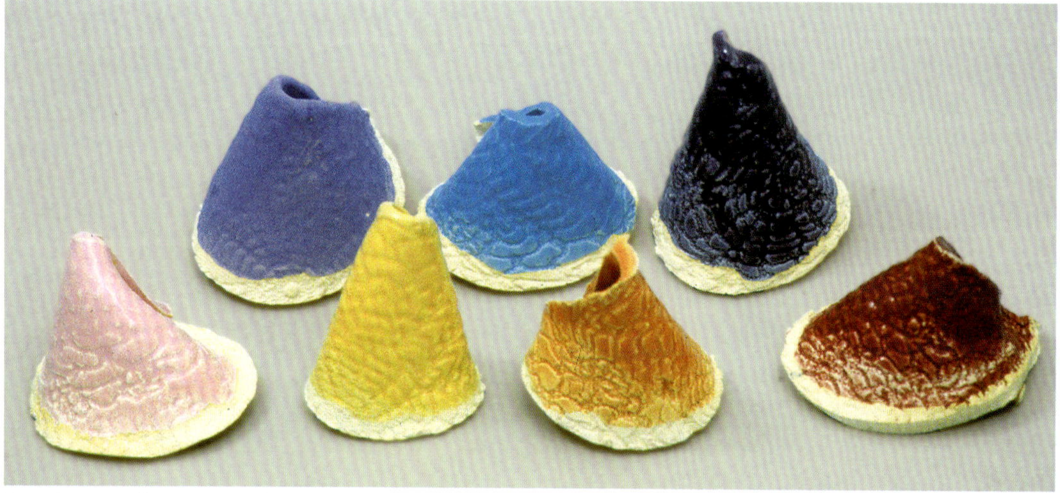

Test glazes, each consisting of 8 parts Sumi's Volumetric Clear to 1 part Mason stain. Back row, left to right: stain 6319 (Lavender), 6364 (Turquoise) and 6387 (Mulberry). Front row, left to right: stain 6000 (Shell Pink), 6407 (Marigold), 6121 (Saturn Orange) and 6006 (Deep Crimson). Tests are on cones made from slabs rolled out on lace to show how the glaze looks on a textured surface.

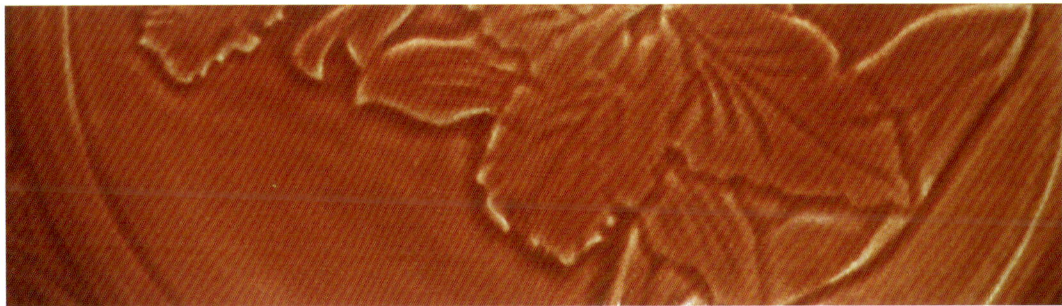

Detail of carved orchid plate with Sumi's Volumetric Clear Glaze mixed with commercial stain.

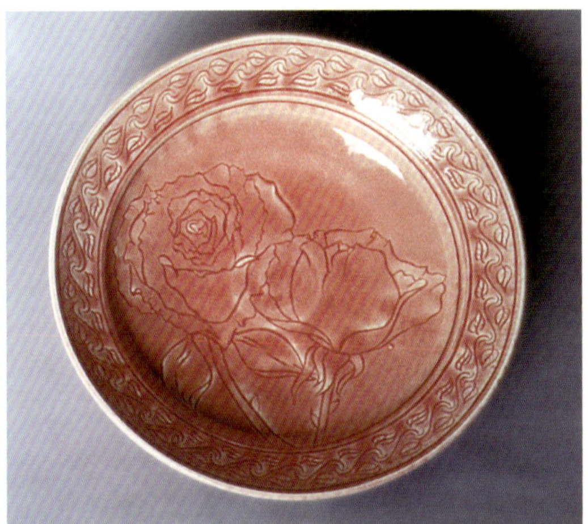

Plate glazed with Sumi's Volumetric Clear Glaze with commercial stain, fired to cone 6 oxidation.

SUMI'S VOLUMETRIC CLEAR GLAZE
Cone 6

Colemanite	3 parts
Magnesium Carbonate	2
Whiting	1
Minspar 200 Feldspar	5
Silica	3
	14 parts

Add stain in amounts between 1 and 2 parts. The pink and red stains work nicely in a ratio of 8 parts base mix to 1 part stain. To test several colors, mix up a batch using large units such as cups. Mix the dry ingredients together thoroughly by shaking them in a large sealable bag or in a bucket with a tight lid; allow to settle before opening. Use 2 tablespoons of stain to each standard (8-ounce) cup of glaze mix.

you'll gradually add to your store of knowledge, and develop familiarity with the many glaze materials in a fun and nonstressful way.

While such experimentation isn't likely to satisfy any potter forever, it offers an easy way to play with mixing and using glazes at home without requiring a large investment in equipment and materials or a great deal of space. Eventually, a gram scale will probably find its way into your studio, and you'll be on your way to having a collection of 5-gallon buckets and filling the cupboards with raw materials.

Mixing a Glaze

A glaze screen, preferably about 80 mesh, is an essential piece of equipment for straining wet glaze before use. It's helpful to screen the glaze through a 40-mesh screen first to eliminate large lumps. You can purchase screens from pottery supply stores. You can also make one from window screen, though you won't be able to get a fine mesh.

The easiest way to work the glaze through the screen is with your fingers, wearing rubber gloves. It's also very helpful to dry-mix the ingredients, then wait at least a day after adding the water before stirring or screening the mixture.

Volumetric Recipe

The nice thing about this glaze recipe is that not only is it easy to mix, but with stains you can mix up several different colors of glaze, using only five basic ingredients.

The stains can also be mixed into the clay body or into engobes and painted onto the pot before bisque firing. This glaze can then be applied as a clear base. It can also be applied to a pot and decorated with stains mixed with a little glaze.

The Basics

FLOATING STRAW HYDROMETER

by Roger Graham

If you mix your own glazes, you will already have discovered that it is a mixture of science and magic. Probably you make use of an accurate scale for weighing out ingredients. Maybe you consult a glaze calculation program, and work out expansion coefficients. That's science (with a small s). But when it comes to actually mixing the glaze, how much water do you add? Does your recipe say, "Mix to the consistency of thin cream?" Or do you just dip your hand in and see how thick a coating clings to your fingers? That's Magic (with a capital M). One way to bring glaze consistency assessment back to the realm of science is to use a hydrometer, which measures the specific gravity of a fluid. You can buy one, but let me share with you the design for a version you can make for the price of a milkshake.

Making the Hydrometer

The idea is to fix the little weight (1) inside one end of the straw, and seal it in with something waterproof. Then you can float the straw upright in the glaze, and the numbers on the straw will show the specific gravity of the fluid. Floating in pure water, the straw should sink to the mark 1.0, meaning that 1 milliliter of the liquid by volume would be 1 gram by weight. If the straw sinks to the mark 1.4 in your glaze, that means 1 milliliter of glaze weighs 1.4 grams, and so on.

If you don't have scales suitable for measuring in grams, you can just do it by trial and error. A 20 mm length of ¼-inch steel rod is a good

MATERIALS LIST

- A McDonald's drinking straw (these are wider than others)
- A dab of silicone sealant, or hot glue
- A 4-gram scrap of lead or steel rod (or a nail or a bolt—but about 4 grams)
- A waterproof felt-tip pen to write marks on the straw

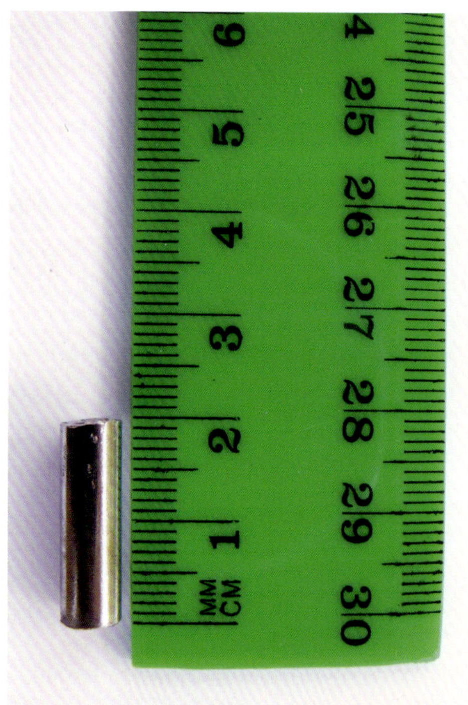

1

This is one possibility for the 4-gram weight, made from a 20-mm length of 6-mm steel rod. A nail or bolt, cut to size will also work.

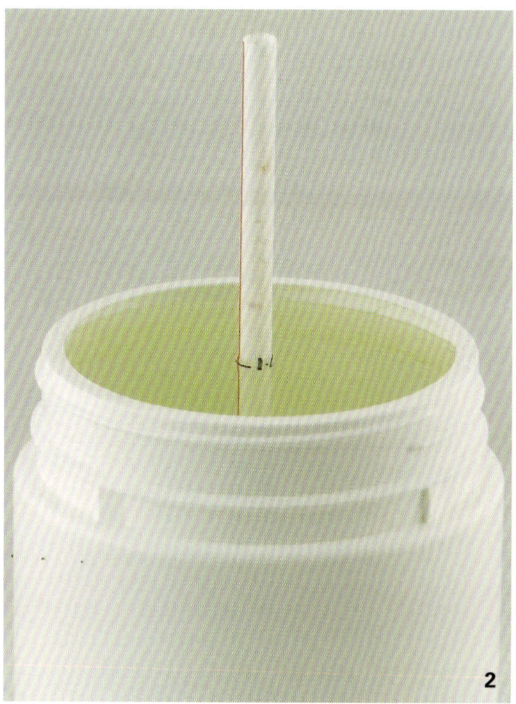

Float the hydrometer upright in water and use an indelible pen to mark the water level on the straw at 1.0.

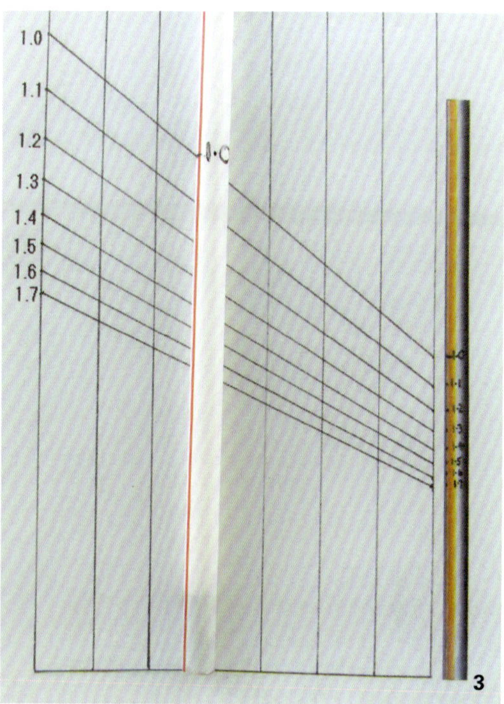

Now lay the straw against the chart so the bottom of the straw is lined up with the bottom chart line, and add the other calibration marks.

starting point. Just trim it down to about 4 grams using a hacksaw or grinder. A scrap of sheet lead just over a millimeter thick, and about 15 x 20 mm in size, is about right, if that's what you've got. Roll it up into a little cylinder and secure it into the end of the straw with the sealant.

Whatever little object you use, it must go completely into the straw (no bits sticking out) and the end of the straw should be closed completely by the sealant. Leave the top of the straw open if you wish, but don't get liquid inside the straw when in use.

Float the newly made hydrometer straw in water. It should sink a bit over half way, and float upright. Make a mark at the water level (2). Now dry the straw and line it up with the calibration chart (available at http://bit.ly/HydroChart) so the bottom end of the straw is on the bottom line, and the mark you've made on the straw is against the chart line marked 1.0 (3). The sloping cross-lines on the chart show where to mark the other numbers, 1.1, 1.2 , 1.3, 1.4, 1.5, 1.6, 1.7 (4).

A value of 1.3 to 1.5 is typical for most pottery glazes (5). The exact value probably matters less than being able to get it the same next time, or every time.

If you prefer not to use the calibration chart, it's easy math to calculate where to put the calibration marks. Just float the newly made straw in water, and mark the water level as 1.0

Now measure the length from the bottom of the straw to the water-level mark, in millimeters. Call that length x. With a calculator, work out a value for (x / 1.1). That tells you the measurement in millimeters where you should add the calibration mark 1.1. Calculate a value for (x / 1.2), and mark the straw 1.2, then do it again for (x/1.3) and so on.

Using the Hydrometer

I know that some potters cling to the view that hydrometers just don't work for measuring glazes, and cannot be persuaded otherwise.

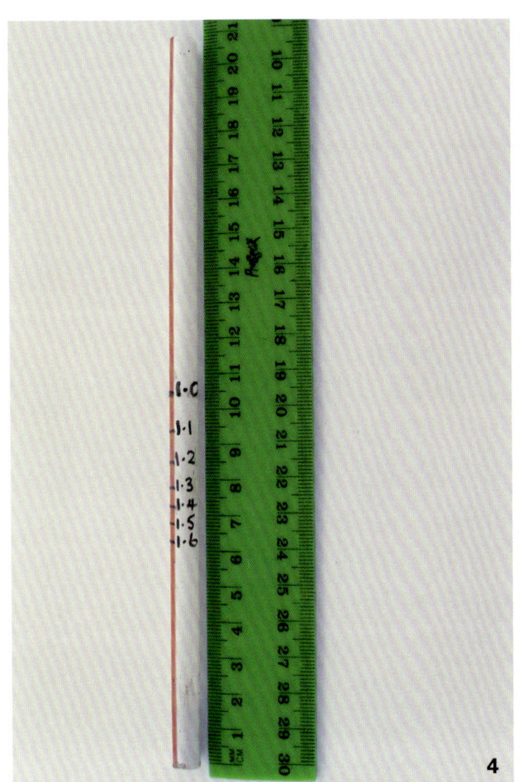

The finished hydrometer, with calibration marks in place. You can just barely see the 4-gram weight inside the bottom of the straw.

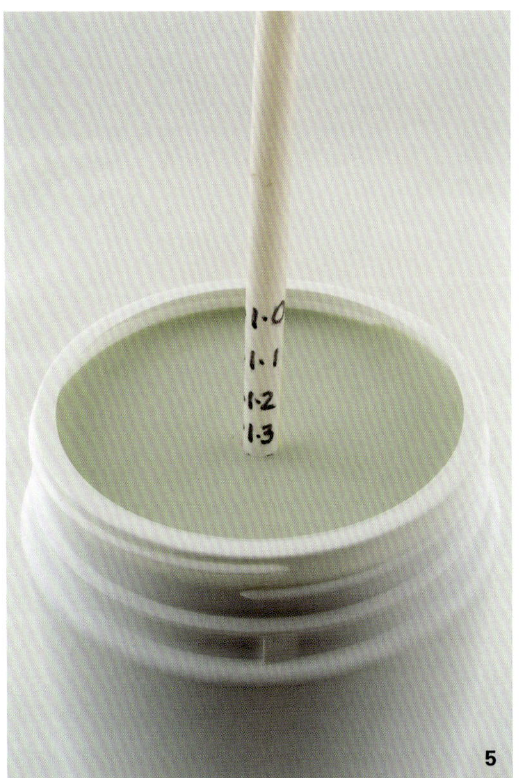

Now float the hydrometer in a well-stirred glaze. Read the specific gravity directly from the straw's scale.

The main objection raised seems to be that, if the liquid being measured is viscous, this will somehow prevent the hydrometer from sinking to the correct level. True perhaps for thick creamy casting slip. But for normal glazes, just whack the side of the container to agitate the fluid a bit, and the hydrometer sinks fine. Try it and see.

Another objection maintains that a hydrometer will only work if the liquid is a true solution, but not if it is a suspension of solid particles like a glaze; however a glaze suspension is a fluid and therefore principles of buoyancy still apply. (See Archimedes principle.)

To calm concerns, I spent time taking measurements on a selection of glazes used in our workshop. The specific gravity of each glaze was measured by the traditional, relative-density bottle method, involving weighing a narrow-necked container, then re-weighing it when filled with water, and again when filled with glaze. Having done that, the specific gravity was measured again using the floating straw hydrometer. The results were the same or similar in every case, with a maximum difference of less than 2%.

Note that we are referring to *specific gravity*, and not *density*. The term density requires that you then state the unit involved—kilograms per cubic meter, or grams per cubic centimeter, or pounds per cubic foot. If you want to express the density relative to that of water, the term *relative density* is okay. But our purposes, let's agree to stick with specific gravity.

I expect that some potters will utter a cry of disbelief and will claim to know better. And I can only repeat, don't just argue about it, take some measurements, try it and see.

CRAZING

by Deanna Ranlett

Crazing is a glaze defect where a network of cracks appear in a fired glaze surface. It raises issues of discoloration and the possibility for increased bacterial growth—something you don't want in dinnerware you use regularly. Perhaps you have a favorite teacup that has crazed and you've noticed a change in glaze color over the years as a brown residue works its way through the crazed lines into the clay body. Even commercially made dishes can grow mold when shut in a dark cabinet after a spin through the dishwasher without a heated cycle.

WATER BLUE—ORIGINAL RECIPE

Cone 6

Gerstley Borate	6 %
Ferro Frit 3110	77
EPK Kaolin	7
Silica	10
	100 %
Add: Copper Carbonate	2 %
Bentonite	3 %

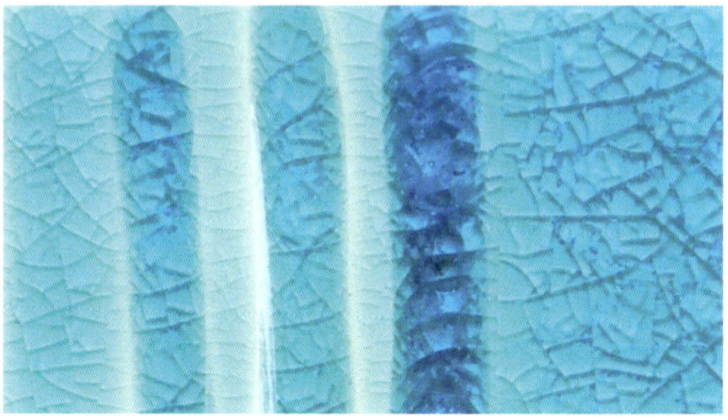

Original Water Blue that creates small, delicate crazing throughout glaze.

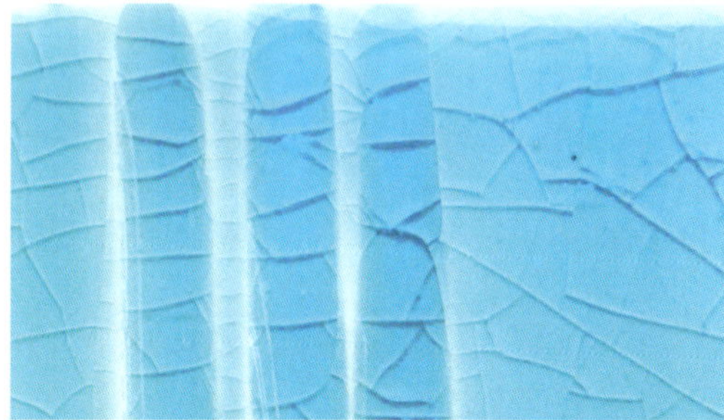

Water Blue with 3% Zircopax added and 10% less Ferro frit 3110. Results: Larger, more spaced out crazing.

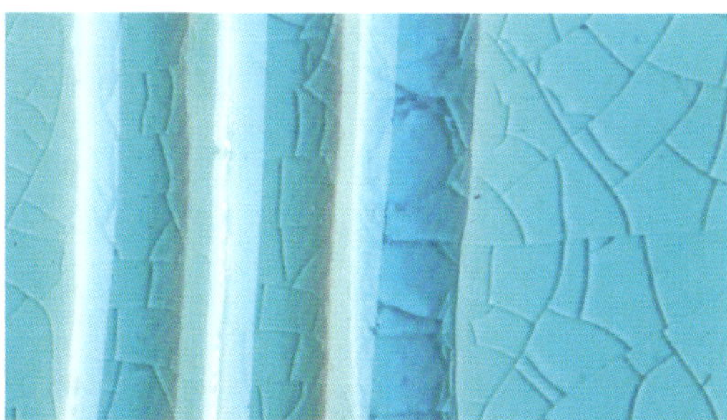

Water Blue with 5% silica added and 5% less Ferro frit 3110. Results: Larger, more spaced out crazing.

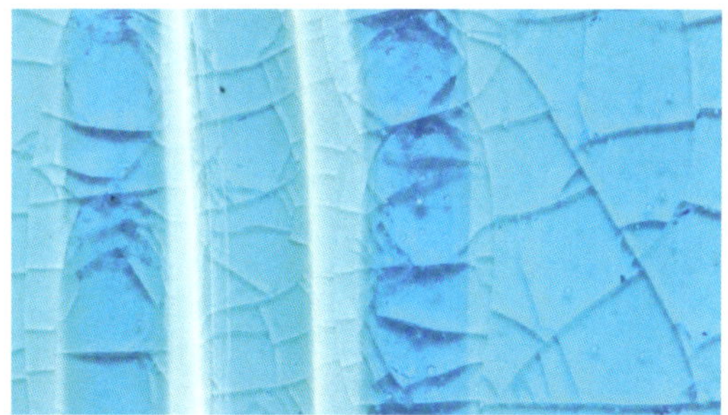

Water Blue with 5% Zircopax and 5% silica added. Results: Largest pattern of crazing.

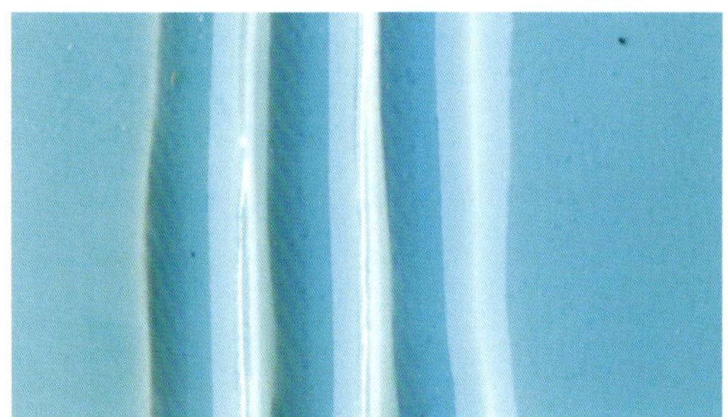

Results: No crazing. Slightly less transparent due to the addition of the Zircopax.

WATER BLUE REVISION 1
Cone 6

Ingredient	%
Gerstley Borate	10 %
Ferro Frit 3110	55
EPK Kaolin	15
Silica	15
Zircopax	5
	100 %
Add: Copper Carbonate	2 %
Bentonite	3 %

Results: No crazing. The added EPK kaolin shifts the glaze to a more greenish color.

WATER BLUE REVISION 2
Cone 6

Ingredient	%
Gerstley Borate	6 %
Ferro Frit 3110	59
EPK kaolin	22
Silica	13
	100 %
Add: Copper Carbonate	2 %
Bentonite	3 %

Glaze crazing also impacts the fired strength of finished ware. I have several customers making beer growlers and the pressure of bottling beer necessitates a solid liner glaze so the vessel doesn't explode. You may not be bottling beer, but the strength and longevity of your work is something to care about. Additionally, if you want to produce ware for the restaurant industry, food inspectors will check food storage and serving ware for this type of defect because crazed glazes can hold bacteria.

Cause and Effect

There are several reasons why glazes craze and several approaches to fix it. Crazing can be aggravated by application and firing—making even a good glaze craze. If you have a glaze that crazes, try testing that involves varying your application from thinner to thicker and compare the results. This will tell you if the glaze is sensitive to thickness. I use a great clear glaze from college but when it's applied too thick, it crazes and when applied thinly, it doesn't.

Clay bodies with high absorption rates can also contribute to crazing. Firing a cone 10 clay at cone 6 can aggravate crazing because the fired ware is still porous and can absorb water and physically swell and expand, causing the glaze to craze. Beyond just firing temperature (to avoid crazing), the coefficient of expansion

(COE) must match between the glaze and clay. The most common kind of crazing involves the COE of the glaze being higher than the COE of the clay body.

Firing a near empty kiln or opening the kiln too early can also aggravate crazing. We've all taken work out of the kiln that appears fine only later to find it crazed, or worse yet, to have a customer or friend tell us something is wrong after we've sent the piece on its way.

Glaze Troubleshooting

So, if you've standardized your firings and application methods and you've checked your clay's firing range, now what? I recommend you keep your clay body constant and start testing glazes. Using glaze calculation software can be very helpful to keep track of results and make suggestions because some changes are very complex, especially in the case of frits and feldspars. There are many great software programs that can help you learn a lot about materials and how to make successful substitutions like Glaze Insight, HyperGlaze, GlazeMaster, etc. But, if you just want to mix up a few tests, here's where to start:

- *Increase the silica.* Start with 3% and increase incrementally after that. Estimating dry weights can be tricky once a glaze is already mixed, so make sure you measure carefully when testing! The addition of the silica lowers the COE of the glaze, bringing it closer to your clay body's COE. Commercial glazes can also be altered with extra silica, just remove a small amount of glaze from the container, add the silica, and take good notes.
- *Decrease the feldspar.* Sometimes you'll need to adjust the ratios of fluxes, alumina, or silica when you do this—this is where glaze software can be helpful!
- *Decrease the sodium or potassium.*
- *Increase the boron* (found in some frits, Gerstley borate, or other boron containing substitutes).
- *Increase the alumina or clay content,* which generally improves the glaze mixture in the bucket as well. Remember that adding more alumina may change the gloss level of your glaze.
- *Add small amounts of Zircopax.* This may cause your glaze to become more opaque, but a 5% or less addition shouldn't impact translucency in most transparent glazes that melt well. If you're starting with an opaque glaze, you can still add a little more Zircopax than you're already using.

My Tests and Results

I decided to test a cone 6 Water Blue glaze. Water Blue is a very popular studio glaze that has made the rounds on many online forums as well as in publications. It does, however, craze severely, but many use it anyway because of its beautiful color. For my tests, I wanted to keep the formula as close to the original as possible to preserve the intense turquoise color.

In my tests, I manipulated the recipe following the same steps as above—I found that even small additions of clay, silica, and Zircopax or a combination of these stabilized the glaze and reduced the crazing. All test tiles were fired to cone 6 in an electric kiln, cooled slowly inside the kiln, then left at room temperature for 48 hours prior to taking photos. Time and various conditions will tell if the glazes continue to craze.

The Basics

PINHOLING

by Dave Finkelnburg

A pinhole marring a fired glaze is possibly the most troublesome of all glaze faults, disrupting an otherwise smooth surface. Slow firing at peak temperature helps heal pinholes, but preventing them in the first place is the holy grail of a smooth glaze.

The root cause of any pinhole is a large glaze bubble. If no bubbles form in the glaze, no pinhole faults will blemish the glaze.

A pinhole starts as a bubble at the contact point between a glaze and the surface it's being fired on. During the firing, the bubble grows so large its diameter is greater than the thickness of the glaze and the bubble bursts at the surface of the glaze. At that point, either glaze flows into the crater left behind by the bursting bubble, or it doesn't. The latter case produces a pinhole.

The gases that form bubbles, leading to pinholes, have many potential sources. Decomposition of oxides in the body or glaze and gases trapped in pore spaces in both are obvious culprits. Because bubbles can come from many sources, most efforts to prevent pinholing focus on making glazes runny enough, and with low enough surface tension, so molten glaze fills the craters left by bursting glaze bubbles. To make runny, low-surface-tension glazes requires managing glaze composition.

Adjusting the proportion of clay in a glaze is the most common starting point. Alumina atoms raise glaze viscosity and thus also raise the surface tension. Adding clay, an alumina silicate mineral, will make a molten glaze "thicker," or more viscous. Reducing clay content thus makes the glaze runnier or less viscous.

An increase in the proportion of the flux element magnesium also raises glaze surface tension. In high quantities, magnesium makes a glaze with an excessively high surface tension (for example, crawl glazes). Flux, colorant, and glass-former atoms all influence glaze viscosity and surface tension to some degree. Given the virtually infinite number of possible combinations of these elements in a glaze, testing is necessary to balance glaze fluidity and surface tension for a given application.

In general, adding any flux element or colorant (with the exception of some commercial stains) will reduce glaze viscosity and surface tension. Since colorants are ordinarily used in small quantities, their effect is usually small. Cobalt may become an exception. When used to make an extremely dark blue, cobalt can make a glaze quite runny.

Increasing the proportion of fluxes in a glaze lowers its melting temperature. Adding the glass-former boron to a recipe, or substituting it for some of the silica in the glaze, has a similar effect. Both permit a glaze to remain molten longer during a firing, and that extra time can heal potential pinholes.

Adjusting a glaze formulation can help heal pinholes, but it's better to prevent them from forming in the first place.

Studio glazing is typically done with glazes applied to work that has been fired to a sturdy but still porous state. The porous ware absorbs water from the glaze, assuring that a glaze coating of adequate thickness adheres to the body.

The process of producing porous ware in the first firing makes later glaze application convenient, but also guarantees there will be air under the glaze in the pore spaces in the body. If the glaze melts before all air is driven out of the body by densification, the air coming from the body is trapped as bubbles in the glaze and can produce pinholes. To compound the problem, air can also be trapped between the applied glaze and the body.

Industry fights the first of these problems by firing hotter in the first firing, which is typically to full body density. However, the dense clay cannot absorb moisture so glazing is typically done by spray application onto heated ware. The heated ware dries the water from the glaze rapidly before the glaze has a chance to run off.

Industry also commonly uses some kind of surfactant or low-foaming soap as a wetting agent in the glaze mix. This helps the glaze wet the body and minimizes air trapping between the glaze and body.

In the glaze mixing studio one can also use a surfactant in the glaze mix. If twice-firing, wetting the surface of the ware before glazing can also be helpful. This will permit the glaze to more completely wet the surface of the ware. It is most convenient to do this while washing the ware to remove dust which may have accumulated during or after the first firing.

When using a fuel-heated kiln and firing to cone 10, firing in reduction up to peak temperature will reduce iron and prevent high-temperature off-gassing of oxygen from iron oxide. This is essentially preventing oil-spotting (created by thermal decomposition of iron oxide beginning around cone 8) by reducing the iron before the glaze melts in a thick, high-iron glaze. The oxygen given off creates craters that heal so the surface is relatively smooth but has a characteristic look.

In the final analysis, slowing the glaze firing near peak temperature to allow time for pinholes to heal over can be helpful. If the last 15 to 30 minutes of the peak cone bending occurs at a constant temperature and pinholing still occurs, then a less viscous glaze may be required.

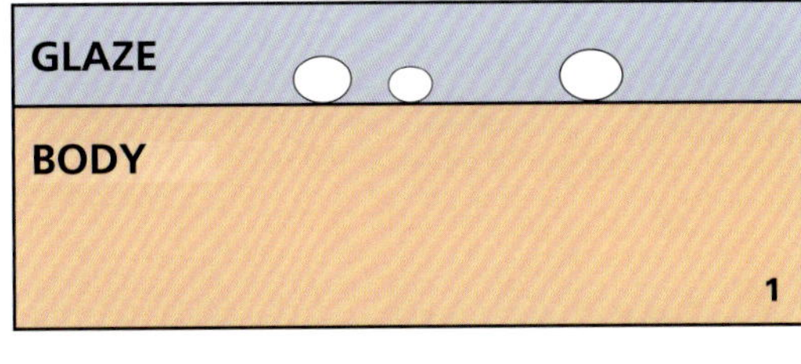

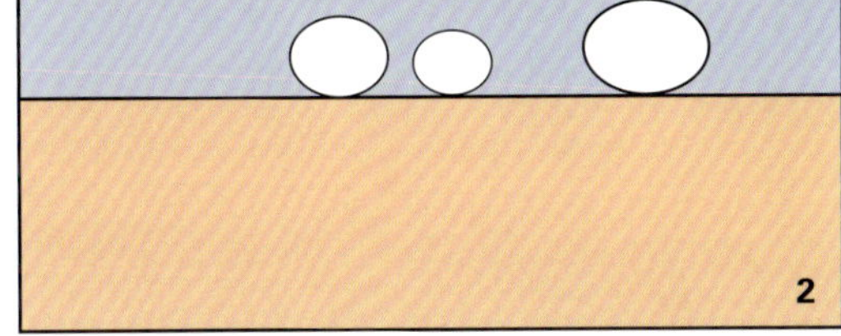

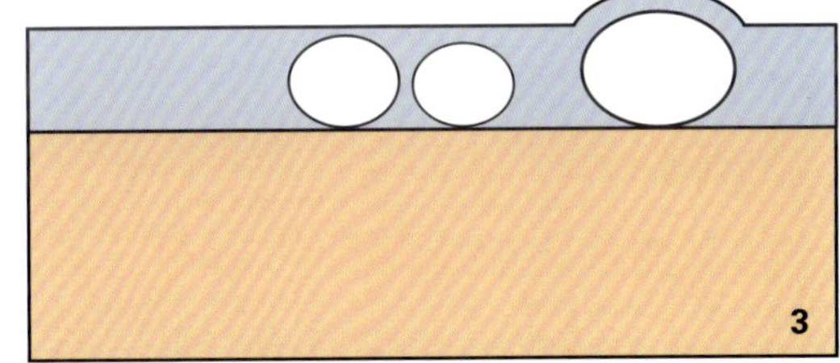

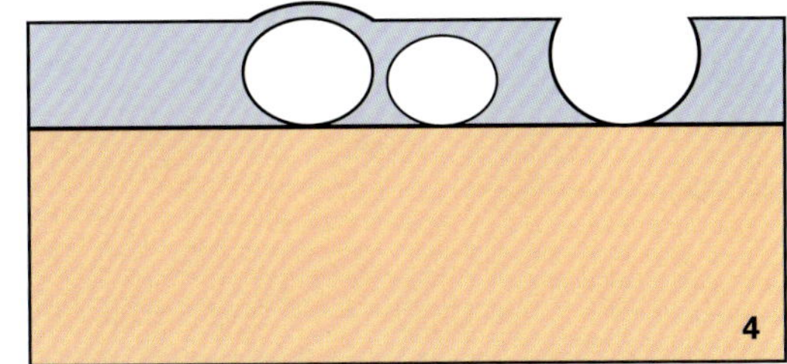

1 A bubble forms at the glaze/body contact surface. **2–3** The bubble grows, pushing through the melted glaze. **4** The bubble bursts, leaving a crater and exposing the clay body. Glaze surface tension and viscosity keep glaze from flowing into the void left by the bubble.

2

Materials

FLUXES

by Dave Finkelnburg

A firm appreciation of fluxes is key to understanding how clay and glazes fire into ceramic art. Fluxes help things melt. Ceramic fluxes lower the melting points of other ceramic materials to temperatures that allow us to use affordable amounts of energy and common equipment and materials. To understand fluxes, though, we need to know what fluxes are and how they work.

Clay, for pottery and ceramic art, is mostly the mineral kaolinite. If pure, kaolinite will not melt unless heated to 3200°F. However, if kaolinite is mixed with a flux, it will begin to melt at a much lower temperature. Fluxes let us fire work at temperatures as low as 1200°F— about what you'd find in an open bonfire. Developing clay bodies and glazes that will fire to specific temperatures requires understanding and controlling the use of fluxes.

Science

As soon as any ceramic material starts to melt, atoms making up the material are freed to move about within the liquid formed. Atoms of any given element within the liquid will move from areas of high concentration of the element to areas of lower concentration. It's like they try to get away from all the neighbors who are just like them and go where the nearest neighbors are not like them. This is the driving force that causes flux elements to diffuse and help dissolve quartz particles in a clay body. There's a lot more going on, of course. Melting of ceramic materials is a complex process. It's important to understand, though, that the chemical composition of the materials in a clay body or glaze ultimately control the temperature and speed of melting.

We often use chemical nomenclature—RO and RO_2—to define our materials (where the letter R is user defined). Since R is not used by any element on the periodic table, it can be used to denote an unknown element in a chemical formula. In ceramics, R refers to one or more of the flux, glass forming, or glass modifying elements we most commonly work with.

We classify flux elements generally as alkali and alkaline earths, and while some fluxing characteristics are specific to each group, many are not. The alkaline earth fluxes fire at a higher temperature while the alkali fluxes melt at a lower temperature and promote brighter colors.

Alkali fluxes are grouped under the label R_2O because it takes two alkali atoms to balance the electrical charge of one oxygen atom. Thus lithium, sodium, and potassium (abbreviated Li, Na, and K) form the oxides Li_2O, Na_2O, and K_2O. Alkaline earth fluxes are labeled RO because it takes only one alkaline earth atom to balance the electrical charge of one oxygen atom. Thus magnesium, calcium, strontium, and barium (abbreviated Mg, Ca, Sr, and Ba) form the oxides MgO, CaO, SrO, and BaO.

Because characteristics beyond general melting temperatures and color response are not particular to one group or another, use these chemical associations carefully. The chart below provides an overview of the effects of the different fluxes. Be aware that the influence of a flux element on glaze color defies classification. For example, magnesium-containing flux materials turn cobalt powerfully purple. In a typical NaKCa-silicate glaze cobalt produces blue. If you begin to remove Ca and replace it with Mg, though, the color will shift to purple. Eventually one can produce a very gorgeous bubble gum grape color without changing the amount of cobalt a bit! Copper is sensitive to different combinations of a number of different fluxes, producing at times blue, yellow, or green. These and other color effects of fluxes must be learned, studied and tested one flux at a time.

FLUXING OXIDE	MELTING TEMP.	CHARACTERISTICS	COLOR AND SURFACE	SOURCE MATERIAL
Li_2O (Lithium Oxide)	1333°F 723°C	can reduce the viscosity and increase fluidity, most reactive flux, strong color response, low expansion/contraction, small particle size	blue with copper, pinks and warm blues with cobalt, textural, variegated effects	lithium carbonate, petalite, spodumene
Na_2O (Sodium Oxide)	1688°F 920°C	strong flux, high expansion/contraction rate causing crazing, begins to volatilize at high temps	copper reds in reduction and copper blues in oxidation	soda feldspar, nepheline syenite, frits
K_2O (Potassium Oxide)	1305°F 707°C	stable, predictable, and active flux, a heavy oxide, high expansion/contraction, crazing in high amounts	promotes bright colors in a broad range	potash feldspar, frits
CaO (Calcium Oxide)	5270°F 2910°C	very active flux in medium/high temp glazes, can harden glaze, intermediate expansion, not an effective flux below cone 4	glossy brown/black to yellow, generally matt surfaces	whiting, wollastonite, feldspars, dolomite
MgO (Magnesium Oxide)	5072°F 2800°C	refractory at lower temps, low expansion and crazing resistance, poor response in bright colored glazes	matt, 'fatty matt' and 'hare's fur' tactile surface	magnesium carbonate, dolomite, talc
SrO (Strontium Oxide)	4406°F 2430°C	useful at lower temps for high gloss and craze resistant glazes, similar expansion and behavior to calcium	satin matt surfaces through a fine crystalline mesh	strontium carbonate
BaO (Barium Oxide)	3493°F 1923°C	very active in small amounts, larger amounts can be refractory and leachable	blues with copper, milky streaks and cloudy effects	barium carbonate, frit
ZnO (Zinc Oxide)	3272°F 1800°C	auxiliary flux in oxidation atmospheres, dramatic color response, low expansion/contraction rate	can produce opacity due to the development of a crystal mesh surface	zinc oxide

LITHIUM

by Dave Finkelnburg

Lithium is the lightest chemical element used in ceramics. In fact, hydrogen and helium are the only known elements that are lighter. Because lithium is such a powerful flux, adding even a small amount to a glaze recipe can produce a big change in the fired result.

The Well Rounded Flux

Lithium is a powerful, useful, alkaline glaze flux. It brightens glaze colors much like sodium and potassium do. However, lithium also promotes clearer transparent glazes and lowers both the melting point and the viscosity of glazes even more than sodium or potassium. Lithium also contributes to a harder fired glaze surface than either of those fluxes. It's well known as a flux in flameware clay bodies.

Lithium dramatically lowers the linear coefficient of thermal expansion (CTE) of glazes and clay bodies. This is part of why lithium is so useful in reducing susceptibility of flameware to thermal shock. However, the amount of lithium used must be carefully controlled. Too much lithium in a glaze is certain to cause that glaze to shiver from most ordinary clay bodies. Too much lithium also causes the formation of crystals, effectively turning a clear glaze opaque.

Magnesium is the only flux that has a lower CTE than lithium. Potassium and sodium, have CTEs on the order of five times larger than that of lithium, and the alkaline earth fluxes (calcium, barium, and strontium) have CTEs twice as large as lithium.

Chemically, lithium is termed an alkali metal. It occurs in the same group of flux elements as the familiar sodium and potassium. When lithium reacts with other elements to form chemical compounds, covalent bonds result. These very strong bonds are the reason lithium contributes higher hardness to glazes than either sodium or potassium.

As a rule of thumb, use no more than 0.2 moles of Li_2O per mole of total fluxes on any functional glaze at any firing temperature. However, even half that amount can cause shivering, so glaze fit (the degree of mismatch between glaze and clay body CTE) will usually determine how much lithium is too much.

Successfully using lithium as a glaze ingredient requires careful control of the glaze chemistry. The chart to the right shows three glaze recipes that illustrate this. The first glaze, 4-3-2-1, was made popular by Bernard Leach. The Lithium A and Lithium B recipes are, chemically, almost identical to the Leach 4-3-2-1. They differ only in that the Lithium A recipe replaces about half of the sodium and potassium of the 4-3-2-1 with lithium, while the Lithium B recipe replaces more than three quarters. Simple substitutions, right? Look at how dramatically different the Lithium A and Lithium B recipes are from the original.

Only 3% lithium carbonate was added to Lithium A, but to remove a molar equivalent amount of sodium and potassium, collectively, it was necessary to remove two thirds of the Custer feldspar from the original 4-3-2-1 recipe. Silica and alumina, which had been supplied by the feldspar, were then added back in the form of silica (about 50% more) and kaolin (more than doubled).

Just over 20% spodumene was added to Lithium B. To remove a molar equivalent amount of sodium and potassium, collectively, it was necessary to remove 85% of the Custer feldspar. Because spodumene is similar to feldspar, the silica and kaolin amounts in the recipe changed little.

The point of the glaze chart is not to present recipes for studio use, but rather to show how easy it can be to substitute a small amount of lithium carbonate and produce a dramatic change in the recipe and the fired results. The CTE of the recipes indicate the original 4-3-2-1 recipe is likely to fit most stoneware clay bodies. Lithium A, however, might shiver off those same stonewares but will fit many porcelains which are formulated to have lower CTEs similar to glazes. Lithium B may even shiver off some porcelains.

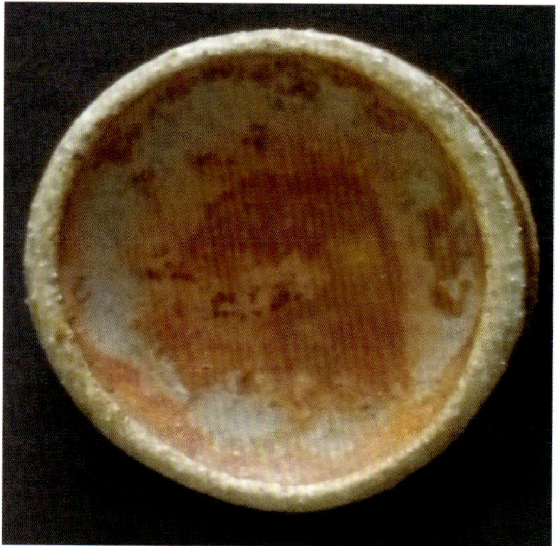

Lithium Carbonate—A synthetic, slightly water soluble lithium source most often produced by reacting concentrated lithium chloride brine with a carbonate. Lithium carbonate contains about 40% Li_2O.
Fired results: At cone 6, $LiCO_3$ fully melts and is extremely reactive; and is mottled in color at cone 6.

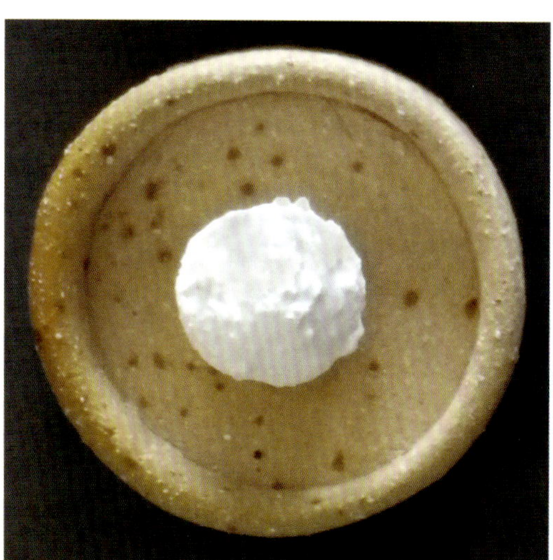

Petalite—A naturally occurring lithium feldspar typically containing between 3.5 and 5% Li_2O.
Fired results: Remains white, does not melt and is nonreactive at cone 6.

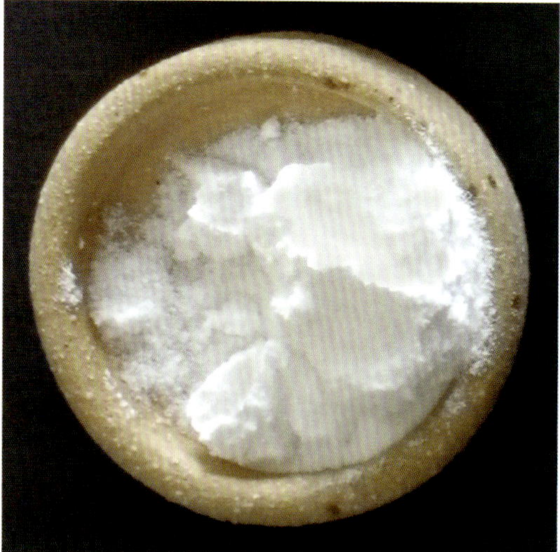

Spodumene—the most readily available naturally occurring lithium source, a lithium aluminum silicate mineral typically containing between 5.5 and 8% Li_2O.
Fired results: At cone 6, no melting occurs, is non-reactive and remains similar to the raw material.

Materials

FELDSPAR

by Dave Finkelnburg

Except for clay and silica, feldspar is the most common raw material in ceramics. It's also the most common mineral on earth—making up more than half the earth's crust. Most feldspar has an almost perfect ratio of flux, alumina, and silica to make a glass at high-fire temperatures.

A Natural Frit

As a crystalline mineral precipitated from molten rock over geologic time, feldspar is definitely not a designer material. Feldspar is sometimes called a natural frit and is composed entirely of crystals, but a commercial frit is made up of a finely ground glass manufactured with a specific composition. More energy is needed to melt crystals than glass, so to give it time to melt, feldspar requires a somewhat slower firing, most often to higher temperatures. While a frit can be manufactured with any desired ratio of flux, alumina, and silica, with feldspar what you mine is what you get. Thus feldspar is a sort of good-news bad-news story.

The good news is that the natural laws controlling how silicon, aluminum, and oxygen link to form the feldspar crystal ensure that the ratio of silica and alumina in pure feldspar is fixed.* More good news is that the flux elements exist in a fixed ratio to the alumina and silica.

Part of the bad news, however, is that nature permits sodium and potassium to occupy that flux amount in infinitely variable proportions to one another. The amount of either in a given feldspar depends entirely on what was handy when the feldspar precipitated from the molten rock in the earth's crust. Virtually every alkali feldspar deposit on earth has at least some difference in analysis.

In scientific terms, albite and microcline/orthoclase can form a solid solution. That is, an alkali feldspar can theoretically vary from 100% sodium to 100% potassium as its flux constituent. Soda feldspars actually tend to have at least 30% of their flux as potassium, while potash feldspars usually have at least 15% of their flux as sodium.

The rest of the bad news is that feldspar most commonly occurs as a rock, usually along with mica, quartz, and other minerals. In a feldspar mine, the rock is ground to a powder and sophisticated techniques are used to separate the minerals. How well and how consistently mining companies clean and concentrate the feldspar that artists use has virtually nothing to do with artists and focuses on the folks who buy 100-ton rail-car loads of feldspar to make literally millions of tons of glass per year. Quality control good enough to make beer bottles may not be as good as we would like

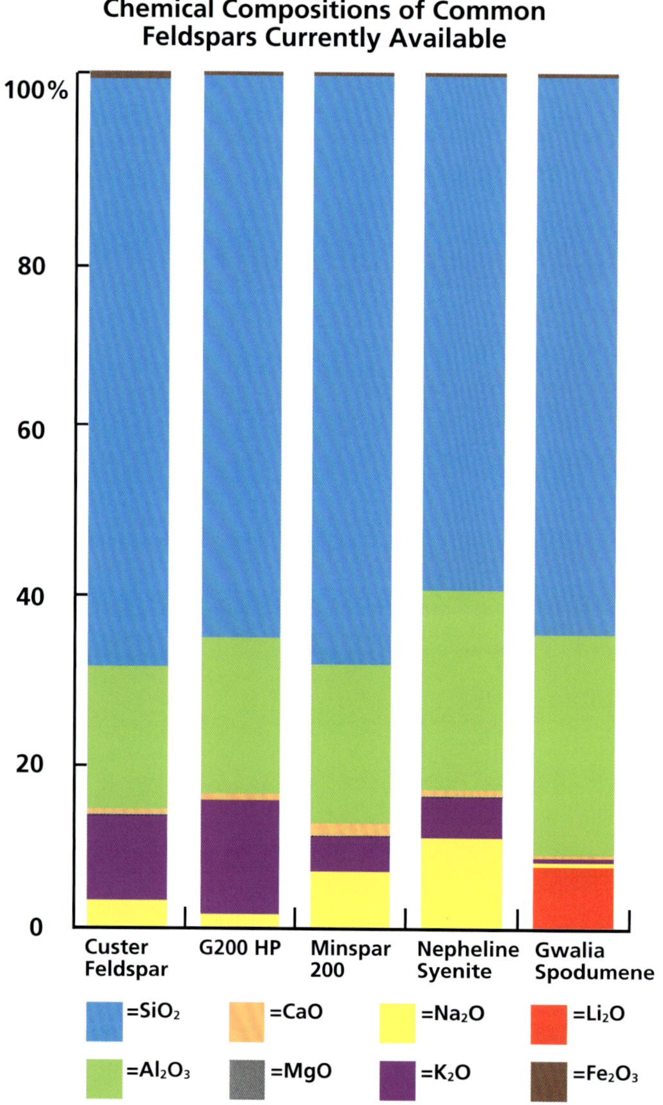

in the studio, but who is ultimately the bigger end user of feldspar—studio artists or folks molding beer bottles? Feldspar is ultimately an industrial mineral and we have to accept that its quality is controlled by what's good enough for industry.

Note: the difference in the ratio of silica and alumina between feldpars, spodumene, and nepheline syenite. There is less silica in the latter two. The crystal structure explains this. This also explains the differences between potash feldspars to nepheline syenite and spodumene.

Making Adjustments

Commercial frits have generally consistent analyses. Naturally occurring feldspars are less consistent and subject to change over time. While all raw materials should be tested before use, this needs to be a requirement before using each new batch of feldspar in the studio.

When feldspar is added to a clay body, it helps to melt very fine quartz into a glass phase that provides strength in the fired body. The amount of feldspar needed in a stoneware body depends entirely upon the flux level of the clays composing the body. For a fixed recipe of clays, various amounts of feldspar are tested to achieve a body with the desired level of vitrification from a given firing cycle.

The difference in silica content between Custer and G-200HP feldspars (see graph) is enough to change glaze fit. While these two potash feldspars can generally be substituted one-for-one, if one wants precise control of glaze chemistry, then a more accurate substitute for Custer is G-200HP plus 3% silica. When an existing feldspar disappears or a new one enters the market, some substitution such as this is likely to be necessary to achieve consistent results.

Time is also a factor. The landscape varies and as industry excavates from one mine to another the composition of feldspar changes along with it. The feldspar you used five or ten years ago is most likely not exactly the same as what you are using today, even if it's the same brand name. Fusion button tests of the new and old material will guide you in whether and how to substitute other materials to accommodate the new feldspar's chemistry.

Testing Procedure

- *Step 1.* Get a full chemical analysis of the new and old feldspars, if they are available.
- *Step 2.* Fire fusion buttons (a few grams of feldspar pressed into a small mold such as a crucible) of both materials side by side to get a visual indication of the differences in the two materials. Note color changes, melting temperatures, opacity, and surface effects.
- *Step 3.* Adjust recipes as these differences indicate and fire recipe tests to confirm that the adjustments are correct.

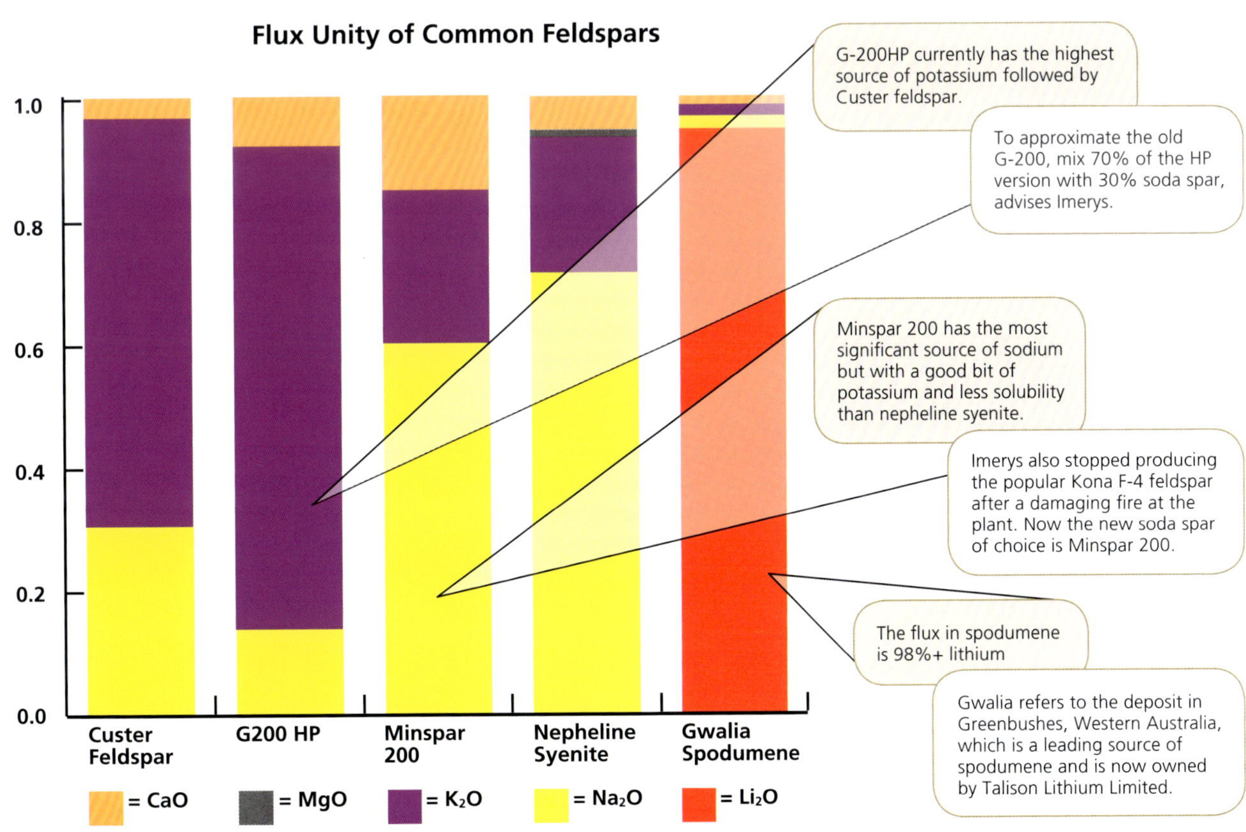

FRITS

by Dave Finkelnburg

Frits are wonderful glaze ingredients. Getting familiar with frits can help solve problems and improve glazes. The challenge of frits lies in discovering which ones to use in a given situation, and why. What are Frits?

What is a frit?

Most simply, it's a ground glass. However, it's a glass of a special composition—typically high in flux elements, low in alumina, usually with enough silica to make a stable glass, and sometimes containing boron.

Fluxes that dissolve in a glaze slurry can cause problems during glaze firing. That's why glaze recipes seldom use soluble fluxes. Frits can be wonderful glaze ingredients because they incorporate soluble elements in a glass matrix, thus rendering those elements insoluble.

At high temperatures (around cone 10) a useful source of insoluble fluxes that melts rapidly is feldspar. However, feldspars are slow to melt at low- and mid-range temperatures. Frits were originally developed to provide an insoluble source of fluxes for low and mid-range glazes and/or to permit formulation of faster melting glaze recipes.

Every frit has a particular ratio of flux elements to each other and, when used, to alumina and also to boron. Enough silica is included to make the frit stable and insoluble in the glaze slurry.

The remainder of the glaze recipe depends on the firing method, peak firing temperature, and the clay body the glaze is applied to. However, all fritted glaze recipes require enough clay or other viscosity modifier to suspend the glaze ingredients. Typically at least 10% of a white-burning ball clay or kaolin is used in the recipe. When kaolin is used, the dry glaze surface will be softer and glaze dusting may be a problem. Additional silica may be required in the recipe, since increasing proportions of silica are required as the firing temperature is increased.

Pros

Renders soluble materials insoluble: Soda ash (sodium source), pearl ash (potassium source), and borax (boron source) are good sources of the pure elements but are all very soluble unless melted into the glass matrix of a frit.

Supplies boron: Boron (B_2O_3) is a very effective melter at low temperatures in ceramic glazes, but its raw forms are mostly soluble and often inconsistent.

Batch consistency: Unlike mined raw materials, commercial frits have specific, known chemical compositions. This makes the effect of a frit on a glaze dependable from batch to batch.

Ability to blend oxides otherwise difficult or impossible with raw materials: A frit can supply a specific chemistry that a raw material cannot. For example, a frit can supply all the elements found in feldspar and can be formulated to melt at a temperature too low to melt feldspar itself.

Reduces melting temperature and improves melt predictability: Since frits have been premelted to form a glass, remelting them requires less time and energy and permits firing a glaze at a lower temperature. A magnesium oxide frit can be more effective at lower temperatures than sourcing the flux from talc or dolomite.

Faster firing: Frits can be formulated to melt quickly and evenly after body gases have been expelled, thus greatly reducing glaze imperfections. The cost of the frit can be offset by the energy saved when firing faster to the same temperature. Fast firing also makes it economically feasible to go to higher temperatures.

Wider firing range: In the presence of frits, many stains soften over a wide temperature range as opposed to having a sudden melting temperature.

Cons

Expensive: Frits are more expensive than raw materials. However the advantages often out-weigh the costs, such as fewer pieces per firing lost due to glaze faults, or energy savings due to faster firings. So, the processing that leads to the expense is as much a pro as it is a con.

Glaze Settling: Glaze recipes must contain enough clay, bentonite, cellulose gum, or a combination of these to keep the relatively dense, coarse frit particles from settling out. When a frit is used in the glaze recipe, careful attention must be paid to the suspending qualities of the glaze slurry.

Which Frit to Use

A great way to quickly gain familiarity with a variety of frits is by firing a small amount of each frit side by side in the same firing and then comparing the fired samples to each other. It is best to weigh the same amount of each frit and put each sample in a separate small, unglazed, deep tray or bowl.

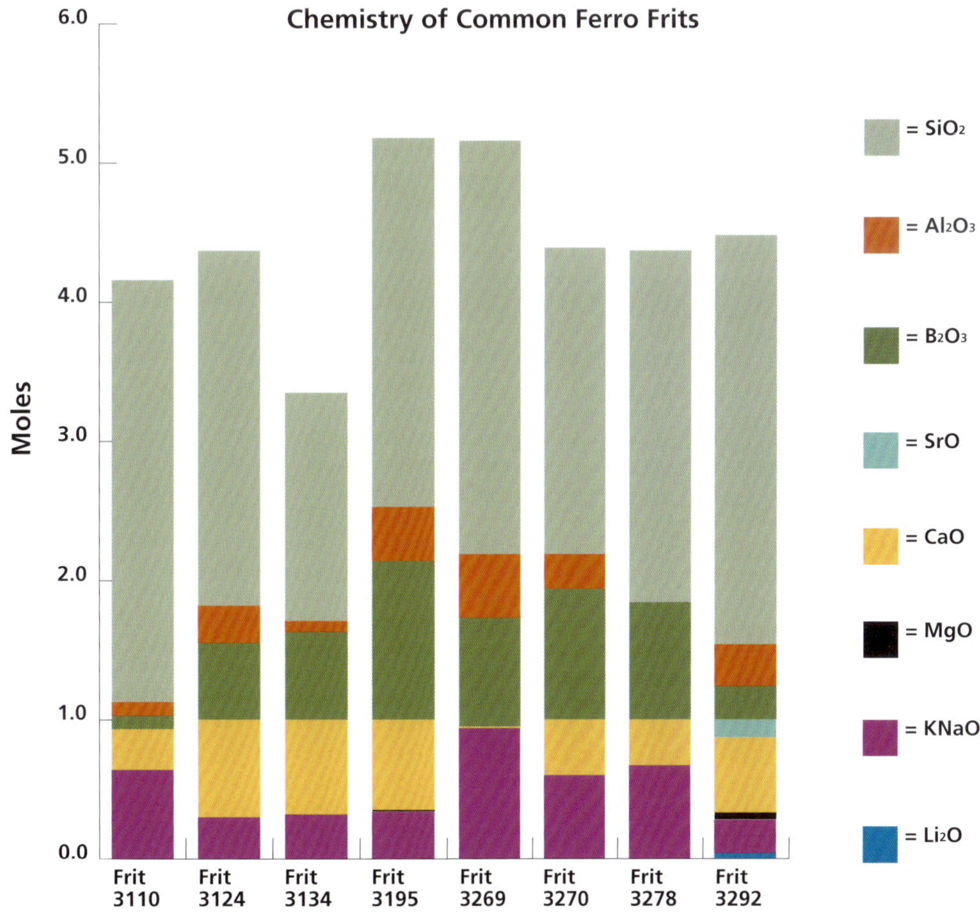

Compare the visual characteristics such as fusibility, melt, opacity, transparency, fluidity, and stiffness of these fired samples to each other and to their published chemical compositions. Now you have information about the chemistry of each frit and the physical attributes that chemistry produces, information that will help you pick a frit for your glaze.

- Ferro frit 3110—high in sodium, plus a small amount of boron and alumina and quite a bit of silica. A high expansion flux, it will easily produce a crackle glaze.
- Ferro frit 3124—calcium borate frit very similar to 3134 but melts at a higher temperature.
- Ferro frit 3134—a calcium borate frit with little alumina so it can be used with a significant amount of clay. Because of its high calcium content it will bleach iron and mute other colorants.
- Ferro frit 3195—high in boron and very fluid. Not good for use in underglaze colors, has a wide firing range from cone 06-02, and needs the addition of a little kaolin to suspend.
- Ferro frit 3269—borate frit, contains more sodium than potassium, a bit of zinc but no calcium. Brightens colors.
- Ferro frit 3270—range from cone 06–04 for many colors, particularly cobalt.
- Ferro frit 3278—high borax frit similar to 3134 but melts at a lower temp.
- Ferro frit 3292 works well from cone 1–4.

Developing a Fritted Glaze

The easiest way to incorporate or substitute a frit into a glaze recipe is to use glaze calculation software—this software is readily available and has dramatically simplified this task.

However, if you want to develop a glaze simply by experimentation, start with the basic materials.

All glazes require silica. It's what forms the glass network. By itself, silica will not melt at ordinary kiln temperatures (silica melts at 2577°F (1414°C)). However, a frit provides necessary flux elements which, when mixed with silica, will make a combination that does melt readily in the kiln. Boron can also be used to speed up silica's melting so the glaze melting temperature falls into the range suitable for your clay body.

When choosing a frit, decide whether you want a glaze that is transparent or opaque, what firing range you will use, and whether you want to brighten or mute any added colorants, then refer to your button tests and the frit chemistry to choose which frits to test.

Next, you'll want to add some alumina to the mix, and alumina is usually sourced from clay. Alumina stiffens the melted glaze, stabilizes and hardens the fired glaze, and increases durability of the fired surface.

Additional raw materials can also be added depending on what you want the glaze to look like. Adding an excess of calcium can produce an opaque satin to matte glaze. This is because calcium compounds crystallize from the melted glaze as it cools. Alkali fluxes—sodium, potassium and lithium—all produce brighter colors.

Finally, test how well the glaze stays in suspension. If enough clay was added to provide required alumina, the glaze may suspend well on its own. If no more alumina is desired, a high-quality bentonite (used sparingly) can be a good alternative. Bentonites have extremely small particles, thus hold a great deal of water, and in excessive amounts may cause an applied glaze to dry too slowly. Glaze suspension can be improved, and the glaze surface hardened simultaneously, by adding a cellulose gum. A common gum is CMC (carboxymethyl cellulose) VEEGUM® CER is a commercial blend of bentonite and CMC. Ball clay or kaolin can also be used, in small amounts, in combination with CMC, to suspend a glaze.

A useful rule of thumb is to use between ¼–2% of bentonite and around ½% CMC. Begin testing at the low end of the addition rate. These ingredients will have a noticeable effect, so test small amounts of glaze carefully to avoid ruining an entire batch.

Note: When adding bentonite, either mix the dry ingredients very well with all other dry glaze ingredients or hydrate it thoroughly with a known amount of water for 24 hours, mix it well, then add it to the slurry as a weight percent of the glaze recipe.

TESTING FRIT SUBSTITUTIONS

by Deanna Ranlett

Pursuing glazes with ingredients that are unknown or unavailable can be frustrating, if not impossible, but with a few tips, you can be successful and possibly make some new glazes in the process. Greg Daly's book, *Developing Glazes*, explores a number of glaze recipes using several ingredients not common in the US, including lead, lead bisilicate frit, and some borosilicate frits. Here is how to choose common ingredients in order to achieve similar results to those in Daly's book when firing to cone 6.

Understanding and Testing Raw Materials

It's fundamental that you know what effects your raw materials have when fired to your ideal firing range. To test raw materials, label a test tile for each material, mix a small amount of each material with water, brush it on the tile, and fire it to your ideal cone. Once you know your materials, making educated guesses when mixing glazes becomes more intuitive and you'll understand what ingredients to use when making changes to glazes. You'll see that some materials have matte surfaces when fired, some glossy, and some satin, so you can start to understand each material's role in a glaze.

When trying to replicate a specific glaze, I normally use my materials knowledge to think of at least two potential recipes, and then I do a quick and easy line blend using those two potential recipes.

Mixing for Line Blends

Weigh out and mix 500 grams of each recipe (this makes a bit extra). Line up 11 cups in a row from left to right. Put 30 grams of glaze A into the cup on the left end and 30 grams of glaze B into the cup on the right end. Next, you'll fill in the cups in the middle with a mixture of the glazes you're testing. Each cup will end up with 30 grams of glaze. Starting with the left cup, the progression in each cup is 10% less of glaze A (see chart below); using a round number makes things easier. You already have 30 grams (or 100%) of glaze A in cup #1, so you'll want 27 grams (or 90%) in cup #2, 24 grams (or 80%) in cup #3, 21 grams (or 70%) in cup #4, and so on. Then work from the right side toward the left side, measuring out glaze B in the same progression. When finished, each cup should have a total of 30 grams of dry base glaze.

For the tests here, we focused on three glazes from *Developing Glazes*: Cu-38 (Copper 38) on

GLAZE A/1	2	3	4	5	6	7	8	9	10	GLAZE B/11
	90 10	80 20	70 30	60 40	50 50	40 60	30 70	20 80	10 90	

Line blend percentages for mixing Glaze A with Glaze B.

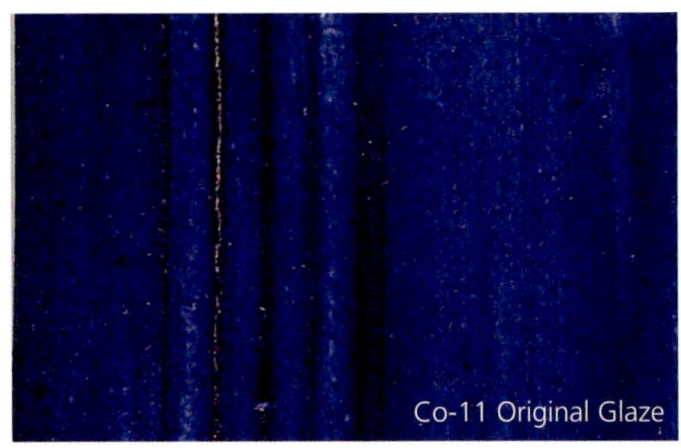
Co-11 Original Glaze

ORIGINAL CO-11

Barium Carbonate	60 %
Soft Borosilicate Frit (Ferro Frit 3110)	20
EPK Kaolin	20
	100 %
Add: Cobalt Carbonate	1 %

CO-11 GLAZE A

Strontium Carbonate	60 %
Ferro Frit 3110	20
EPK Kaolin	20
	100 %
Add: Cobalt Carbonate	1 %

CO-11 GLAZE B

Strontium Carbonate	45 %
Ferro Frit 3110	35
EPK Kaolin	20
	100 %
Add: Cobalt Carbonate	1 %

p. 100 (figure 1), Co-11 (Cobalt 11) on p. 94 (figure 2), and Ti-19 (Titanium 19) on p. 122 (figure 3).

In addition to lead, the book also uses a soft borosilicate frit—some substitutes are researchable online, but often too many options come up, so my advice is to test the frit you have on hand first before investing in others.

Ferro frit 3110 is a great substitute for a soft borosilicate frit as it has a low-melting point, supports great color, and can aid in crystal formation. It can be tricky in glazes for functional ware because it can craze when used in high percentages so some adjustments may be necessary to make the glazes food safe.

Glaze Recipe 1

There are also viable alternatives to some toxic ingredients, like barium. One I regularly use is strontium at 75% of the original barium content. For the Co-11 glaze below, I use a 1:1 ratio substitution of strontium instead of barium for Glaze A. And in Glaze B, I used the recommended 75% substitution but added more frit. I did this to show that the strontium doesn't melt as easily as the original barium, thus necessitating the reduction in overall percentage. You can see the progression of the melt in the tiles, although the original barium softness is harder to capture—future tests might include using some strontium and some lithium carbonate to gain some of the softness back.

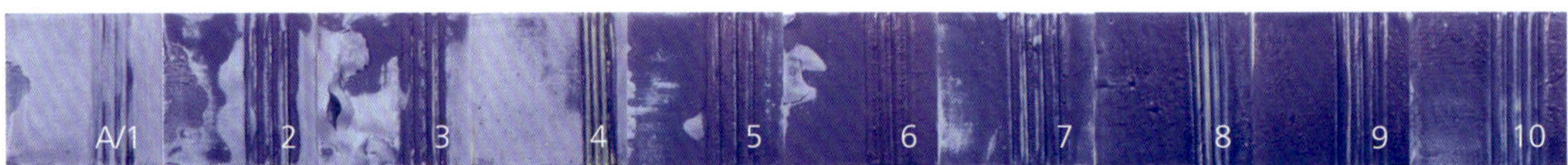

Line blend of Co-11 Glaze A with Co-11 Glaze B fired to cone 6.

Glaze Recipe 2

For the Cu-38 tests, there is no direct substitution to replace the lead bisilicate frit. This is where the test on raw materials comes in handy. I know that sodium content is often important in color development and that some sodium fluxes have a lower melting point, making them good candidates for substitution. In reviewing the frit composition of lead bisilicate frit 3403, I found it has a very low melting point of 1350°F. This tells me that Ferro frit 3110 is a good candidate but it's already a large portion of the recipe. One option was to go with increased Ferro frit 3110 and add in nepheline syenite (a powerful feldspathic flux high in sodium content) in Glaze A. And in Glaze B I added borax, which I know to be a low-melt flux common in many glazes. Regarding the frit content, I knew we also needed to add some silica, as frits are manufactured and are compositions that are fused or melted, then quenched to form glass and granulated and powdered. This process is helpful because it renders any soluble and/or toxic components insoluble by causing them to combine with silica and/or other materials. So, note the addition of silica where there was none in the original recipe. The original surface of this glaze was matte but my results are more semi-gloss with great color. The addition of a slow cooling cycle could further crystallize the surface and give even more similarity to the original glaze.

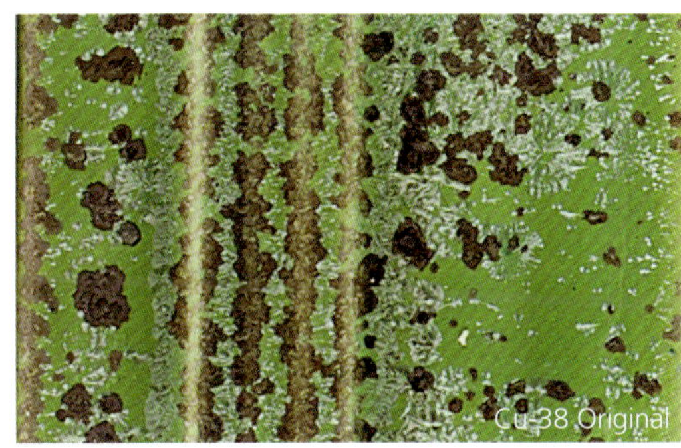

Cu-38 Original

ORIGINAL CU-38

Nepheline Syenite	20 %
Lead Bisilicate Frit	35
Soft Borosilicate Frit (Ferro Frit 3110)	30
Whiting	5
Talc	5
EPK Kaolin	5
	100 %
Add: Rutile	10 %
Copper Carbonate	4 %

CU-38 GLAZE A

Nepheline Syenite	30 %
Ferro Frit 3110	50
Whiting	5
Talc	5
Silica	10
	100 %
Add: Rutile	10 %
Copper Carbonate	4 %

CU-38 GLAZE B

Nepheline Syenite	40 %
Whiting	10
Talc	5
EPK Kaolin	10
Borax	15
Silica	20
	100 %
Add: Rutile	10 %
Copper Carbonate	4 %

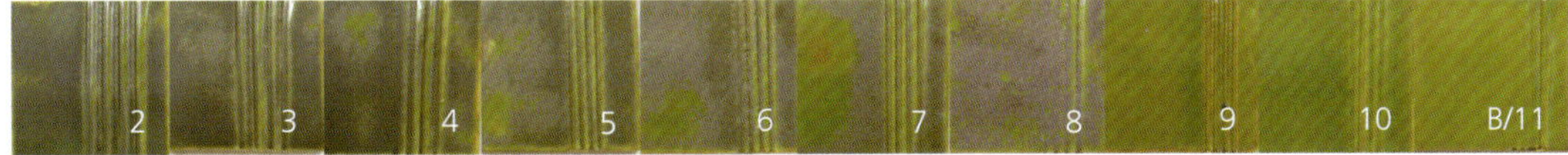

Line blend of Cu-38 Glaze A with Cu-38 Glaze B fired to cone 6.

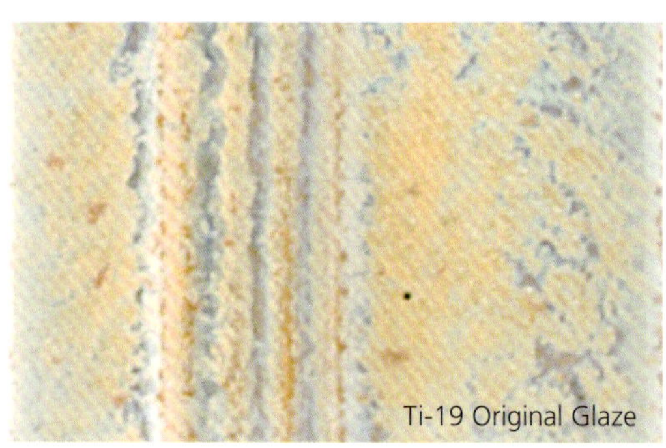

ORIGINAL TI-19

Nepheline Syenite	15 %
Lead Bisilicate Frit	40
Soft Borosilcate Frit (Ferro Frit 3110)	30
Whiting	5
Talc	5
EPK Kaolin	5
	100 %
Add: Rutile	10 %

TI-19 GLAZE A

Nepheline Syenite	15 %
Whiting	5
Talc	5
Ferro Frit 3110	30
Minspar 200	35
Silica	10
	100 %
Add: Rutile	10 %

TI-19 GLAZE B

Nepheline Syenite	28 %
Whiting	5
Talc	5
Ferro Frit 3110	38
EPK Kaolin	12
Silica	12
	100 %
Add: Rutile	10 %

Glaze Recipe 3

For Ti-19, I knew from my research on the Cu-38 glaze that I would need to add some silica and also that I would need to change the amounts of some of the other fluxes or add new fluxes. In Glaze A, I chose soda feldspar (Minspar 200), which my raw materials test shows will yield a crystalline effect. The surface of the original tile showed a rutile float and small crystals. I then manipulated Glaze B using other additional fluxes in the original recipe and increased the nepheline syenite. Again I am using sodium in both glazes to boost the color from the lead in the original formulas. In this particular test the versions were very close to each other. Some tiles had more crystals on the surface than others but the overall color was not as satisfying as the original tile. As a group, the glazes were good candidates for layering glazes.

I find that when you are interested and have a little fun with glaze chemistry it doesn't seem so daunting. Materials substitutions don't have to be a headache—just make sound educated guesses! And remember, if you can't have the frit you love—love the frit you have!

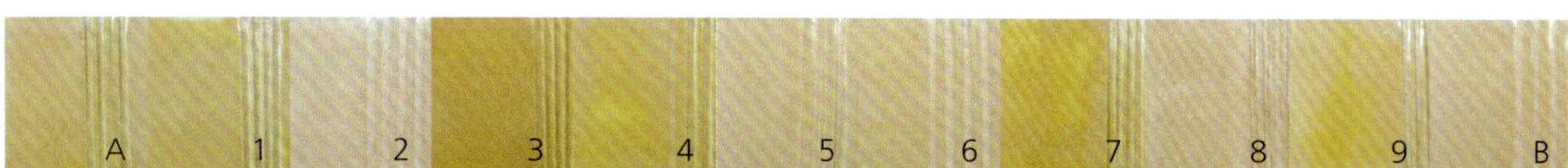

Line blend of Ti-19 Glaze A with Ti-19 Glaze B fired to cone 6.

BORON

by Matt Katz

Boron is one of the most, if not the most, misunderstood material in ceramics but it doesn't need to be. What exactly does it do? Where does it come from? How should we use it? These questions permeate the mysteries of boron but are easily answered.

Glass Former or Flux?

Boron is very basic in function and it performs in a predictable manner. However, boron usage in the US for the last 50 plus years has been dominated by Gerstley borate, a raw material that is prized for its unpredictability. This has left at least a couple generations of ceramists with varying levels of confusion about the true nature of boron and a collection of recipes that don't work without this particular material.

Boron is found primarily in Turkey as an element in the mineral borax ($Na_2O{\cdot}3B_2O_3{\cdot}10H_2O$), and Boron, California, where the largest mine in the state produces half of the world's boron.

All glazes are based on only eleven oxides. These are the oxides of silicon, aluminum, lithium, sodium, potassium, magnesium, calcium, strontium, barium, zinc, and boron. There are others, but they are all relegated to the role of colorants, additives, or the relatively unused, such as the dreaded lead. These basic eleven elements make up 99% of glazes. The first ten can be simplified further into two groups—glass formers and fluxes. This leaves us with boron. Which is it, a glass former or a flux?

If you look at the version of the periodic table of the elements below, as used by glass scientists, boron is grouped with silicon and four other glass formers. It is above aluminum, which can substitute, within limits, for silica in a glass network.

All of the fluxes (except for zinc) are found in the first two columns of the table. They are the alkalis in the first column and the alkaline earths in the second. The elements in each column act similarly to each other and slightly different than the elements in the other column, yet all are fluxes. The function of true fluxes is to lower the melting temperature of glass formers. In the process, fluxes also influence color, strength, and the chemical and mechanical durability of glazes.

Historically, many have declared that boron is a flux because we use it to make glazes melt at low (cone 04) and mid-range (cone 6) temperatures. Here's where the confusion comes from. The fact is that boron is a glass former. We know this because pure boron oxide will make a glass on its own, just like pure silica will. Where boron differs from silicon is that boron oxide forms a glass at a dramatically lower temperature than silica.

All glazes require silica, and it is by leaps and bounds the most prevalent material in all glazes,

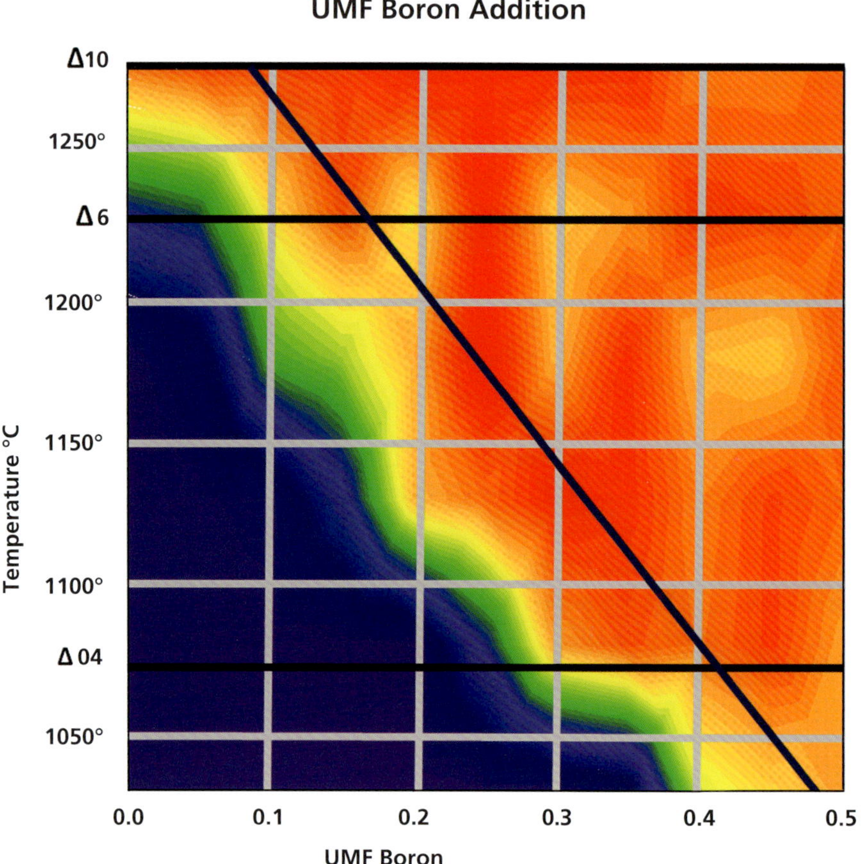

Boron Glaze Limits. The above chart indicates amounts of boron needed to make a glaze melt based on the desired firing temperature. Orange/red suggests a glossy melt, purple/blue areas indicate underfired surfaces.

regardless of temperature or type. Silica is the second most abundant material on earth after iron, making it cheap and plentiful. Boron, on the other hand, is a minor player. Boron is not pragmatic as a primary glass former for many reasons; material sources are all limited for reasons such as solubility, common availability, and cost. There are no glazes that are composed exclusively of boron; it is, at best, an accessory. Yet understanding boron for mid- and low-temperature glazes (even high-temperature), is very useful.

Sources

For many years, the major source of boron has been Gerstley borate. This is a naturally occurring deposit of the minerals colemanite ($2CaO{\cdot}3B_2O_3{\cdot}5H_2O$), ulexite ($NaCaB_5O_9{\cdot}8H_2O$) and bentonite ($3Al_2O_3{\cdot}SiO_2{\cdot}H_2O$). Gerstley borate is an exciting material for ceramists as the two borate materials (colemanite and ulexite) melt at different times in the firing, leading to the "breaking" effect of the glaze.

When it was feared that Gerstley's availability would be limited (the mine was closed for safety reasons) a variety of materials sold as Gerstley substitutes came onto the market. There are also two other types of borate materials: frits, and soluble sources. The soluble materials, boric acid ($B_2O_3{\cdot}3H_2O$) and borax, are very effective boron sources. The problem with these materials is they are very soluble in water, meaning that the boron dissolves in the water of the glaze. As glazes dry, the water is absorbed into the bisqued clay body rather than remaining in the glaze. This can change the melting performance of the body (over melting) and the glaze (under melting).

For this reason, frits are the favored sources for boron. Frits are wonderful materials as they provide all the boron required in a stable, minimally soluble form. Frits are essentially glazes that have been batched, melted, and then ground to a powder by the frit manufacturer. There are a huge number of frits out there, but in the US our palette is often limited to Ferro's 31XX series, including 3110, 3124, 3134, and 3195. Each of these frits does something different but they are all very simple and bring in various amounts of boron.

Boron and UMF

The function of silica, alumina, and fluxes are well understood in the unity molecular formula (UMF) or Seger formula, thanks to the work of R.T. Stull. However, boron, as a bit player, did not receive any attention in his work. All high-temperature glazes require silica, alumina, an alkaline earth, and an alkali. Boron is not required for a cone 10 glaze. At Alfred University, Dr. Bill Carty and I have put a lot of effort into defining how to best utilize boron from a UMF perspective. We believe that one can predict the amount of boron needed to make a glaze melt based on the desired firing temperature.

The graph on this page shows the amount of boron required at any temperature. The purple-blue areas are underfired, while the red/orange areas are very glossy. The vertical axis is temperature in celsius and the horizontal axis is UMF boron additions to a standard glaze. By finding the desired temperature and determining the position on the oblique line, you can figure out the corresponding required UMF boron level at that temperature. This chart applies from cone 06 to cone 10. As a general rule, we define the required amount of boron as an additional 0.1 mole (via UMF) of boron for every 50°C below cone 10. Boron is an exceptionally good material for adding to glazes as it makes glasses at lower temperatures that are just as strong and resistant to wear and chemical leaching as the best cone 10 glazes.

Cone 10 to Cone 6: The First Step

A glaze temperature conversion is no easy feat. It takes knowledge and experience to successfully convert a glaze recipe that works at one temperature so it works as well at another. There are a lot of subtle factors in the chemistry of a glaze that dictate its color, texture, and performance. That said, here is a quick start with fast results, helped in part by boron.

- *Step 1.* Take a cone 10 glaze and mix three 100 gram batches of it.
- *Step 2.* Add Ferro frit 3124 to the cups: 5% to one, 10% to the second, and 15% to the third.
- *Step 3.* Apply each test recipe to its own flat test tile and place in a disposable unglazed clay run catcher.
- *Step 4.* Fire the tiles, propped at a 45° angle, to cone 6.
- *Step 5.* Select the glaze that ran the least in the kiln.

This is just a first step to adjusting a glaze to a lower temperature, but it should be a good starting place for creating a glaze that looks similar. By using a frit, you're introducing boron as a material that will not alter the basic nature of the glaze but will still contribute the boron needed to lower the firing temperature.

Materials

IRON OXIDE

by John Britt

Iron oxide is the most common colorant in ceramics. It's so ubiquitous that it's very difficult to find a material without some iron—it's found in almost everything from feldspars to kaolin to ball clays, earthenware clays, and many colorants. Many materials require expensive processing to reduce the amount of iron to acceptable levels.

Iron is a very active metal that combines easily with oxygen. That means it is very sensitive to oxidation and reduction atmospheres, producing a wide range of glaze colors and effects from off white, light blue, blue, blue-green, green, olive, amber, yellow, brown, russet, tea-dust, black, iron saturate, iron spangles, iron crystalline (goldstone/tiger's eye), oil spot, hare's fur, kaki (orange), leopard spotted kaki, tan, black seto, pigskin tenmoku, shino, gray (Hidashi), iridescent, silver, gold, etc. Iron also plays a major role in clay bodies, slips, terra sigillata, and flashing slips.

There are three major forms of iron used in ceramics: red iron oxide (Fe_20_3), black iron oxide (FeO or Fe_3O), and yellow iron oxide ($FeO(OH)$). There are different mesh sizes and grades, and each contains varying degrees of impurities that can make a significant difference in the results you get. There is a synthetic red iron that's produced by calcining black iron oxide particles in an oxidation atmosphere. They are then jet milled, which produces "micronized" red iron oxide particles that are approximately 325 mesh. This type of red iron is very heat stable, up to 1832°F (1000°C). This differs from black iron oxide, which changes color at 365°F from black to brown to red as it oxidizes. The color of red iron oxide changes from light pinkish to red to dark purplish red as the particle size increases.

Iron in Glazes

The most interesting thing about iron is that it can act both as a refractory and a flux. As red iron oxide, Fe_20_3, it is an amphoteric (refractory/stabilizer) similar in structure to alumina (Al_2O_3). But if it is reduced to black iron oxide (FeO) it acts as a flux similar in structure to calcium oxide (CaO). What this means is that a tenmoku glaze with 10% red iron oxide will be a stiff black glaze if fired in oxidation because the iron oxide acts as a refractory. But, if the same glaze is fired in reduction that 10% Fe_20_3 will be reduced to FeO, changing it to a flux, which will make it a glossy brown/black glaze that may run.

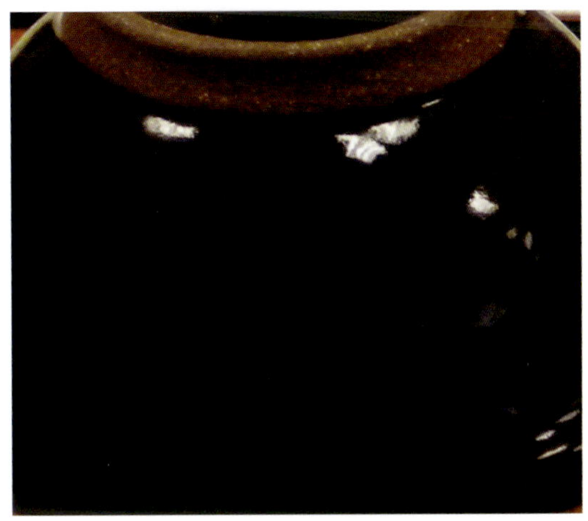

RON ROY BLACK

Cone 6

Talc	3 %
Whiting	6
Ferro Frit 3134	26
F-4 Feldspar	21
EPK Kaolin	17
Silica	27
	100 %
Add: Cobalt Carbonate	1 %
Red Iron Oxide	9 %

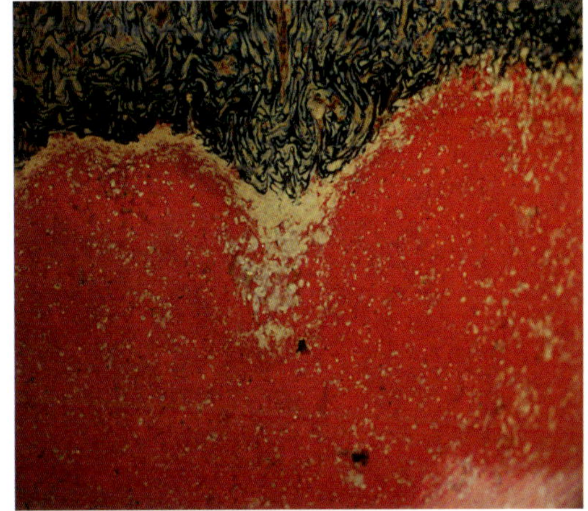

KETCHUP RED (JAYNE SHATZ)

Cone 6 oxidation

Gerstly Borate	31 %
Talc	14
Custer Feldspar	20
EPK Kaolin	5
Silica	30
	100 %
Add: Spanish Red Iron Oxide	15 %

Works best on dark colored stoneware. If used on a buff clay body, the red is less intense.

Another interesting property of iron oxide is that if it is fired in oxidation it will remain Fe_2O_3 until it reaches approximately 2250°F (approximately cone 8) where it will then reduce thermally to Fe_3O on its way to becoming FeO. The complex iron oxide molecule simply cannot maintain its state at those temperatures. This results in the release of an oxygen atom that will bubble to the surface of the hot glaze and pull a bit of iron with it. When it reaches the surface the oxygen releases the iron as it leaves the glaze, creating spots with greater concentrations of iron oxide. This is what creates an oil spot glaze. This reaction can easily be seen through the spy hole of a kiln or with draw tiles. There is an obvious and unmistakable bubbling. If heated further, these spots begin to melt and run down the pot, creating a distinctive "hare's fur" effect.

FORM	CHEMICAL NAME	CHARACTERISTICS	MOST COMMON USE
Red Iron Oxide	Fe_2O_3 ferric iron, Hematite	Most common form of iron and is a finely ground material that disperses well in glaze slurries, contains 69.9% Fe in the chemical formula, sold as: • Natural Red Iron Oxide or Brown 521 (85% purity) • Spanish Red Iron Oxide* (83–88% purity) • Synthetic Red Iron Oxide* (High Purity Red Iron or Red 4284) (96–99% purity). Very fine 325 mesh. Sometimes sold as the brand name Crocus Martis or Iron Precipitate.	Used in glazes, washes, slips, engobes, terra sigillatas, and clay bodies, used to make celadons, tenmoku, kaki, iron saturates, etc. Normally used from 1–30% in glazes.
Black Iron Oxide	FeO ferrous oxide, Wustite	Strongest form of iron, containing 72.3% Fe in the chemical FeO, sold as: • Natural Black Iron Oxide (85–95% purity) 100 mesh; is black in color and has a larger particle size. In glazes it's prone to speckling but is easily eliminated by ball milling. • Synthetic Black Iron Oxide* (99% purity) 325 mesh	Used in glazes, washes, slips, engobes, and terra sigillatas; used to make celadons, tenmoku, kaki, iron saturates, etc.
Yellow Iron Oxide	FeO (OH) ferric oxide hydrate, Geothite	Weakest form of iron, containing 62.9% Fe in the chemical formula, has a high LOI of 12%, sold as: • Synthetic Iron Oxide* (96% purity) 325 mesh • Yellow Ochre or Natural Yellow Iron Oxide (35% purity) contains impurities of calcium carbonate, silica, and sometimes manganese dioxide	Used in glazes, washes, slips, engobes, terra sigillatas, and clay bodies; used to make celadons, temmoku, kaki, iron saturates, etc.; sometimes yellow ochre is added to porcelain to make "dirty" porcelain (5–9%)
Umber, Burnt Umber		Calcined Umber which is a high-iron ochre material containing manganese	Used in glazes, washes, slips, engobes, terra sigillatas or claybodies to make a range of reddish-brown colors; darker than sienna and ochre (yellow iron)
Sienna, Burnt Sienna		Calcined Sienna, which is a high-iron ochre material with less manganese than umber	Used to make browns in glazes, washes, slips, engobes, terra sigillatas or clay bodies
Iron Chromate	Cr_2FeO_4	Contains chrome and iron oxide (ferric chromate); toxic— absorption, inhalation, and ingestion	Used to make dark colors in glazes, slips, engobes or clay bodies; can give gray, brown, and black; can give pink halos over tin white glazes
Ferric Chloride/ Iron Chloride	$FeCl_3$	Water soluble metal salt; toxic—corrosive/ caustic, affects liver, inhalation and ingestion	Used in low-fire techniques, like pit firing, aluminum foil saggars, horse hair and raku techniques; also used in water coloring on porcelain techniques
Iron Sulfate (Copperas)	$FeSO_4$	Water soluble metal salt, soluble form of iron, (aka Crocus Martis)	Salt used in water coloring on porcelain, raku, and low-fire soda
Iron Phosphate	$FePO_4$		Rarely used but can be used to develop iron red colors; sometimes used instead of bone ash as a source of phosphate without the calcium in synthetic bone ash (TCP or tri-calcium phosphate)
Rutile (light, dark, and granular)	TiO_2	Most common natural ore of titanium, containing various impurities including iron (up to 15%)	Used in glazes, washes, slips, engobes, and terra sigillatas to give yellows, tans, greens, blues, and milky, streaky, mottled textures; also used to produce crystalline glaze effects
Illmenite (powdered and granular)	$FeTiO_3$	Naturally occurring ore containing iron and titanium, higher in iron than rutile (when 25% or more iron is present)	Commonly used to produce speckles in glazes or clay bodies
Iron Clays		e.g., Redart, Albany slip, Alberta Slip, Barnard Slip (aka Blackbird Slip), Michigan slip, Lizella, laterite, and other assorted earthenware clays	Used in glazes, slip glazes, slips, engobes, terra sigillatas, and claybodies to make a range of reddish-brown colors
Magnetic Iron Oxide	Fe_3O_4 Magnetite	Iron scale or iron spangles—coarse, hard particles that resist melting and chemical breakdown	Gives speckles in clay bodies and glazes

Materials

THE MANY FACES OF IRON

by Dr. Carol Marians

One of the more fascinating, sometimes frustrating parts of ceramics is learning to balance the innumerable factors that affect the outcome of a firing. Glaze ingredients, the clay body used, firing cycles, atmospheres, kiln-stacking techniques and geography (to name a few variables) can all affect firing results.

This may be frustrating if you don't control those variables, but if you do, there is opportunity for new discoveries. By changing just one variable, the same glaze recipe can be deliberately manipulated to yield different results. In this instance, I decided to investigate one variable in an iron-rich glaze: the cooling period.

I achieved greatly differing results in a single glaze with a single clay body, consistent glaze thickness and application, and the same heating schedule for all of the firings. The differences in the resulting appearance of the glaze on the pots came exclusively from their heat treatment after they reached maturity.

When the witness cone bends, the glaze should be fully vitrified. The kiln has reached temperature, but has not yet begun to cool. I studied what happens between that point and the return of the kiln to room temperature. I found that I could get a glossy black surface, a densely textured rough surface, a golden red/mud color, or anything in between, just from different cooling schedules.

How Does This Happen?

At the top of the firing cycle, the glaze is matured, but not watery; it doesn't flow off the pot. At this point, the glaze is not a homogenous melt, but a mixture of several melts. It is not fully blended.

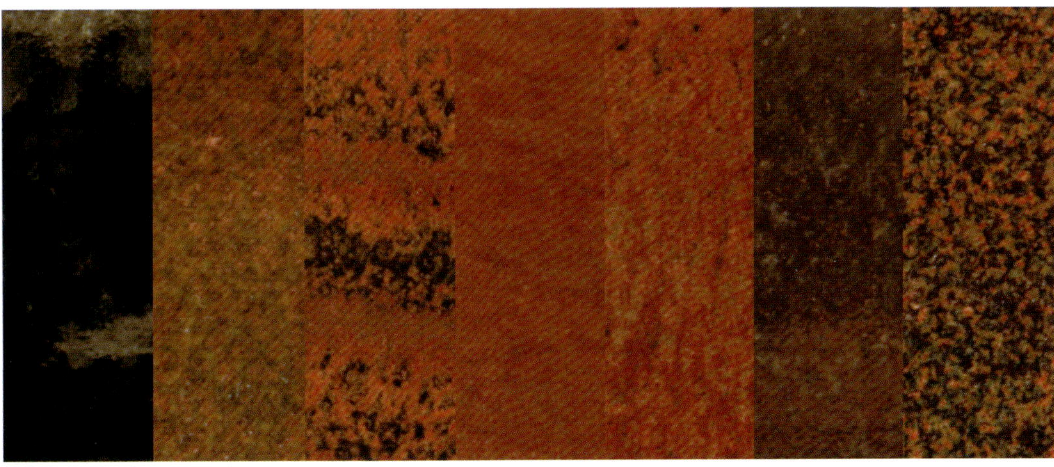

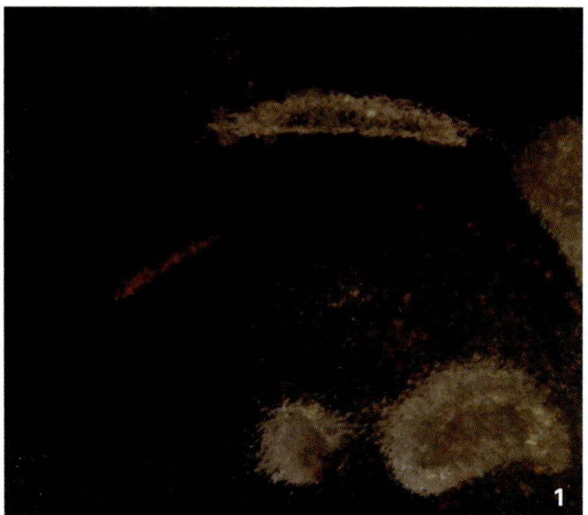
1

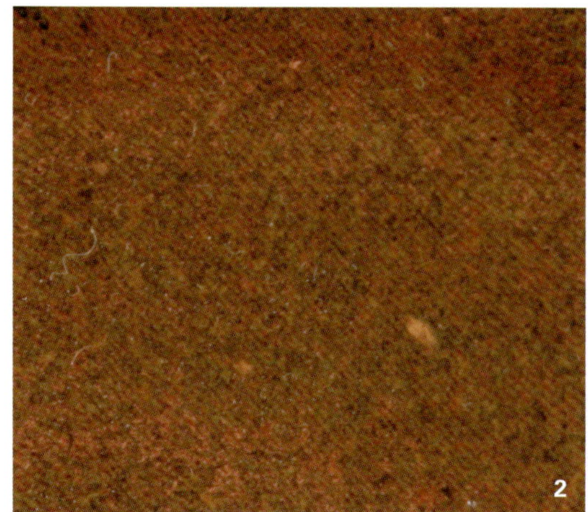
2

It may contain a dissolved second phase—in our case an iron compound—analogous to sugar dissolved in hot tea. More sugar dissolves in hot tea; less as the tea cools. The sugar precipitates as crystals as the tea cools. Our glaze, when melted, has a dissolved iron compound—the "sugar" in the tea. The iron precipitates as the glaze cools. So how does the iron form in the glaze?

Glaze is more complex and more viscous than tea, inhibiting motion. The iron crystals cannot precipitate and sink to the bottom of the glaze, nor can they grow very large, as the iron ions do not congregate in the same location. Instead, as the glaze cools, the dissolved iron separates out, forming numerous small crystals suspended in the glaze. The number of particles, and their eventual size, is affected by the surface texture of the underlying clay body, the cooling speed of the melt, the thickness of the glaze application and several other factors. The competition between the number and size of particles as the glaze cools results in the variety of desirable effects (see accompanying figures).

As it cools, the glaze becomes progressively more viscous and less mobile, until it reaches a temperature at which it "freezes" and nothing can move or precipitate within it. If the glaze is held at a temperature high enough to permit continued mobility of the iron into progressively larger crystals, but low enough that the glaze doesn't run off the pot, the surface will become matt. The multitude of tiny iron particles disrupt light transmission. Otherwise, the glaze solidifies with the same smooth, glossy surface as it had while fully melted. If the glaze is cooled quickly, few visible, very small particles form. Most of the visible color is the reflection off the smooth surface. This gives an aesthetically pleasing clear glossy black glaze, somewhat akin to a temmoku (see test 1). The opacity and depth of the glossy black show that the glaze can dissolve quite a lot of iron.

As the glaze cools and becomes more viscous, crystals begin to form at edges and imperfections in the body. If the glaze layer is thin, different kinds and shapes of crystal will form. If the crystals are stuck to the clay body at the bottom of a thick opaque glaze layer, they will be largely invisible. Crystals that float on top of the glaze give the appearance of sandpaper, which can present utilitarian problems. We want the crystals near the

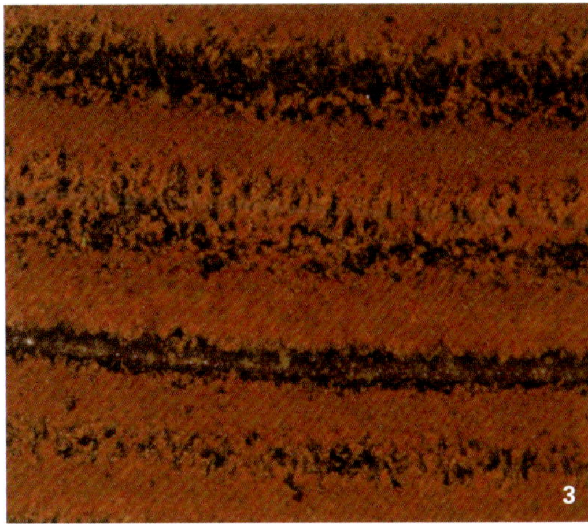

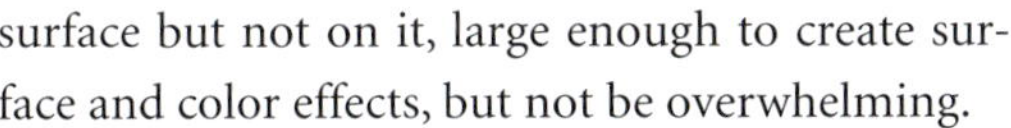

surface but not on it, large enough to create surface and color effects, but not be overwhelming.

A series of cool-down profiles with lots of jigs and jags showcases a different phase, exposing a range of surface effects. This translates into profiles with one or more narrow temperature ranges with extreme slow cooling and/or long holds, and possibly no retarded cooling outside the selected ranges. Since extended firing cycles can be costly, I framed my experiments with a maximum extension to 4-hour firing cycle.

I started out with the firing profile in Hesselberth and Roy's *Mastering Cone 6 Glazes*. The ramp for reaching temperature was a fast rise (200°F in the first hour, then 500°F per hour to 2100°F) until the last three hours, which had a rise of approximately 30°F per hour. Orton cones showed a hard cone 6. These firings were done in a very old Skutt 1227 with a computer controller. I examined the results of my firings and based my next firings on those results, only changing one factor with each firing. I chose 1450°F as a low end for controlled cooling, selecting intervals for markedly slow cooling in the 2200°–1450°F range.

Speculation

With this limited series of tests, I produced a variety of textures and colors, by "poking" the cool-down profile. Each firing included several identically glazed test pieces distributed throughout the kiln. I obtained an encouraging indication that the different results were caused by the cooling-down profiles and not extraneous effects. I next will explore whether maximal particle size growth takes place "hotter" than the temperature at which the greatest number of particles is formed. Cooling to approximately 1600°F, then reheating to around 1800°F should obtain both good numbers and development of microcrystals.

Test 1

Cool down: A continuous cool from cone 6 to 1500°F at –150° per hour.

Results: This is the cool-down profile from Hesselberth and Roy. It gave a predominantly glossy black glaze, not greatly different from the quick cool, but with a hint of variegated color. I could see isolated metallic bronze and red flecks, but no crystals breaking the surface.

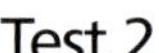

Test 2

Cool down: An uncontrolled drop from 2200°F to 1750°F, then –50° per hour from 1750°F to 1500°F.

Results: The cooling was slower from 2200°F down to 1450°F. Because the solubility of iron in glaze decreases at lower temperatures, I cooled at 1/3 the speed between 1750°F and 1500°F. The result was a substantially textured surface, with much visible variation, and crystals of a variety of colors breaking the surface. The glossy black was gone, and the surface variation uniformly distributed. There were a relatively small number of largish particles. The color was intermixed red, bronze and mud brown. Bronze predominated where the glaze was thickest. I interpreted this as substantial particle growth below 1750°F, with little precipitation of new particles.

Test 3

Cool down: An uncontrolled drop to 1750°F, then –50° per hour to 1600°F, a hold at 1600°F for one hour, then –50° per hour to 1500°F.

Results: By adding a one-hour hold at 1600°F, the color shifted from gold/brown to red/gold. The red and brown regions followed the throwing lines, indicating that glaze thickness has significant influence. The strength of this effect showed there is a critical region for this glaze's development somewhere near the temperature 1600°F.

Test 4

Cool down: An uncontrolled drop to 1750°F, hold at 1750°F for half an hour, then –50° per hour to 1650°F, hold at 1650°F for one hour, then –50° per hour to 1500°F.

Results: Adding a half-hour hold at 1750°F and a one-hour hold at 1650°F gave smaller particles and a near-smooth, lustrous satin, variegated bronze glaze with small specks of red and brown. The original glossy black was completely gone. Color variation in the throwing line showed the considerable effect that glaze thickness has. The half-hour hold at 1750°F facilitated the formation of a large number of small particles, leaving little free iron to add to crystal growth later. This uniform result was much like a pointillist painting, with exceedingly fine points. Moving the hold from 1600°F up to 1650°F could have a similar

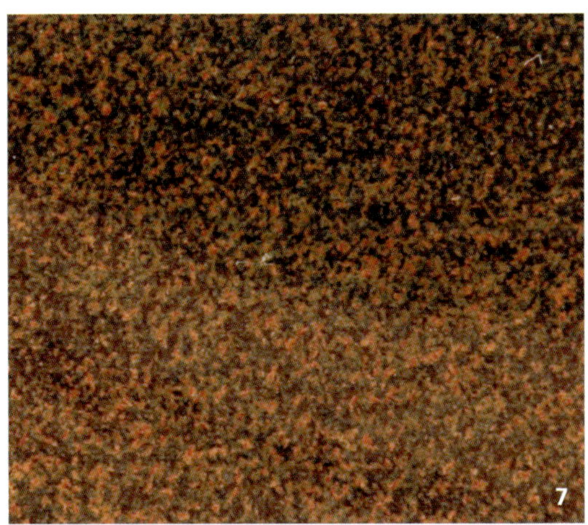

GA16 VARIATION
Cone 6

Ingredient	%
Bone Ash	4.6 %
Dolomite	13.6
Lithium Carbonate	4.6
Red Iron Oxide	9.1
Unispar	22.7
Bentonite	1.8
OM 4 Ball Clay	20.9
Silica	22.7
	100.0 %

The glaze used in these tests is a minor modification of the glaze GA16 from Michael Bailey's Cone 6 Glazes, poured thick on Georgies Ceramic Supply's G Mix 6 clay body.

effect. Alternatively, we could see this change as a result of the glaze spending more time in the critical temperature interval for crystal development.

Test 5

Cool down: An uncontrolled drop to 1800°F, then –50° per hour to 1450°F.

Results: As the previous test result could have come from extended time in the crystal growing range, or specifically from the hold at 1650°F and 1750°F, I gave this firing just as much time in the sensitive zone, but uniform decrease in temperature over the extended region. The results were similar to the previous test, but with larger grain size and a lizard-skin feel to the texture. The glaze was mottled and less uniform. The smooth satin look was gone. I concluded one of the holds in the previous test hit the "sweet spot," at which point many small particles form. I did not know at which level.

Test 6

Cool down: An uncontrolled drop to 2000°F, then –50° per hour to 1650°F.

Results: The slow cool from 2000°F to 1650°F gave a surface and color as in test 1, with a much greater number of gold particles. This also shows that the effects of test 4 depended on the 1650°F hold. This critical test showed that the greater color effect I wanted needed two holds.

Test 7

Cool down: From cone 6 to 2100°F at –50° per hour, then uncontrolled cooling to 1700°F, then –25° per hour to 1600°F.

Results: To test a second slow-cooling region, the kiln was cooled quickly from a peak of 1700°F, then slowly to 1600°F. The result was an intensely variegated effect with relatively few but larger particles in red and brown. The throwing lines were not prominent, so glaze thickness was not as important. The texture is lizard-skin satin, not the gloss of tests 1 and 5, nor the smooth satin of test 4. This result was related, but not quite like anything previous. This could be a jumping off point for a new series of tests.

Materials

CHROME OXIDE

by John Britt

Chrome oxide is a very powerful colorant that can at times be fickle. It mostly gives a wonderful range of strong greens, but it can also produce blues, browns, and even reds.

Properties and Characteristics

Chrome produces a wide range of greens, from a transparent glossy lime green to the more iconic, opaque, satin kelly green. The strong green color can often be modified by very small amounts of other oxides, like cobalt oxide, copper oxide, iron oxide, manganese dioxide, rutile, tin oxide, etc. In addition to green, chrome oxide also produces gray, brown, red, pink, and orange colors. It is also used in black glazes and stains to give a strong, true black color.

Chrome oxide comes to potters as a bright green powder derived from iron chromate. It is a very powerful colorant—even 0.1% can give a green color. Chrome is unaffected by oxidation and reduction but sometimes glazes that use chrome oxide appear to be affected by reduction because they also contain other oxides to influence their color and those are affected by reduction (like tin oxide, copper oxide, etc.)

Chrome oxide is an amphoteric oxide, which means it plays an intermediate role between fluxes and silica. It is generally very refractory and not very soluble in a glaze melt but sometimes it acts as a flux, e.g. as with the acidic tin oxide. The exact color it produces depends on the role chrome is fulfilling in the glaze. For example, in high alkaline or high boron glaze bases, when less than 1% chrome is added, it can dissolve well and give bright glossy transparent greens, (see Odyssey series 0.15/0.5%). In a zinc (zinc chromate) base it produces browns (see Chun glazes). In a high calcium or high strontium base without zinc, it can produce pinks, or crimson to burgundy colors (see Raspberry and Cranberry glaze). In a glaze that contains tin oxide, adding chrome pushes it toward shades of pink. The colors of chrome-tin pinks can be quite variable but consistent chrome-tin colors can be achieved by using commercial stains where the chrome and tin combination have been pre-melted together.

Because chrome oxide is volatile, placing a chrome green glaze next to a tin white glaze will often produce pink flashes on the tin white glaze. A good kiln vent can help to pull out the chrome fumes before they have time to latch onto the tin whites. But chrome flashing is best avoided by not mixing the two glazes in the same firing. Alternatively, if you like the pink flashing, this can be encouraged by mixing chrome greens and tin whites in a firing or even firing pieces in a partially closed saggar with a chrome green glaze painted on the inside wall of the saggar.

RASPBERRY AND CRANBERRY
Cone 6

Whiting	20.0 %
Ferro Frit 3134	14.0
Nepheline Syenite	18.0
Kentucky OM4 Ball Clay	18.0
Silica	30.0
	100.0 %

RASPBERRY

Add: Tin Oxide	7.5 %
Chrome Oxide	0.2 %

CRANBERRY

Add: Tin Oxide	3.8 %
Chrome Oxide	0.2 %

From *Mastering Cone 6 Glazes* by John Hesselberth and Ron Roy.

Raspberry base

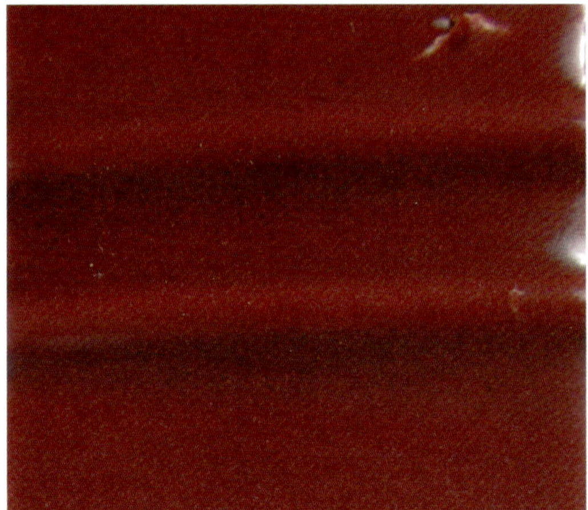
Raspberry base with 0.25% cobalt carbonate

Raspberry base with 8% Mason 6006 Stain

Chrome oxide gives a burgundy/red when combined with tin oxide at cone 6 in oxidation (see Raspberry, Cranberry or Chrome Red glazes). This iconic cone 6 glaze needs a specific formulation to be successful. First, there needs to be a specific ratio of tin oxide to chrome oxide. Start with 0.1–0.5% chrome oxide and 7.5–9.0% tin oxide. Remember that these are targets that should help you, but you can get red colors to develop with less amounts of tin oxide (see Cranberry glaze with 3.5% tin oxide). Varying the amounts will give a variety of pinks to deep burgundy colors. The calcium content of the glaze should be high (10–15% or 0.7–0.9 moles). It is also important to have no zinc in the recipe or the glaze will turn brown. Alumina is also best if kept low. Some recommend no magnesium oxide (talc, dolomite, or magnesium carbonate) in the base recipe while others use small amount of MgO to achieve interesting red/burgundy colors (see Burgundy/Red glaze). A thin application is best as a thicker coating may produce a gray glaze.

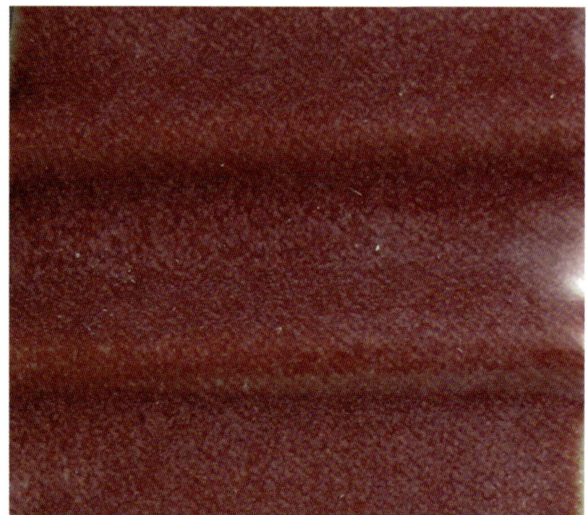

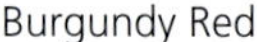
Burgundy Red

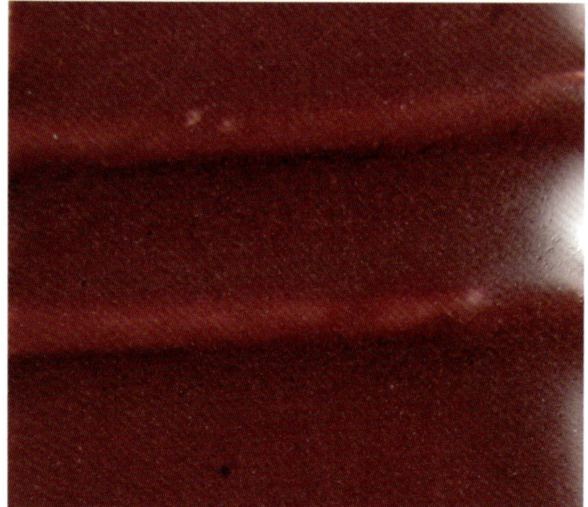

Chrome Red with 0.25% cobalt carbonate

BURGUNDY/RED
Cone 6

Gerstley Borate	8 %
Talc	4
Whiting	21
Ferro Frit 3134	9
Custer Feldspar	31
EPK Kaolin	9
Silica	18
	100 %
Add: Tin Oxide	5.00 %
Chrome Oxide	0.20 %

CHROME RED
Cone 6

Gerstley Borate	21 %
Whiting	20
Nepheline Syenite	16
EPK Kaolin	11
Silica	32
	100 %
Add: Tin Oxide	5.00 %
Chrome Oxide	0.15 %

You can also get chrome/tin reds at low-fire temperatures but they don't work well above cone 8. If you don't want to mess with the ratio of tin to chrome, an easy way to get cone 6 burgundy reds is to simply add 5–8% stain, such as Mason Deep Crimson 6006, (which contains calcium, chrome, tin, and silica), to a high-calcium base glaze (see Cranberry glaze).

Adding cobalt carbonate to a chrome/tin or burgundy/red can push the glaze toward purple but adding too much will overpower the red (see Raspberry and Chrome Red glaze tiles with added cobalt carbonate). You can also alter the tone of the burgundy/red glaze with small additions of iron oxide, rutile, or manganese dioxide.

Toxicity: While there is no legal limit set for safe leaching of chrome in glazes, potters should be aware that the legal level of allowable chrome oxide deemed safe for drinking water is 0.1 mg/L (ppm). Because chromium can have different valences, its toxicity and carcinogenic effects vary greatly. It is volatile at higher temperatures and is a toxic fume (fugitive chrome). Care should be taken when handling and firing chrome compounds.

CHUN BASE

Cone 6

Ingredient	%
Whiting	14 %
Zinc Oxide	12
F-4 Feldspar	38
Kentucky Ball Clay	6
Silica	30
	100 %

A great cone 6 electric base that is a nice clear and gives excellent colors except with chrome because it contains zinc, which turns brown.

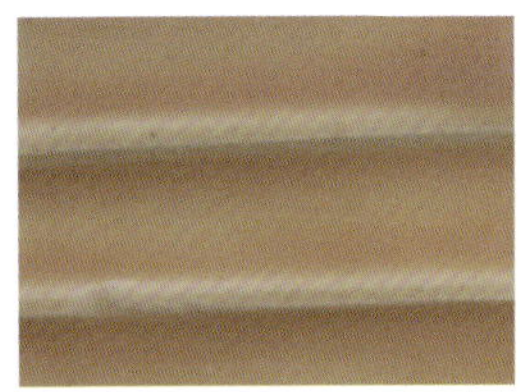

Chun Base with 0.15% chrome

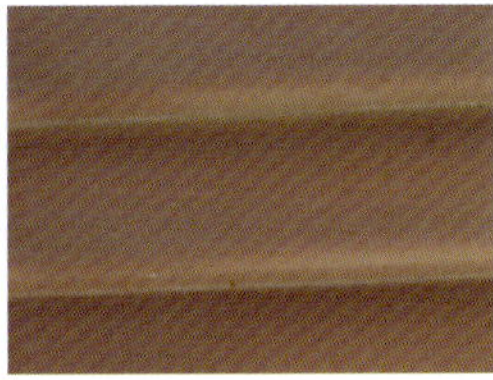

Chun Base with 0.5% chrome

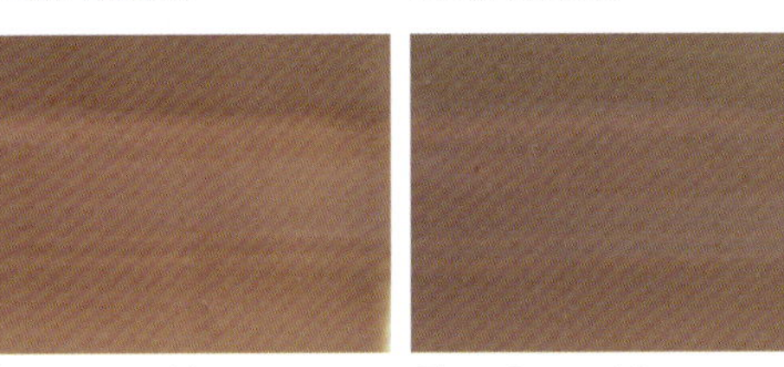

Chun Base with 1.0% chrome

Chun Base with 2.0% chrome

ODYSSEY BASE

Cone 6

Ingredient	%
Gerstley Borate	20%
Whiting	10
Nepheline Syenite	30
EPK Kaolin	10
Silica	30
	100%

A standard base from the Odyssey Center in Asheville, North Carolina. Contains high boron, calcium, and sodium, gives bright, glossy, transparent colors.

Odyssey Base with 0.15% chrome

Odyssey Base with 0.5% chrome

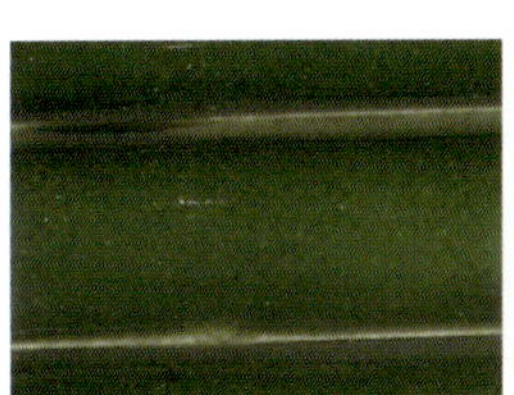

Odyssey Base with 1.0% chrome

Odyssey Base with 2.0% chrome

RANDY'S BASE

Cone 6

Ingredient	%
Gerstley Borate	31.7 %
Talc	13.8
F-4 Feldspar	19.8
EPK Kaolin	5.0
Silica	29.7
	100.0%

An excellent and popular base (originally from Randy's Red). Contains a lot of boron and low alumina, gives bright, glossy, transparent colors.

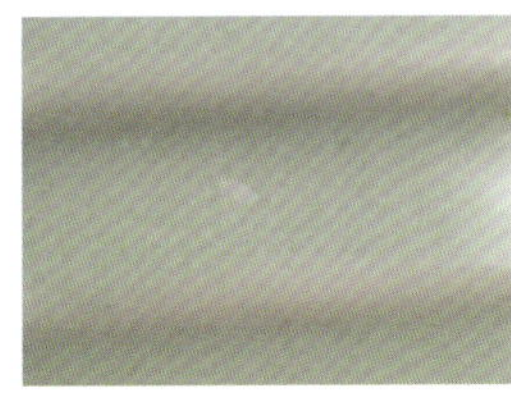

Randy's Base with 0.15% chrome

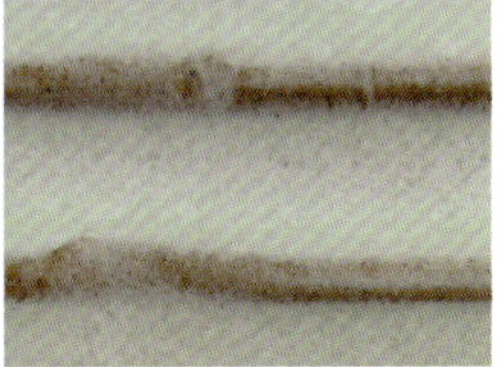

Randy's Base with 0.15% chrome on stoneware

Randy's Base with 0.5% chrome

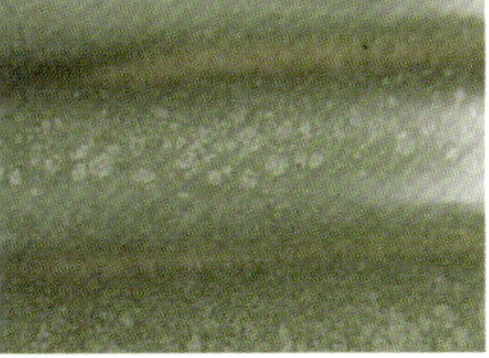

Randy's Base with 1.0% chrome

Materials

COBALT

by Dave Finkelnburg

Why Cobalt Is Blue

When a fired glaze is exposed to light, the color of the glaze depends entirely on which wavelengths of the light are absorbed by the valence electrons in the glaze colorants. The energy level of the valence electrons determines which photons it will absorb (absorb them all and you have black) or emit (emit them all and you have white). Emit only one wavelength and you have that color. Cobalt in a fired glaze usually absorbs all wavelengths of visible light except blue and thus a glaze containing cobalt is blue; however, two or more colorants in a glaze interact so that the wavelengths of light absorbed are different for the combination than for either colorant by itself. The interaction between atoms of one colorant, say cobalt, and another, say chrome, alters the energy level of the valence electrons of both elements. That is why we may add both cobalt (blue) and chrome (green) to get a glaze that is turquoise.

Cobalt in Use

If we use lots of talc, dolomite or another source of magnesium in a cobalt glaze, a beautiful bubble-gum purple glaze can be the result! Magnesium oxide (MgO) shifts the wavelengths of light emitted from our fired cobalt glaze from blue to purple. Every mole of flux should include more than 0.2 moles of MgO to get purple. Make a line blend varying MgO content to test for the shade of purple desired. Lesser amounts of MgO will produce lavender, larger amounts combined with an opacifier will produce a strong grape purple.

Alumina and titania in a cobalt glaze will shift the fired glaze color from blue to green. Because a significant amount of alumina can be dissolved from the clay body by the glaze during firing, glaze thickness can cause the same glaze to turn blue (where thick) and green (where thin) on the same piece. Glaze layering can have a similar effect with layering of the cobalt glaze over a white glaze firing blue but the cobalt glaze alone firing green. Cobalt greens are invariably satin to matte rather than glossy glazes. These glazes are typically flux saturated and the matteness comes from precipitating crystals of the flux in combination with aluminum and silicon. The amount of titanium oxide used, either as rutile or titanium dioxide, influences the green color. While cobalt greens have been reported using as much as 7.5% rutile in a cone 9 glaze, 2% rutile is far more typical. Less rutile also helps avoid pinholes in the glaze. Cobalt's spectrum of effects can be seen at all temperatures.

Black glazes are typically achieved using cobalt oxide or cobalt carbonate plus a blend of iron and other metallic oxides. Typical cobalt levels are between 1 and 3% and iron levels up to 9%. The total of all the colorant oxides need not be more than 10 or 11%. Cobalt should be used with care—it is expensive, and in thick applications, too much cobalt can make a glaze fluid enough to flow off the ware. Iron is not required to make a black glaze, but as an alternative, it is inexpensive, readily available, and non-toxic. One or more of the oxides of copper, manganese, and chrome are added in many black glazes. Black glazes high in iron tend to fade brown and glazes with high amounts of cobalt tend to fade blue over white glazes. A simple black glaze can be made with 9% red iron oxide plus 2% cobalt. If other oxides are used, a good starting point is 4% iron, 2% cobalt, 2% manganese dioxide, and 2% copper oxide.

BLACK MATTE GLAZE

Cone 6

Whiting	17.9 %
Zinc Oxide	8.0
Potash Feldspar	49.2
EPK Kaolin	19.9
Silica	5.0
	100.0 %
Add: Red Iron Oxide	6.7 %
Cobalt Oxide	1.3 %

Materials

SILICON CARBIDE

by Mark Chatterley

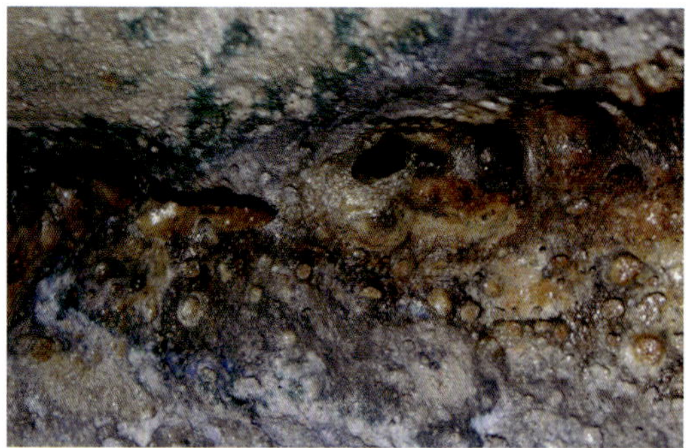

Silicon carbide (SiC) is found naturally in a rare material called moissanite that comes from meteors, but the silicon carbide we use is synthetic. Used in small amounts (0.5%, 500 mesh) in copper red glazes, it enhances reduction. In larger amounts, it creates bubbles from carbon gas coming through the glaze. The larger the grit size, the bigger the craters will be. It can cause glazes to spit in the kiln. Placing a layer of sand down makes it easy to clean the shelves. If you fire an electric kiln, you will need to put silicon carbide glazed work in an unsealed saggar to protect the elements (and other work, for that matter).

It only takes one coat of cream consistency glaze covering the work to get a bubbly, crusty surface. If you apply more than one coat, larger reactions happen. The faster you cool the glaze the more you "freeze" the bubble effect. These glazes are not food safe. They can also have sharp edges on the ends of the craters so caution should be used when handling the work.

CHATTERLEY GLAZE
Cone 6

Gillespie Borate	50.0 %
Kaolin	17.5
Silica	32.5
	100.0 %
Add: Silicon Carbide (180 grit)	20.0 %
Sand	12.0 %

M & M ALTERED
Cone 5–6

Gerstley Borate	18.0 %
Whiting	16.0
Custer Feldspar	40.0
EPK Kaolin	10.0
Silica	16.0
	100.0 %

BOB'S ALTERED
Cone 6

Bone Ash	9.1 %
Dolomite	9.1
Gerstley Borate	9.1
Talc	9.1
Nepheline Syenite	18.2
EPK Kaolin	18.2
Silica	27.2
	100.0 %

Control (no additions) | **20% Silicon Carbide** | **1.5% Cobalt Oxide** | **20% Silicon Carbide 1.5% Cobalt Oxide** | **10.5% Copper Oxide** | **10.5% Copper Oxide 20% Silicon Carbide**

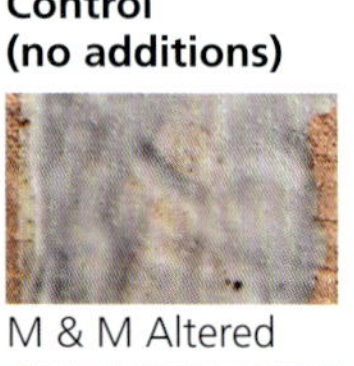
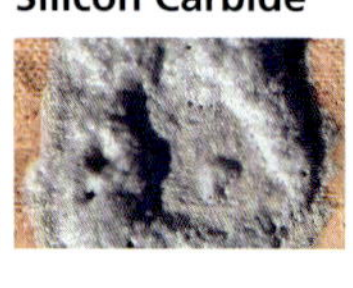
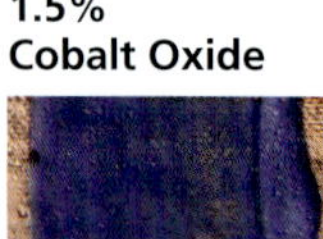
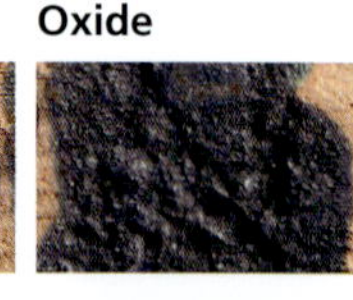
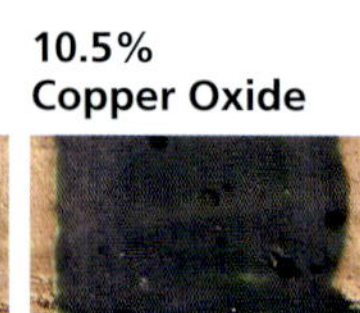
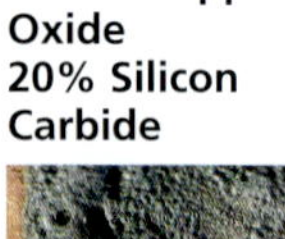
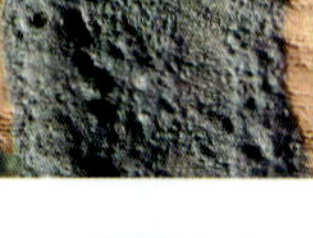
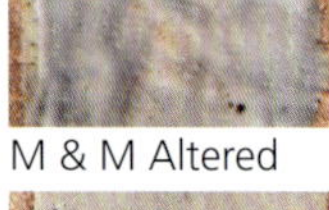

M & M Altered

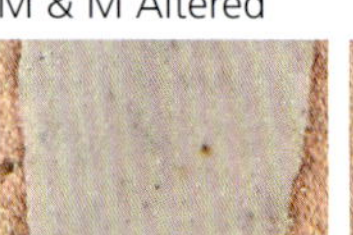
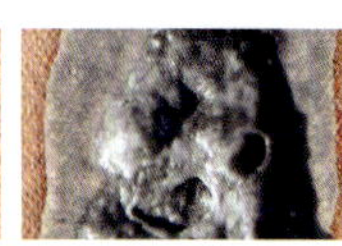

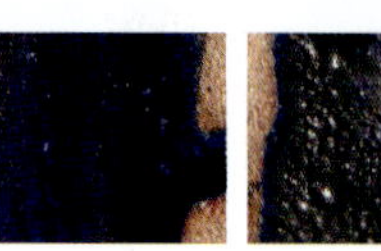
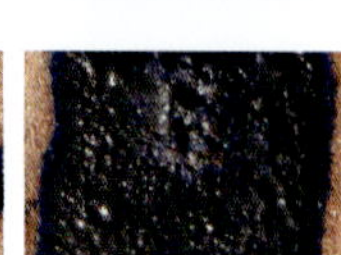

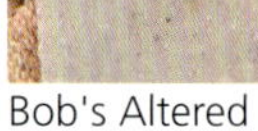

Bob's Altered

Materials

CERAMIC STAINS

by John Britt

Ceramists today are spoiled. It wasn't that long ago that getting the colors and surfaces you wanted took a lifetime of work to achieve. But today because of the developments in modern stain technology, we have practically every color in the rainbow at our finger tips.

Properties and Characteristics

Historically, potters made glaze from feldspar, ash, and whatever iron-rich clays were available locally. This usually meant brown pots, or occasionally another earth-tone color. Then they began using metal oxides—like copper, chrome, manganese, iron oxides—and blending them with opacifiers to create colors. There is historic evidence that colored frits were used at least as early as 2600 BCE. Egyptian blue was a combination of silica, limestone, sodium, and copper oxides. This required a great deal of knowledge about glaze chemistry and firing to achieve the desired colors. And this knowledge was something that was in short supply, so potters basically accepted the glazes they stumbled upon and liked enough to build a body of work around.

Stains are a mixture of ceramic oxides and coloring metal oxides that are melted in kilns, quenched, ground to specific mesh size (some are acid washed), and colored with organic dyes to simulate the fired color. Essentially they are fritted colorants. They are made and manufactured for several reasons: to provide a consistent and stable form of colorant that doesn't dissolve in the glaze melt as easily as coloring metal oxides; to make colorants safer to use than raw metal oxides (commercial stains are less soluble in water); to allow

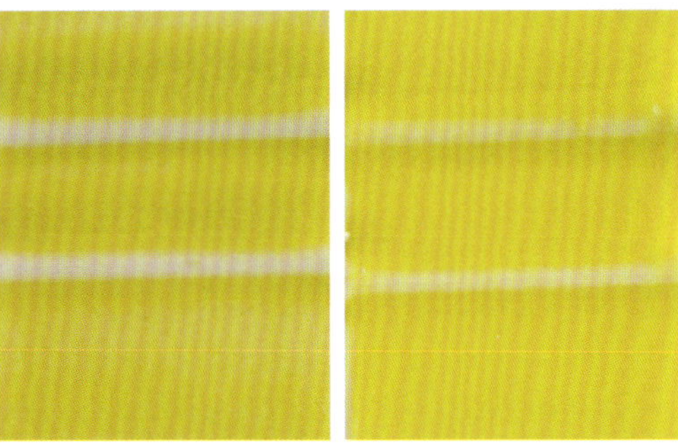

Degussa Yellow 239496 stain 4% in 5 × 20 Base Glaze on porcelain, fired to cone 6 in an electric kiln.

Degussa Yellow 239496 stain 8% in 5 × 20 Base Glaze on porcelain, fired to cone 6 in an electric kiln.

Praseodymium Yellow 6433 stain 4% in 5 × 20 Base Glaze on porcelain, fired to cone 6 in an electric kiln.

Praseodymium Yellow 6433 stain 8% in 5 × 20 Base Glaze on porcelain, fired to cone 6 in an electric kiln.

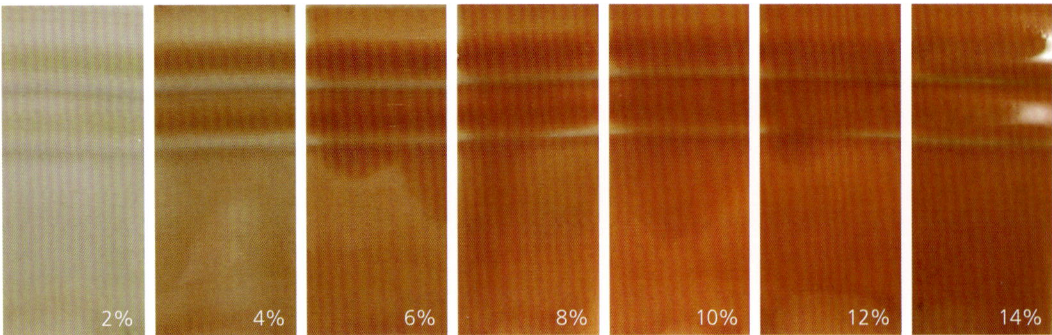

Progression blend of Degussa Orange 239616 stain in 5 × 20 Base Glaze on porcelain, fired to cone 6 in an electric kiln, showing a transparent glaze with only 2% stain and an opaque glaze with 14% stain.

repeatable and consistent results with minimal effort; and to allow you to fine tune your color selection to get the color you want at a reasonable cost. They can appear expensive, but time is money. Consider the countless hours of glaze testing that would be necessary without the consistency of a dependable commercial stain, then the prices are more reasonable.

Commercial stain companies provide a detailed list of what oxides are present in each stain. The exact recipe is proprietary, but knowing what oxides are used in a given stain can give you great clues as to how a color is achieved or how to encourage or prevent particular effects. For example, there are several different black stains. One is Best Black while another choice is Cobalt-Free Black. If you're using a white glaze with a black-stained glaze next to it, you may notice that a blue line develops at the overlap. If you don't want that line, you can look in the stain chart and choose the black stain without cobalt—the cause of the blue line. This chart also tells the base glaze structure that is necessary for each stain to work. Before deciding on a color, it is advisable to look at the reference notes associated with that stain. Sometimes called the Base Glaze Guide, this information indicates the specific requirements to achieve each color. For example, the name is listed, followed by the oxides it contains, and finally a list of numbers such as 3, 5, and 9; each indicating information important to the mixing, firing, etc., to that stain: #3: Maximum firing limit 2300°F, #5: Do not use zinc in glaze, and #9: Glaze must contain 6.7–8.4% CaO (12–15% $CaCO_3$). Each manufacturer will have a full list of reference notes for their stains.

Each color is not guaranteed in all bases, and being aware of these reference notes will help you achieve greater success. Stains are not meant for all firing conditions and are generally designed for neutral or oxidation firing atmospheres (although some may work in reduction atmospheres). Because stains contain coloring metal oxides along with other ceramics materials like opacifiers, silica, and alumina, adding them to certain glaze bases can cause a glossy glaze surface to turn matte.

Stains are generally added at 5–8% in a glaze and 15–25% in slips and clay bodies. At 8% most of the glazes are opaque and flat but if you add smaller amounts of stain (1–3%) it is possible to get transparent colors, including some very nice transparent celadon-colored glazes, when fired in an electric kiln or similar neutral atmosphere.

Encapsulated (Inclusion) Stains

Specialty stains, called encapsulated stains, allow potters to get colors that were once not possible with traditional stains. These stain types, also known as inclusion stains or inclusion pigments, are zirconium silicate with cadmium sulfoselenide crystals (Ca/Se). Dave Finkelnburg explains that the discovery of the encapsulation process (the melting of the colorants into a zirconium

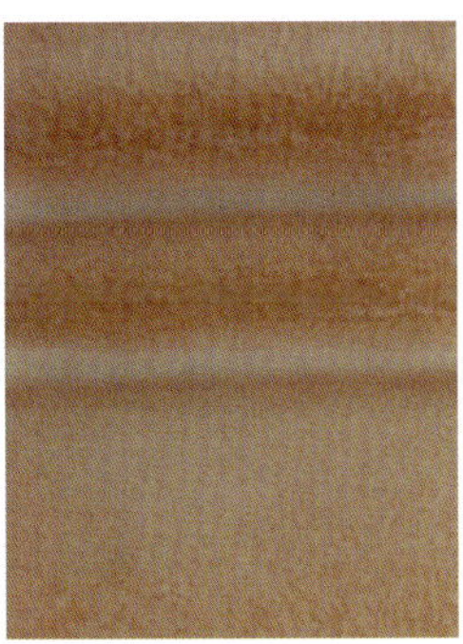
Degussa Intensive Red 279496 stain, 4% in 5 × 20 Base Glaze on porcelain, fired to cone 6 in an electric kiln.

Degussa Intensive Red 279496 stain, 8% in 5 × 20 Base Glaze on porcelain, fired to cone 6 in an electric kiln.

silicate glass at high temperatures) has now made the many hues of yellow through red reliable at temperatures through cone 10 in both oxidation and reduction atmospheres." The addition of 3% zirconium silicate will produce an even brighter color. These stains are refractory at higher temperatures, they do not melt much, if at all.

As Tony Hansen writes on Digital Fire (www.digitalfire.com), "Encapsulated stains are not, as the name suggests and some misunderstand, a zircon capsule around an otherwise unstable compound. Rather they are manufactured by sintering to form a crystalline matrix (in a process called encapsulation)." Inclusion stains have specific firing temperatures and duration of firing protocols as well as warnings about not ball milling the stains (which will allow release of cadmium and/or selenium). If the fired glaze surface is damaged it can release the crystals.

Finkelnburg also states that cadmium stains can produce food-safe colors; however, under certain circumstances, it can be leached from the fired glaze. He adds that a sample of any cadmium-stain-tinted glaze used on potential food surfaces should be tested for leaching by a qualified laboratory.

Washes

Washes made with commercial stains can be used both over and under many glazes. Mason Color Works recommends mixing 85% stain and 15% Ferro frit 3124 as a starting point, but many potters us a 50% stain and 50% frit ratio with good success. When used under a glaze, cover with a transparent or semi-transparent glaze. When used over a glaze, be sure to have sufficient flux in the mix because if the stain or wash is too thick, it can turn into a crusty surface after the firing.

A very popular use of washes is on majolica-glazed work. Potters using majolica often mix 50% stain with 50% frit or Gerstley borate to brush designs on top of the white majolica-base glaze. If the stains are refractory, as listed by the manufacturer, increase the flux—use 1 part stain and 4 parts frit or Gerstley borate.

Discovering New Colors

A triaxial blend is a method of testing three ingredients on a three-axis system similar to a two-ingredient line blend.

Often triaxial blends are used to test the primary ingredients in a glaze base, (for example, feldspar, whiting, and kaolin). It is often employed when you don't have a percent analysis to reference. If you have a percent analysis, you can use a glaze software program to predict glaze surfaces, but if you don't, a triaxial blend is the empirical method to see how they melt.

Another use of the triaxial system is color blending. In this method, you keep the base glaze the same and vary the colorants (oxides or stains or even opacifiers). In this triaxial color blend, I tested various stains to develop different colors. Since we do not know the exact amounts of oxides in commercial stains, blending them in a triaxial can reveal surprising and unusual colors.

A 21-point triaxial is a systematic blending of three variables with 100% of each variable at the three corners. So in this case, Mason Deep Crimson #6006 is corner A at 100%, Mason Sky Blue #6363 is corner B at 100% and Mason Praseodymium Yellow #6433 is corner C at 100%. The flow along the vertices is then 80/20, 60/40, 40/60, 20/80. Instead of using the numbers directly from the triaxial chart, I used 4 grams of stain at each corner. So 100% = 4 grams and then I figured out that 80% of 4 grams was 3.4 grams, 60% was 2.4 grams, and 20% was 0.8 grams. Then I substituted those numbers into the triaxial mixtures. For the triaxial glaze chart shown at the right, I used the 5×20 Base Glaze as shown below.

For additional testing you can also add metallic oxides to stains to change the colors or add visual textures; add 3% Zircopax to brighten a color; add 3% titanium dioxide to make colors slightly more variegated; add 1% copper carbonate to any stain to push it toward green. The list can go on and on.

5 X 20 BASE GLAZE
Cone 6

Wollastonite	20 %
Custer Feldspar	20
Ferro Frit 3134	20
EPK Kaolin	20
Silica	20
	100 %

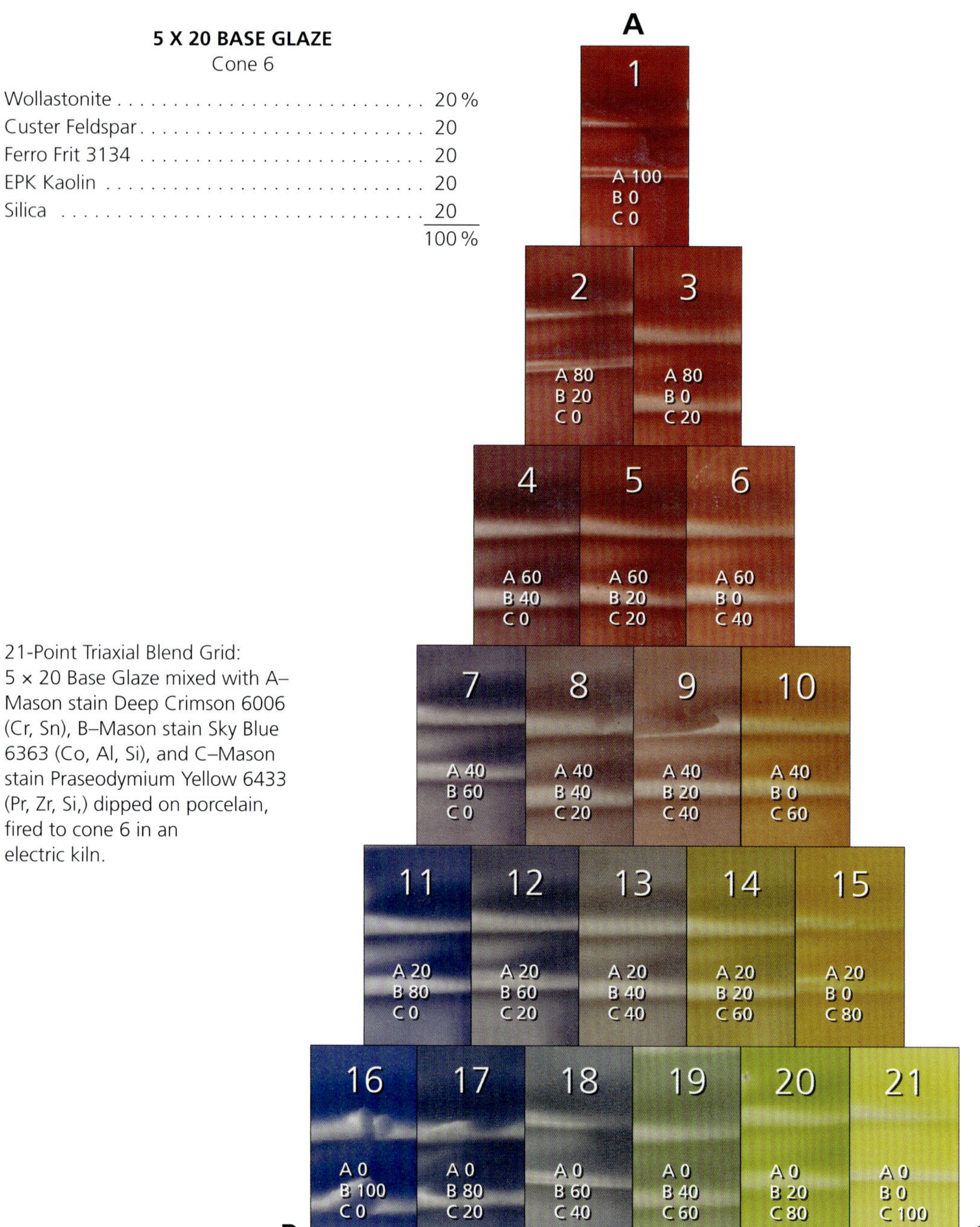

21-Point Triaxial Blend Grid: 5 × 20 Base Glaze mixed with A–Mason stain Deep Crimson 6006 (Cr, Sn), B–Mason stain Sky Blue 6363 (Co, Al, Si), and C–Mason stain Praseodymium Yellow 6433 (Pr, Zr, Si,) dipped on porcelain, fired to cone 6 in an electric kiln.

Materials

SUSPENDERS AND BINDERS

by David Pier

Potent additives can make your life much easier and increase your glazing success. Put the drudgery of extensive stirring and flaws from fragile,unfired glaze coatings behind you.

Gaining Control of the Mix

A suspender is simply any additive whose primary purpose is to slow or eliminate settling. They typically work by absorbing a huge amount of water, thereby thickening (increasing the viscosity of) the glaze. A binder is any additive whose primary purpose is to harden the dry, unfired glaze coat. Binders usually make it easier to apply multiple and thick glaze coats. Most of these materials function as both suspenders and binders; there is only one common material that is exclusively a binder, and that's gum arabic. Only flocculents can sometimes improve suspension while actually worsening binding. Therefore, for the rest of this discussion, the word suspender will mean suspender/binder.

Because suspenders absorb so much water, glazes containing them shrink more when drying. This can sometimes lead to cracking and crawling, especially when using suspenders in quantities exceeding the recommended ranges, but more often suspenders actually decrease cracking because their binding power increases cohesiveness and because they dry slowly, which gives the glaze more time to adjust to the stress of shrinking.

These additives can be broadly divided into organic and mineral categories. Mineral suspenders are clay-like minerals and are, by far, the most frequently used (when added to clay bodies they increase plasticity, but mixed up by themselves they are not plastic and so are not clay). They can be used as the only suspending material in a glaze. Their effects on suspension are more dramatic than on binding, but they do improve binding. They become part of the fired glaze, but because their chemical composition is similar to clay (and they are typically used at only about 2% of dry ingredients) they usually do not noticeably alter the final appearance. The most common mineral suspenders are bentonite and Veegum-T. There are many different sources of bentonite, varying somewhat in strength and quite a bit in iron and other impurity content. In most circumstances the different mineral suspenders can be used interchangeably, perhaps with a small adjustment in quantity to account for different potencies. Mineral suspenders usually exhibit thixotropy, which means they gel when not being stirred. This improves suspension more than simply increasing the viscosity, sometimes completely preventing any settling.

Organic suspenders, usually called gums, are usually even more potent in most ways than the mineral suspenders. They also have the advantage of almost completely burning out and therefore leaving the fired glaze unaltered. Many of them also are more effective binders than the mineral suspenders. One drawback is that they will rot after several days to months if there is no preservative. Not only do they lose effectiveness, but it makes a nasty stink. This rotting is easily prevented by the addition of a preservative. There are some preservatives sold specifically for this, but they are quite toxic to people as well as to the bacteria. I have found the best preservative is one you already have in your studio: copper carbonate. It only requires 0.04% of total dry batch (0.4g $CuCO_3$ per 1000g dry glaze) to indefinitely prevent rotting. This amount of copper, if properly dispersed, is almost never visible in the fired glaze.*

Suspenders, most dramatically the organic gums, also slow the drying of glazes. Sometimes this is an advantage, as it allows easier brushing, or touching up of drips after dipping. Too slow, though, and glazing takes longer, since it is hard to put the piece down until the glaze has dried. If you start your experimentation with usage levels at the lower end suggested in the chart, and then work your way up, you will find the quantity that balances suspending, binding, and drying time to best suit your work habits. CMC gum is particularly potent in slowing drying.

CMC gum is the most common gum and is typically used in brushing glazes, as it is better at binding and slowing drying than it is at suspending. CMC doesn't exhibit thixotropy, and can actually reduce any thixotropy already present, so it only slows rather than prevents settling. Much of CMC's prevalence is due to CMC having been available for many decades before most of the other gums. A recently introduced organic gum, MAGMA, exhibits strong thixotropy and can prevent settling of any glaze, indefinitely, without as much slowing of drying time as CMC. Because of the thixotropy, MAGMA is more or less suitable for different brushing techniques. (MAGMA is suitable for all applications, but CMC is often preferable for brushing since it provides smoother brushstrokes due to slower drying. However, that

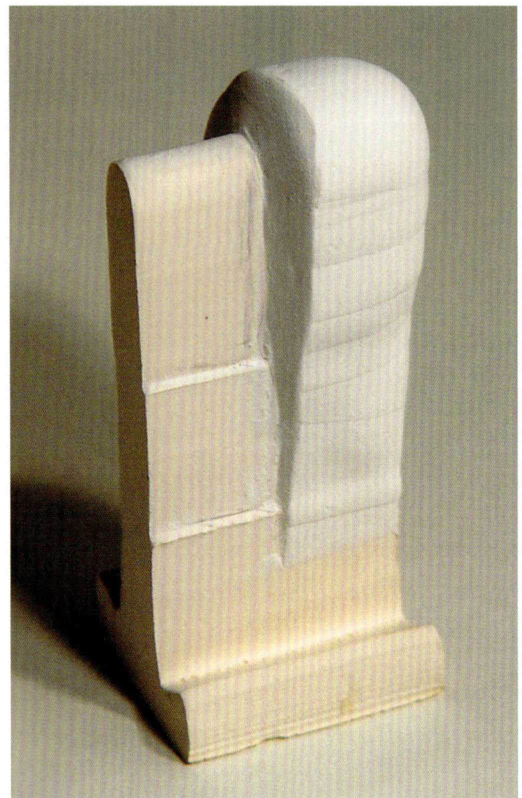

Repeatedly dipped in a simple glaze (100% frit with 3% added MAGMA), the above tile shows how a good binder allows unlimited glaze layering as well as carving. The glaze on the left half of the tile was carved away without chipping the remaining glaze.

should be weighed against the potential for dripping of CMC glazes on dipped pots.)

There are many other organic gums available, although not usually from ceramic suppliers. Most of them behave similarly to CMC gum, although potency varies widely.

Tips for Smooth Mixing

If you leave these additives out of your slips and glazes, they'll look pretty much the same after the firing as if you had put them in. So why bother? Imagine big buckets of glazes that only need a few seconds of stirring, even if they have been sitting unused for over a year. Imagine unfired glazes that never chip because they are as hard as the bisque they are applied to! It isn't magic that makes commercial, ready-to-use glazes so easy to use; it's the additives. Most of these materials are sold as dry powders. If you sprinkle them into your already-mixed glazes, you'll get little globs that will hinder rather than help glazing. If you try to sieve them, you'll be trying all day and night. Below are two basic methods of adding suspenders to your slip or glaze while avoiding clumping and excess water.

ADD TO AN EXISTING WET GLAZE

1. Calculate/estimate the maximum amount of suspender you might end up using in the batch. If you end up mixing more than you need, consider mixing in a preservative.
2. Add suspender powder to hot water. For every 20 gr suspender add 80 ml of hot water, then add a little more water bringing the concentrate to a total of 100 ml.
3. Mix with a hand blender, or wait a few hours for the mixture to thoroughly combine into a gel/syrup; depending on the suspender it might take some time, even overnight.
4. Add gel/syrup in small increments to your glaze.
5. Mix together with an electric mixer until the suspender is thoroughly dispersed.

CMC Gel/Syrup to Wet Glaze	
Mixed Wet Glaze (approximate amounts)	**CMC Gum Gel/Syrup (approximate amounts)**
4 oz.	add 3/4 tsp.
20 oz.	add 3 3/4 tsp.
40 oz.	add 2 1/2 Tbsp.
1 Gallon	add 1/2 cup
3 Gallons	add 1 1/2 cups

ADD SUSPENDER TO A DRY GLAZE BATCH

1. Calculate and weigh out an appropriate quantity of suspender, add preservative if necessary. (Typically 0.5–2%; for the example below we are using 0.75%)
2. Mix suspender (and preservative powders) with the glaze dry ingredients. The combination and mixing of dry ingredients will prevent the suspender from clumping.
3. Use hot water unless contraindicated by another ingredient. The hotter the water, the faster the dispersion will be.
4. Add the dry mixture to a normal amount of water for the glaze batch (the glaze will be thicker than normal). Wait a few hours to ensure full dispersion and absorption then sieve the glaze as usual.

Dry CMC Gum to Dry Glaze	
Mixed Glaze Dry Ingredients (approximate amounts)	**Dry CMC Gum (approximate amounts)**
100 grams	add 0.75 grams
500 grams	add 3.75 grams
1000 grams	add 7.5 grams
3500 grams	add 26 grams
10,000 grams	add 75 grams

Materials

GLAZE ADDITIVES

by Jessica Knapp

Glaze additives are the secret ingredients that make average glazes great. Sometimes the glazes we use are fine for one application method, but disappointing for others. A glaze might perform well when dipping or pouring, but dry so quickly when brushing that your brush sticks to the pot. Commercial glazes might have the opposite problem, brushing easily, but having a consistency that's too thick for pouring or dipping applications.

There are several glaze additives that help solve these various shortcomings, by conditioning your glazes for brushing, dipping, or pouring. They fall into the categories of suspenders and binders. According to Dave Pier (a ceramic artist who is well versed on glaze additives and has even developed one), most glaze additives do a little of both, fixing suspension problems while also enhancing the bond between bisque ware and the raw glaze. Some, like CMC Gum, Magma, and Spectrum Brushing Media, are organic, while others, like Spectrum Suspender, bentonite, Veegum-T, and Bentone MA/Macaloid, are clay-like materials. Spectrum's Glaze Thinner is a sodium hexamethaphosphate solution, and Apt-II Ceramic Enhancer is an acrylic emulsion additive.

The organic materials and products are great binders, and also help with suspension. They need to be used in small glaze batches, or if added to larger ones, a preservative needs to be added as well to prevent them from rotting. The materials listed are best at keeping a glaze in suspension, but also help somewhat in binding.

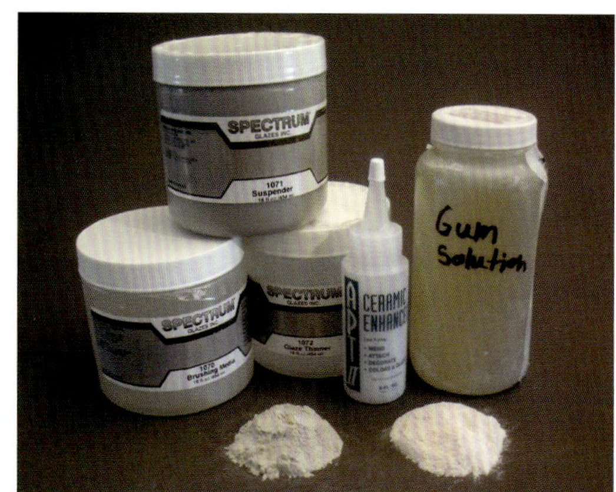

Various glaze additives can help your favorite glazes excel at various application methods. Along with the liquid-based products featured in the back row, bentonite (left front), Veegum-T (right front), and many other powder-based additives are also available.

Testing Methods

To test various additives, I used a transparent clear base glaze to which I added different Mason stains as colorants to differentiate each one.

For the manufactured liquid products, I followed the instructions on the label for how much to add to a specific volume of already mixed glaze. For the dry materials, I used 20 grams of suspender/binder added to 100 ml (100 grams) of water. I allowed the dry material to absorb the water overnight, then mixed it thoroughly. I added it to the glaze at a volumetric ratio of 1 part binder to 8 parts glaze. Some suspenders are more potent than others, so as a general rule use between 0.5% and 2% by weight (of the dry ingredients). Testing is key for figuring out the ratios that work best. For really small quantities of glaze, add the suspender by the drop until it has the desired consistency.

Brushing

Bentonite and Veegum-T are not as beneficial for brushing applications as they don't really change the rate at which the glaze dries. The brush still tended to stick and drag across the surface.

CMC Gum, Apt-II, Spectrum Brushing Media, and Magma all improved the glaze's brushability. They slow the drying time, allowing for more movement of the glaze before it soaks into the bisque-fired pot, and reduce the surface tension of the glaze so that it's more willing to flow rather than just stick to itself. Once the first coat of glaze was dry, a second coat could be brushed on without disturbing the first coat.

Tip: If you don't have any of these materials on hand, a few drops of liquid dish soap added to a glaze can improve brushability by reducing the glaze's surface tension. It won't affect the durability of the dry glaze surface though.

When brushing colored glazes over a raw base glaze, I found that CMC Gum, Apt-II, Spectrum Brushing Media, and Spectrum Glaze Thinner helped, as they dried more slowly and flowed smoothly.

Dipping and Pouring

Bentonite and Veegum-T work well for dipping and pouring, as do Spectrum's Glaze Thinner and Suspension Agent. The glazes required less stirring before use, and adhered well to the test tiles.

For the glazes tested, CMC Gum, Apt-II, Spectrum Brushing Media, and Magma allowed for thicker glaze coatings when dipping. Glazes with Magma added to them can be built up into very thick coatings without chipping.

All of these products are also suited for techniques that call for carving away glaze. Since they improve binding qualities of the raw glaze, the glaze coating is harder, and therefore the carved lines can be very precise.

Re-glazing

CMC Gum, Magma, and Spectrum Brushing Media helped when attempting to re-glaze an already glaze-fired piece. They worked even at room temperature; however, as they take a little while to dry, the process took longer and the coats tended to be thin. Glaze material did build up on the surface though, and so when pieces were pre-heated, the re-glazing process went faster and was an improvement over results without additives.

Apt-II was the only product that enabled a thick layer of glaze to be applied in one coat to the surface of an already glaze-fired piece without preheating the piece. It's an acrylic-based medium and so has different properties than the other three products tried, which are organic gums.

Conclusion

If you apply your glazes in a variety of ways, the best thing to do is to have a large container of your base glaze and pour some into smaller containers then mix in the appropriate additive for this smaller amount. If the larger glaze batch doesn't behave well, you can then add a suspender/binder (and preservative if using an organic binder) to the mix.

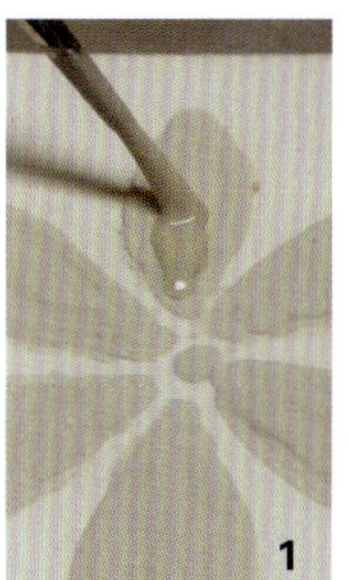
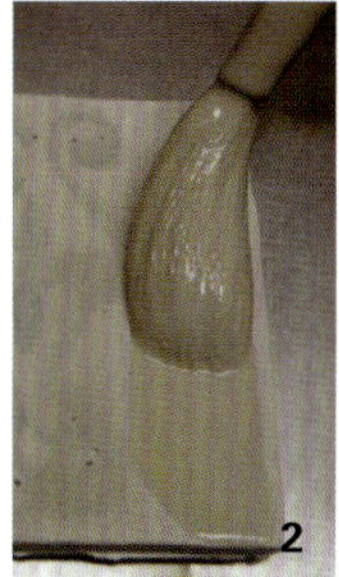
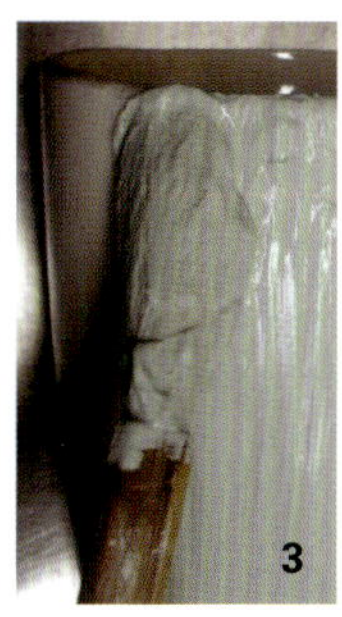

1 Base glaze mixed with CMC Gum allowed for smooth brushing. **2** Bottom layer: A pattern made with the base glaze mixed with Spectrum Brushing Media. Top layer: The base glaze mixed with Spectrum Glaze Thinner to get a thin, even coat. **3** Base glaze mixed with Apt-II Ceramic Enhancer applied over an already glaze fired piece without pre-heating.

Cone 5–6 Glazes

3

Expanding a Palette
ADDING COLORANTS AND OPACIFIERS

by Yoko Sekino-Bové

There are so many wonderful books, websites and even software that feature spectacular glaze formulas; so one may wonder why this article should be introduced to you. The focus of this research was to establish a comprehensive visual library for everyone. Rather than just providing the reader with a few promising glaze formulas, this reference is a guideline. Because it is a guide, there are some test tiles that do not provide immediate use other than the suggestion of what to avoid, or the percentages of certain chemicals that exceed the safe food-serving level, etc., but I believe that this research will be a good tool for those who wish to experiment with, and push the boundaries of, mid-range firing.

Many people may be thinking about switching their firing method from high-fire to mid-range. For instance, students who recently graduated and lost access to school gas kilns, people with a day job and those who work in their garage studios, or production potters who are concerned about fuel conservation and energy savings. This reference is intended as a tool for those people to start glaze experimentations at mid-range that can be accomplished with minimal resources.

There is no guarantee that this chart will work for everyone everywhere, since the variety between the different resources overwhelmingly affects the results, but by examining a few glazes in this chart you can speculate and make informed adjustments with your materials. This is why all the base glazes for this research use only simple materials that are widely available in the US.

Five years ago, when I switched to mid-range oxidation firing with an electric kiln from high-temperature gas-fueled reduction firing, most of my knowledge in high-fire glazes had to be reexamined. Many earth metal colorants exhibited

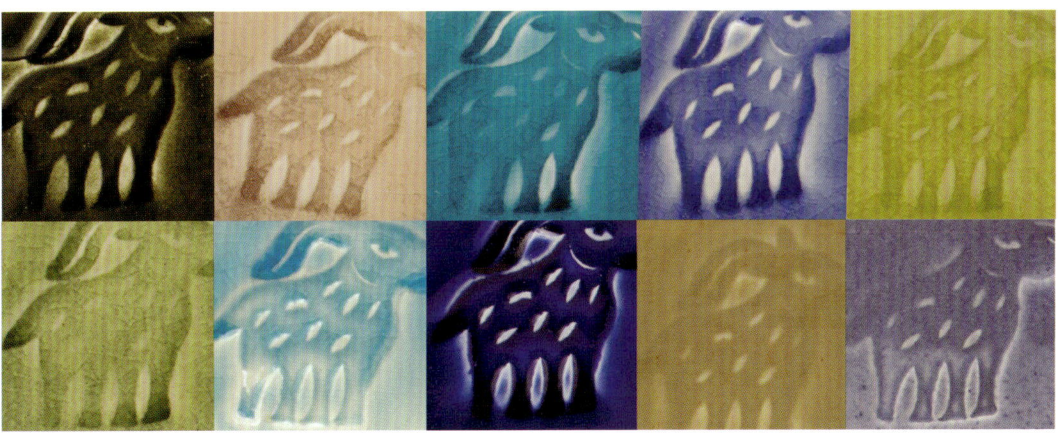

N501 TRANSPARENT
Cone 5

Ferro Frit 3110	90 %
EPK Kaolin	10
	100 %

N502 TRANSPARENT & GLOSSY
Cone 5

Gillespie Borate	30 %
F-4 Feldspar	46
EPK Kaolin	13
Silica	11
	100 %

N503 OPAQUE, GLOSSY & TEXTURED
Cone 5

Gillespie Borate	52.6 %
EPK Kaolin	21.0
Silica	26.4
	100.0 %
Add: Zircopax	10.0 %

N504 SEMI-OPAQUE, SEMI-SATIN WITH TEXTURES
Cone 5

Whiting	9.5 %
Ferro Frit 3124	44.5
F-4 Feldspar	20.0
Zinc Oxide	5.5
Bentonite*	7.5
EPK Kaolin	5.0
Silica	8.0
	100.0 %
Add: Zircopax	9.0 %

N505 SATIN OPAQUE WITH TEXTURES
Cone 5

Dolomite	12 %
Gillespie Borate	14
Wollastonite	10
Ferro Frit 3124	8
Cornwall Stone	46
EPK Kaolin	10
	100 %
Add: Magnesium Carbonate	6 %

completely different behaviors in oxidation firing, and problems in adhesion were prominent compared to high-fire glazes.

The role of oxides and carbonates used for texturing and opacifying were different as well. But compiling the available glazes and analyzing them were not enough. I felt there should be a simple chart with visual results that explained how the oxides and carbonates behave within this firing range. This motivated me to write a proposal for glaze mid-range research to the McKnight Foundation, which sponsors a three-month artist-in-residence program at the Northern Clay Center in Minneapolis.

Most of the tests presented in these experiments were executed at the Northern Clay Center in 2009 using clay and dry materials available at Continental Clay Co. The rest of the tests were completed later at my home studio in Washington, Pennsylvania. For those tests, I used dry materials available from Standard Ceramics Supply Co.

Test Conditions

Clay body: Super White (cone 5–9) a white stoneware body for mid-range, commercially available from Continental Clay Co.

Bisque firing temperatures: Cone 05 (1910°F), fired in a manual electric kiln for approximately 10 hours.

Firing temperatures: The coloring metals increment tests were fired to cone 5 (2210°F) in a manual electric kiln for approximately 8 hours. The opacifier/texture metals increment tests were fired to cone 5 in an automatic electric kiln for 8 hours.

Glaze batch: Each test was 300g, with a tablespoon of epsom salts added as a flocculant.

Glazing method: Hand dipping. First dip (bottom half): 3 seconds. Second dip (top half) additional 4 seconds on top of the first layer, total 7 seconds.

Coloring Metals Increment Chart

Colorants tested: black nickel oxide, cobalt oxide, copper carbonate, chrome oxide, iron chromate, manganese dioxide, red iron oxide, rutile, and yellow ochre. You should note that tests with cobalt oxide and chrome oxide in high percentages were not executed due to the color predictability. Other blank tiles on the chart are because either the predictability or the percentages of oxides are too insignificant to affect the base glazes.

Depending on firing atmospheres, manganese dioxide exhibits a wide variety of colors. When fired in a tightly sealed electric kiln with small peepholes, the glaze color tends toward brown, compared to purple when fired in a kiln with many and/or large peepholes.

Note that some of the oxides and carbonates in this test exceed the safety standard for use as tableware that comes in contact with food. Check safety standards before applying a glaze with a high percentage of metal oxides to food ware and test the finished ware for leaching.

Test tile numbering system: The glaze name is the first part of the identification number, followed by an abbreviation or code that stands for the colorant name. The last part is a two or three digit number referring to the percentage of colorant added. So, for example if a test was mixed with glaze base N501, to which 1 percent cobalt oxide was added, the test tile marking would be: N501COX10.

Depending on firing atmospheres, manganese dioxide exhibits a wide variety of colors. When fired in a tightly sealed electric kiln with small peepholes, the glaze color tends toward brown, compared to purple when fired in a kiln with many and/or large peepholes.

Note that some of the oxides and carbonates in this test exceed the safety standard for use as tableware that comes in contact with food. Check safety standards before applying a glaze with a high percentage of metal oxides to food ware and test the finished ware for leaching.

Test tile numbering system: The glaze name is the first part of the identification number, followed by an abbreviation or code that stands for the colorant name. The last part is a two or three digit number referring to the percentage of colorant added. So, for example if a test was mixed with glaze base N501, to which 1 percent cobalt oxide was added, the test tile marking would be: N501COX10.

Opacifiers were added to glaze bases in increments. The chart at left shows which materials were added for this purpose, and the percentages tested. All glazes in this test batch also had 1% copper carbonate added to increase the visual effect of the chemicals on the glaze.

Note: Some of the oxides and carbonates did not exhibit a significant visual effect by themselves. However, sometimes a combination of more than one chemical can change the glaze characteristics and create spectacular visual effects.

Conclusion

This group of tests has been a great opportunity for me to study the characteristics of oxides and carbonates and how they behave at mid-range temperatures. There are scientific methods for calculating glazes and proven theories, but there are many small pieces of information that can only be picked up when you actually go through the physical experiments. It is important for us to become familiar with a glaze's behavior so that we can better utilize it. Key to that is learning both the theory and application. It is my hope that these tests will benefit many potters by helping them to expand their palette and inspire them to test the possibilities.

Glaze base N501 with coloring oxides and carbonates

	0.1%	0.5%	1.0%	5.0%	10.0%
Copper Carbonate		N501CC05	N501CC10	N501CC50	N501CC100
Red Iron Oxide (regular)		N501ROI05	N501ROI10	N501ROI50	N501ROI100
Cobalt Oxide	N501COX1	N501COX05	N501COX10		
Chrome Oxide	N501CH01	N501CH05	N501CH10		
Manganese Dioxide		N501MD05	N501MD10	N501MD50	N501MD100
Black Nickel Oxide		N501BN05	N501BN10	N501BN50	
Iron Chromate		N501IC05	N501IC10	N501IC50	N501IC100
Rutile (powder)		N501R05	N501R10	N501R5	N501R100
Yellow Ochre		N501Y05	N501Y10	N501Y50	N501Y100

Glaze base N502 with coloring oxides and carbonates

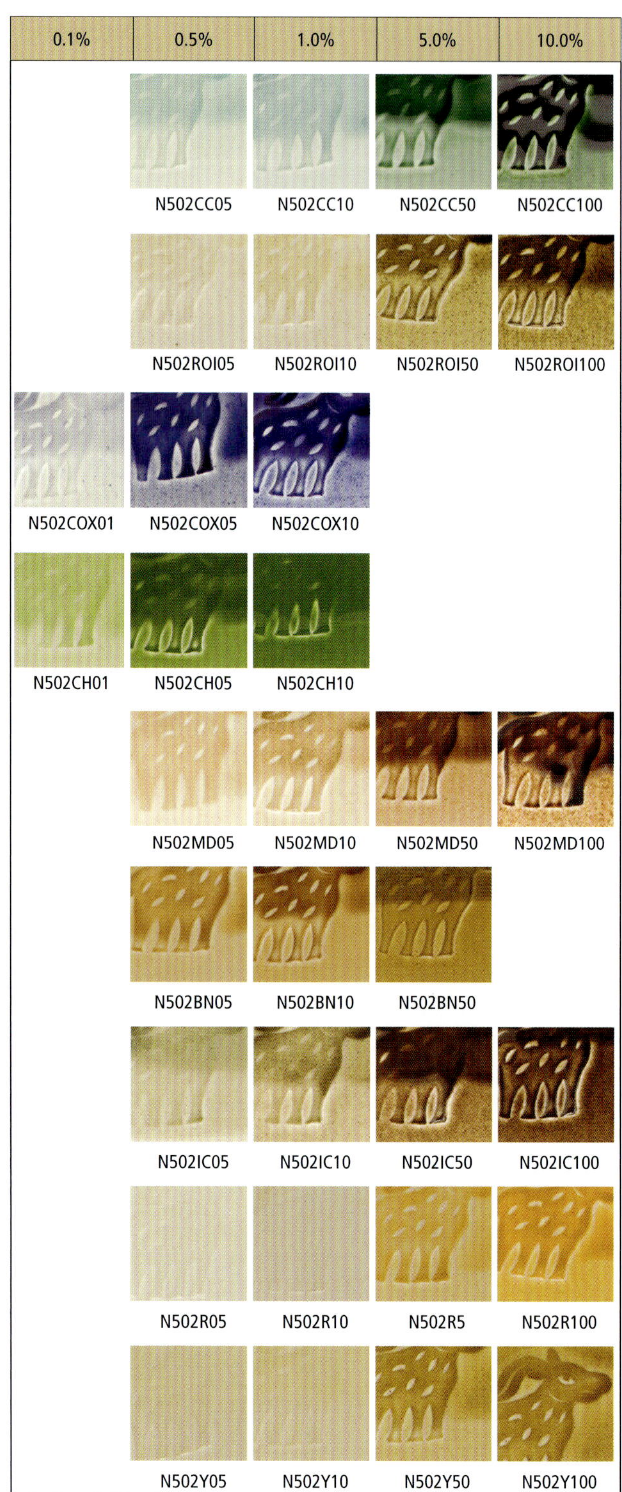

	0.1%	0.5%	1.0%	5.0%	10.0%
Copper Carbonate		N502CC05	N502CC10	N502CC50	N502CC100
Red Iron Oxide (regular)		N502ROI05	N502ROI10	N502ROI50	N502ROI100
Cobalt Oxide	N502COX01	N502COX05	N502COX10		
Chrome Oxide	N502CH01	N502CH05	N502CH10		
Manganese Dioxide		N502MD05	N502MD10	N502MD50	N502MD100
Black Nickel Oxide		N502BN05	N502BN10	N502BN50	
Iron Chromate		N502IC05	N502IC10	N502IC50	N502IC100
Rutile (powder)		N502R05	N502R10	N502R5	N502R100
Yellow Ochre		N502Y05	N502Y10	N502Y50	N502Y100

Glaze base N503 with coloring oxides and carbonates

	0.1%	0.5%	1.0%	5.0%	10.0%
Copper Carbonate		N503CC05	N503CC10	N503CC50	N503CC100
Red Iron Oxide (regular)		N503ROI05	N503ROI10	N503ROI50	N503ROI100
Cobalt Oxide	N503COX01	N503COX05	N503COX10		
Chrome Oxide	N503CH01	N503CH05	N503CH10		
Manganese Dioxide		N503MD05	N503MD10	N503MD50	N503MD100
Black Nickel Oxide		N503BN05	N503BN10	N503BN50	
Iron Chromate		N503IC05	N503IC10	N503IC50	N503IC100
Rutile (powder)		N503R05	N503R10	N503R50	N503R100
Yellow Ochre		N503Y05	N503Y10	N503Y50	N503Y100

Glaze base N504 with coloring oxides and carbonates

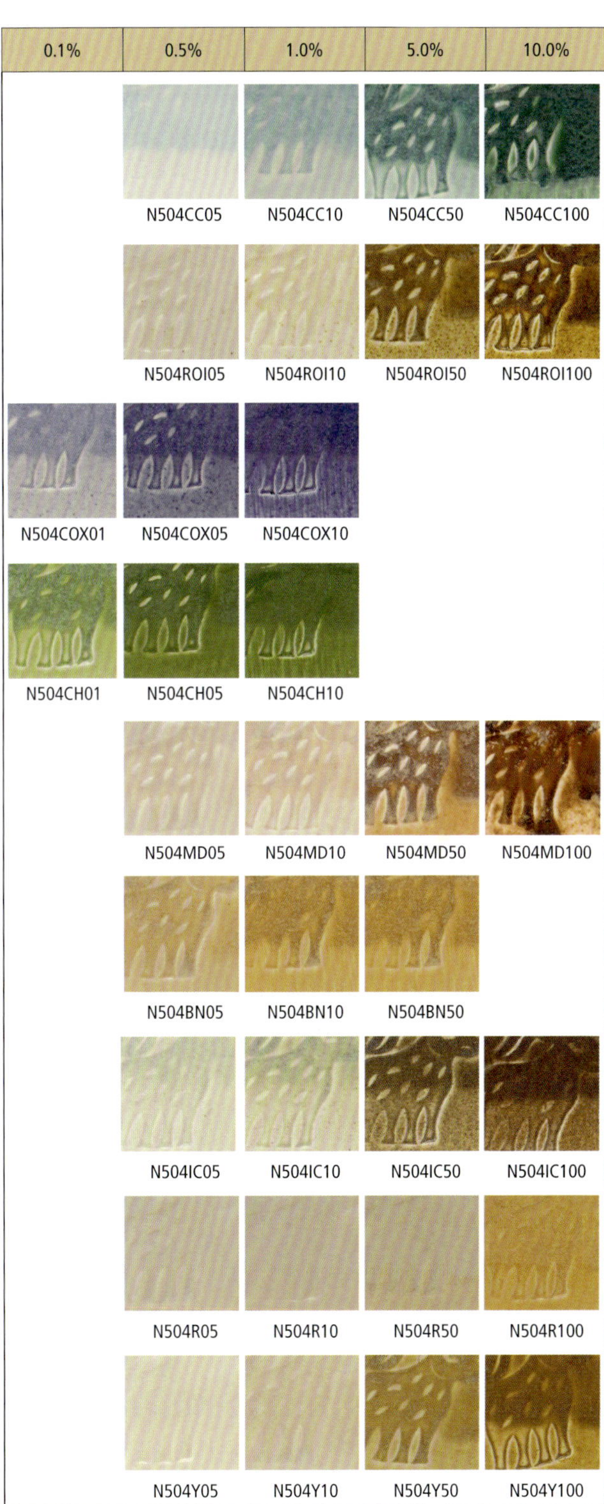

	0.1%	0.5%	1.0%	5.0%	10.0%
Copper Carbonate		N504CC05	N504CC10	N504CC50	N504CC100
Red Iron Oxide (regular)		N504ROI05	N504ROI10	N504ROI50	N504ROI100
Cobalt Oxide	N504COX01	N504COX05	N504COX10		
Chrome Oxide	N504CH01	N504CH05	N504CH10		
Manganese Dioxide		N504MD05	N504MD10	N504MD50	N504MD100
Black Nickel Oxide		N504BN05	N504BN10	N504BN50	
Iron Chromate		N504IC05	N504IC10	N504IC50	N504IC100
Rutile (powder)		N504R05	N504R10	N504R50	N504R100
Yellow Ochre		N504Y05	N504Y10	N504Y50	N504Y100

Glaze base N505 with coloring oxides and carbonates

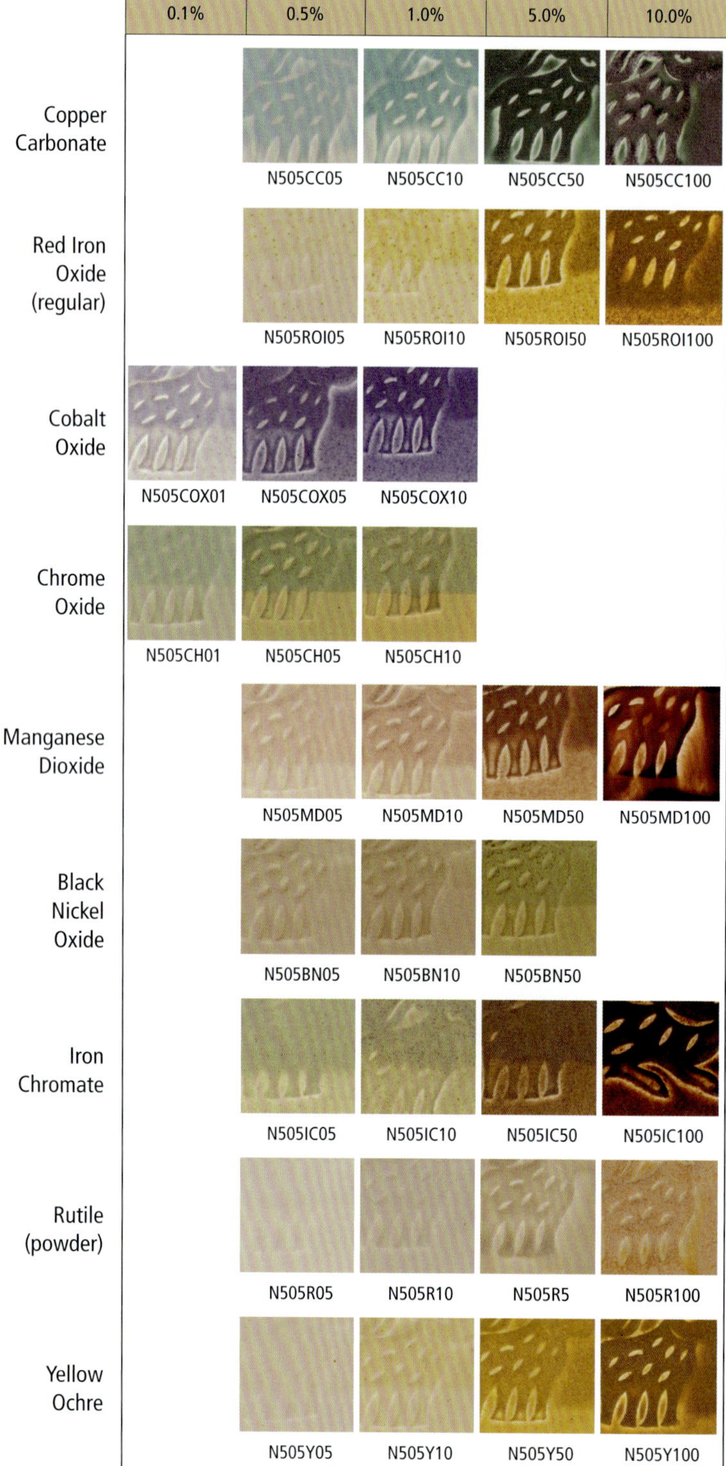

Glaze bases with opacifiers

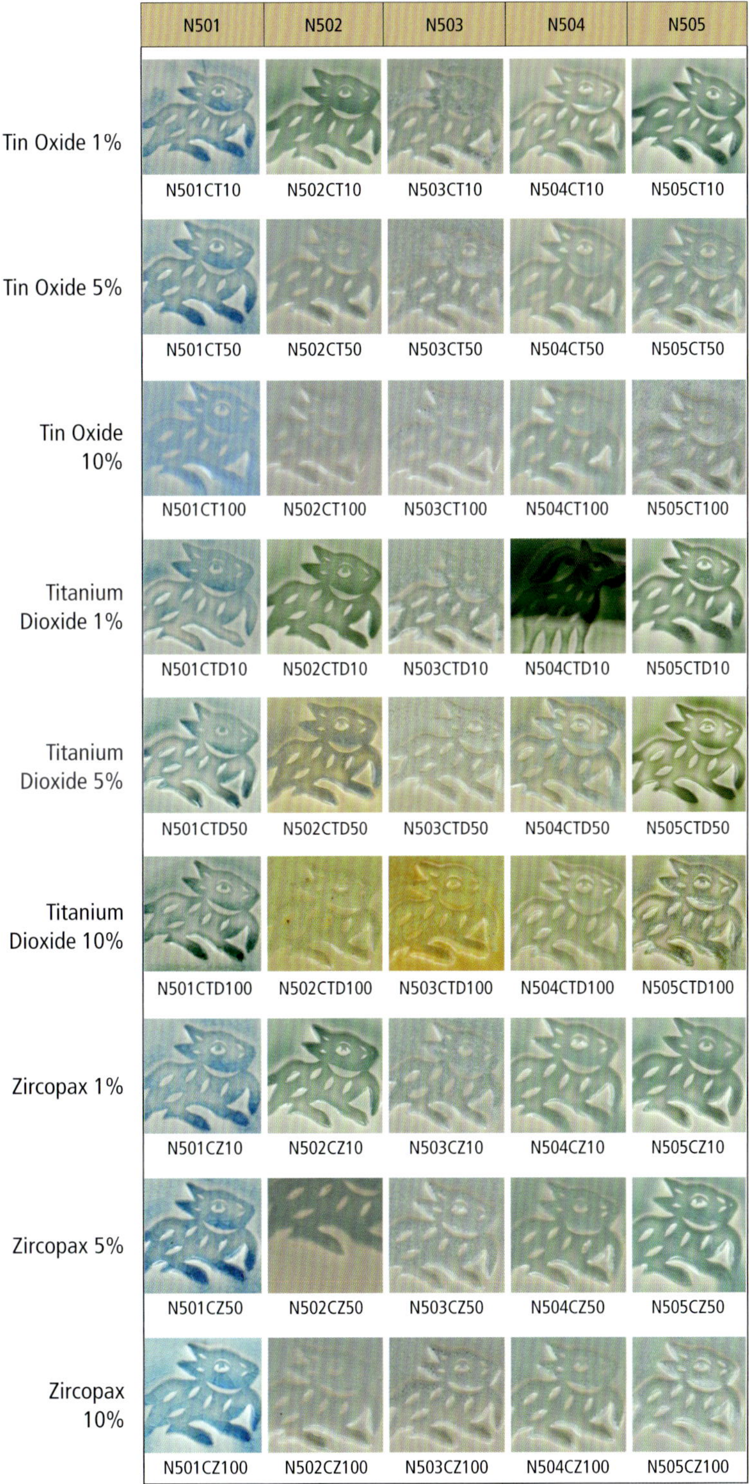

	N501	N502	N503	N504	N505
Tin Oxide 1%	N501CT10	N502CT10	N503CT10	N504CT10	N505CT10
Tin Oxide 5%	N501CT50	N502CT50	N503CT50	N504CT50	N505CT50
Tin Oxide 10%	N501CT100	N502CT100	N503CT100	N504CT100	N505CT100
Titanium Dioxide 1%	N501CTD10	N502CTD10	N503CTD10	N504CTD10	N505CTD10
Titanium Dioxide 5%	N501CTD50	N502CTD50	N503CTD50	N504CTD50	N505CTD50
Titanium Dioxide 10%	N501CTD100	N502CTD100	N503CTD100	N504CTD100	N505CTD100
Zircopax 1%	N501CZ10	N502CZ10	N503CZ10	N504CZ10	N505CZ10
Zircopax 5%	N501CZ50	N502CZ50	N503CZ50	N504CZ50	N505CZ50
Zircopax 10%	N501CZ100	N502CZ100	N503CZ100	N504CZ100	N505CZ100

Expanding a Palette

COMBINING GLAZES

by Lou Roess

If you'd like a bigger selection of glaze colors, but don't have the time or money it takes to mix and test new ones, try one of these four easy methods to add color to your glaze palette.

Method 1

The quickest way to get more colors is to make half-and-half mixes of your current glazes. Combining ¼ cup each of any two glazes will give you enough glaze to cover a test tile, small plate or bowl. Just one example: Mixing a dark glaze half-and-half with a white one gives you a lighter version (figures 1–3).

Now, try it yourself. Six- or eight-ounce yogurt cups make handy containers. Mark the glaze combinations on both the cup and the lid. You can speed up labeling by numbering your glazes so you don't have to write out the full name. After firing, you'll discover some combinations you like.

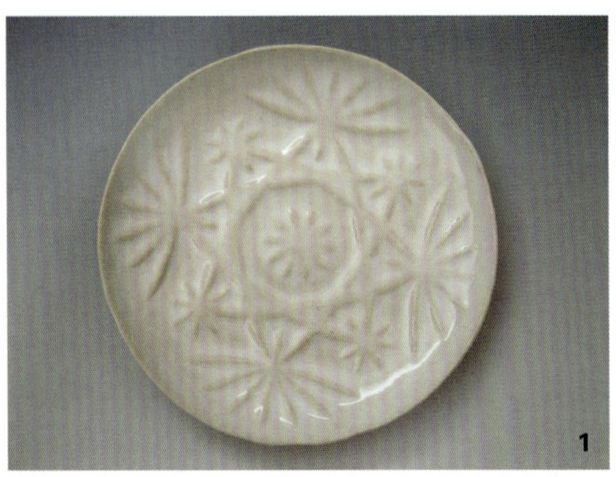
1

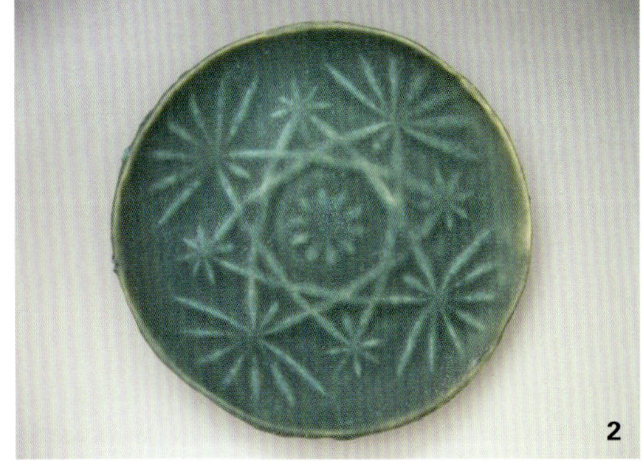
2

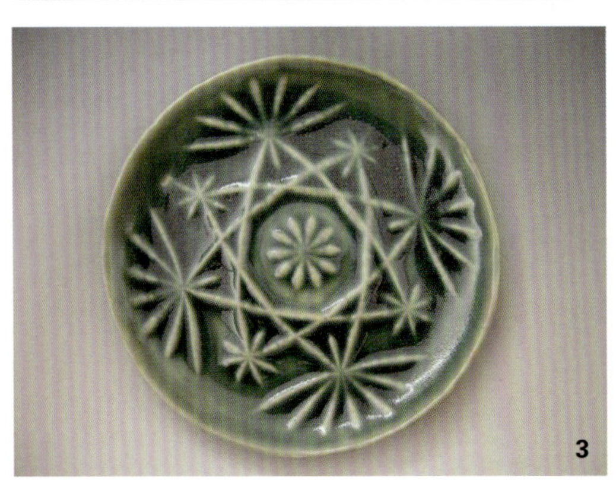
3

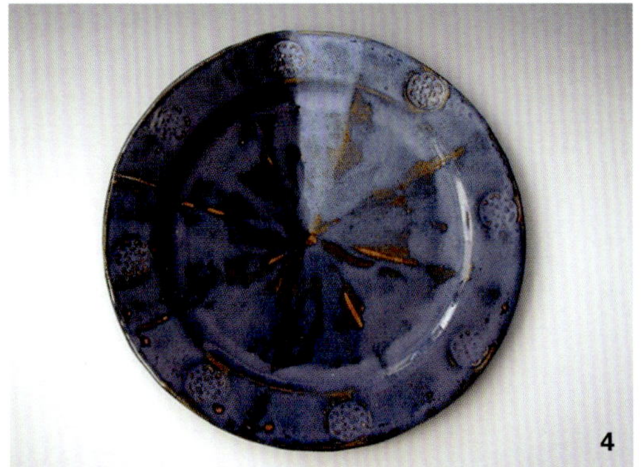
4

Doing a line blend is a good way to see how intermediate colors will look (figure 4). Combine two glazes together in two different amounts. Incrementally increasing the amount of one glaze and decreasing the amount of the other for each segment can produce many variations. Note that most of the change takes place on the right side of the plate. This indicates that after a point the darker color overtook the lighter one. A light version of this combination could be used on the body of a bowl with a darker version on the rim to add interest. Now, try mixing equal parts of three different glazes to discover even more glaze possibilities.

Method 2

Another way to get more colors is to apply different glazes over or under one another. The best way to check out how your glazes will look when applied this way is to make a test grid. Roll out a fairly thick slab of clay, allowing 1 inch each in depth and width for each glaze you want to test. For example, if you have eight glazes, make your grid 8×8 inches. Now, measure out a row with a 1-inch-wide ruler, rolling the edge of the ruler onto the clay to make a line. Repeat for the next row and so on. Make the columns in the same way.

Next, use a stamp to make a design in each individual square or drag a small fork in a wavy line across the width of each 1-inch square. After firing, this will show you how the glaze breaks (figure 5). Mark out an equivalent grid on paper to record your entries; it doesn't have to be to scale.

Bisque your clay slab. (If you're using paper clay you can usually get away with once firing.) Begin by brushing your first glaze in a horizontal line from left to right across the top 1-inch stripe of the grid. Record this glaze on your paper grid. If you make the first stripe a white glaze you will have a good idea of how the other glazes will look over white clay. Brush the second glaze across the next horizontal stripe and record it on your paper grid. Continue brushing different glazes, one to each grid stripe, until all the horizontal stripes are covered.

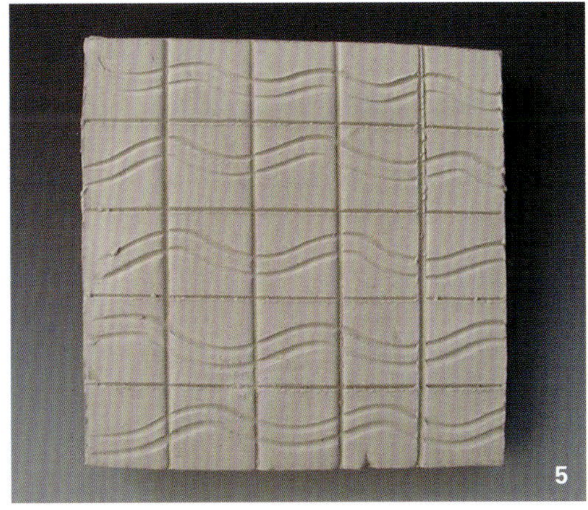
5

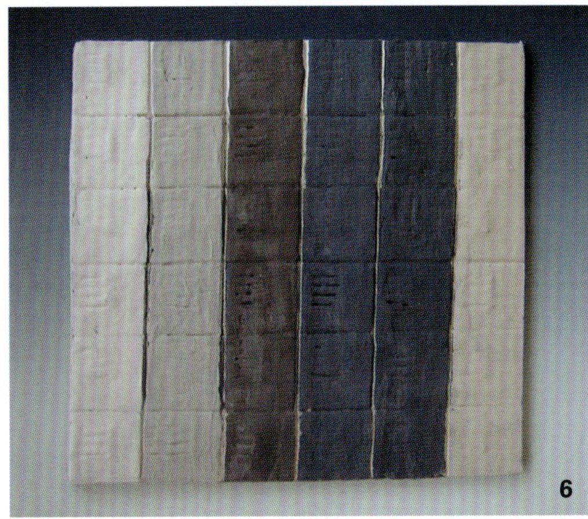
6

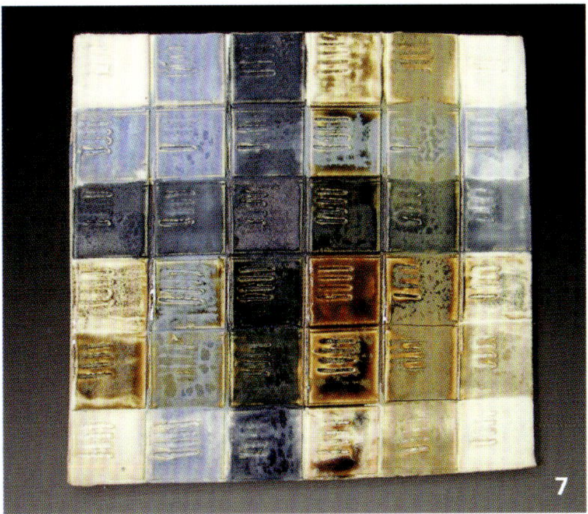
7

Roll out a slab of clay and divide into 1-inch squares. (from left to right) Mark a design in each square. Glaze each 1-inch horizontal strip with a different glaze. Repeat the same sequence of glazes vertically. Fire the grid to see how each glaze looks both over and under all the other glazes.

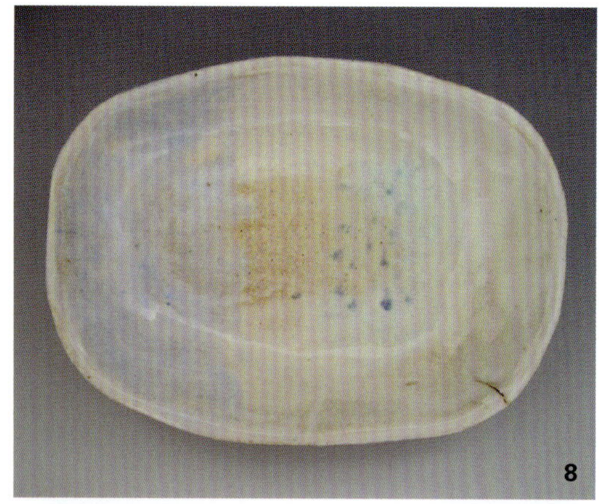

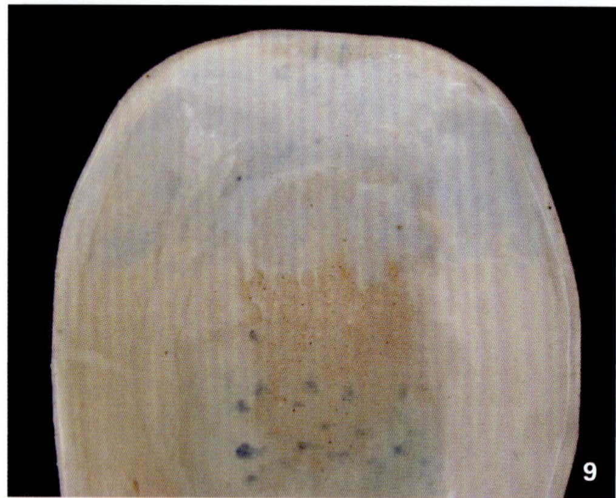

Distribute a pinch of oxide evenly to your glaze. Apply the glaze by dabbing with a sponge. The base color will look speckled after firing.

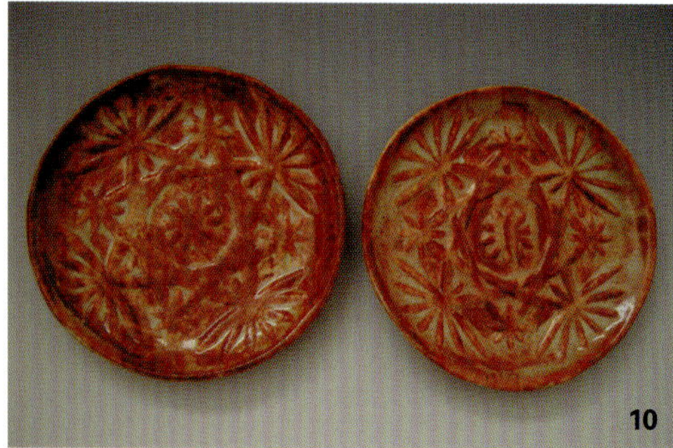

Apply varying thicknesses of the same glaze to achieve subtle differences.

When the last glaze is no longer wet looking, start on the left and add vertical stripes in the same order you applied the horizontal stripes. For example, if you started with white horizontally, start with white vertically. Brush the second glaze vertically in the next column, and so on, until you've applied all the glazes (figure 6). Make sure to record your glazes on the paper grid.

Fire the grid and mount it on a piece of cardboard. It's a good idea to write the glazes in the order used on the back of the cardboard, then attach the finished grid to your studio wall so it's handy for reference.

You will now have a good idea of how each glaze looks both over and under all the other glazes. The vertical stripes will be "over" and the horizontal stripes "under" (figure 7). While this flat method doesn't tell you how the glazes move on a vertical surface, it does uncover colors of interest which you can test further.

Method 3

A third way to get a new look from your glazes involves a base glaze with a small amount of coloring oxide (especially cobalt oxide—notable for being hard to combine in a glaze) distributed evenly in it. Stir thoroughly, but don't blunge or sieve.

Pour or dab it on with a sponge (figure 8). If you brush the glaze on or dip it, you're apt to get streaks. A white base works well with this method. You may want to apply a first coat of the glaze without speckles for better coverage. The fired result is usually a mottled finish with some speckles of oxide (figure 9).

Method 4

Another easy way to add to your color palette is by varying your application. You can often get subtle but noticeable differences in color by applying glazes in varying thicknesses (figure 10). Using some or all of these simple methods, you can easily add variety and interest to your glaze palette.

STRONTIUM BLUE BRONZE
Cone 6

Lithium Carbonate	1.0%
Strontium Carbonate	20.0
Nepheline Syenite	60.0
Ball Clay	10.0
Silica	9.0
	100.0%
Add: Cobalt Carbonate	0.15%
Copper Carbonate	4.0%

This glaze is a variation of Pinnell's Bronze Green and usually has a matt surface. It is not a food safe glaze but would work well on the outside of functional forms or on sculpture.

NARAGON WHITE
Cone 6

Dolomite	4%
Gerstley Borate or Ferro Frit 3134	26
Whiting	6
Kona F-4 Feldspar	31
EPK Kaolin	8
Silica	25
	100%
Add: Zircopax	12%
Bentonite	2%

This has a glossy, opaque surface. The color appears whiter when placed on a white clay body.

BLUE GREEN
Cone 6

Gerstley Borate	22.0%
Strontium Carbonate	4.0
Whiting	11.0
Custer Feldspar	38.0
Silica	25.0
	100.0%
Add: Cobalt Carbonate	0.5%
Chrome Oxide	1.0%
Bentonite	2.0%

This glaze has a glossy surface and the color can be mottled in appearance.

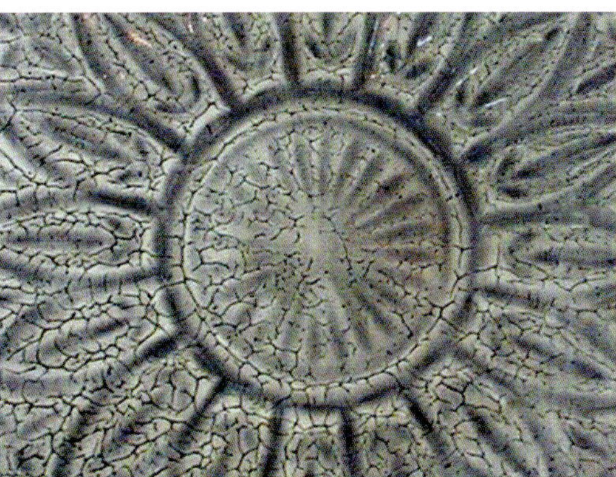

Naragon White glaze over Blue Green glaze. The crackle effect was an unexpected but pleasant surprise.

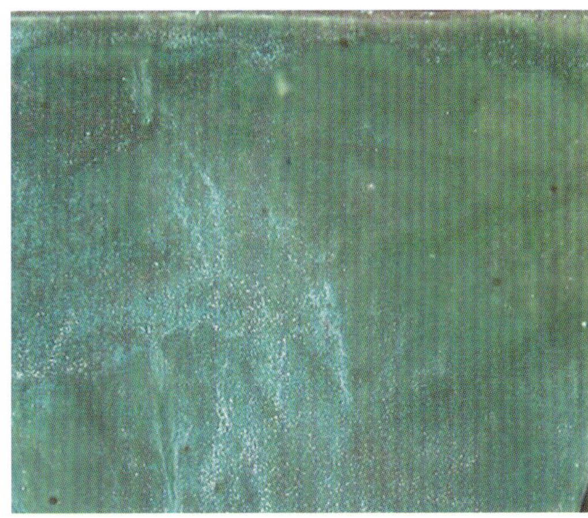

Stoneware vase with Strontium Blue Bronze glaze.

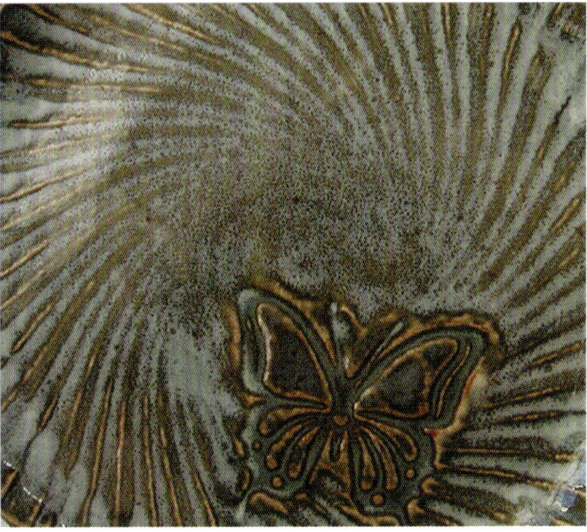

Stoneware plate, with Naragon White glaze over Blue Green glaze. The butterfly area was waxed before the Narragon White glaze was applied.

Expanding a Palette

ALTERING THE FIRING

by Deanna Ranlett

Down firing, or slow cooling, refers to controlling the rate at which your kiln cools. I've programmed my kiln to a slowly cooling rate for a variety of purposes, ranging from slow cooling large work to reduce dunting to cooling slowly and holding at certain temperatures to form glaze crystals. Slower cooling reduces stress on ceramic wares and is well worth the extra time. For glazes containing zinc, rutile, calcium, magnesium, lithium, and iron (to name just a few), slowing the cooling rate can result in some spectacular effects, ranging from feathering to small crystals and in some cases a fully-developed satin-matte surface. The combination of a short soak at peak temperature and then down firing can also eliminate pin holing in some glazes (figure 1).

Many new computer controlled kilns come with built-in preheat or cool-down programs, but I have an older model computer-controlled kiln so I program my own firings. *Tip:* If you plan to use a pre-program set-up, test the program in a typical firing using self-supporting Orton cones to calibrate the kiln. The type of kiln, type of ware being fired, and the size and density of the average ware stack inside the kiln can impact final temperature determinations, but this initial calibration firing gives you a baseline for the length of the firing to reach a specific temperature.

Over the years, I've determined that the preprogrammed cone 6 firings tend to overfire my work. I tend to pack my kiln very full and the result of the pre-programmed firing schedule finishes closer to cone 7 than to cone 6. As a result, I've researched additional down-firing schedules and came across Ron Roy and John Hesselberth's *Mastering Cone 6 Glazes* book. In the appendix, I found a perfect starting point for a cone 6 downfiring. To this initial schedule, I've made adjustments to suit the way the kiln is loaded, and to take into account what the self supporting cones told us about the firing speed, and the end temperature. I've also learned that generally, the slower the climb to temperature, the lower the end temperature, so programming a hold at your desired peak temperature also impacts what the end shut-off temperature should be because heat work continues to occur during those slower periods. A hold at the end of a firing allows a slight soaking effect which allows all work to reach temperature if there's any unevenness inside the kiln from top to bottom. It also allows glazes to move together and flatten a bit, which is great if you're creating a reduction-fired effect by layering multiple glazes. Refer to your kiln manual or manufacturer's website for proper programming instructions.

If you're down firing for crystalline growth, you want to keep the glaze fluid enough so that crystals can form but not so fluid that it starts to run. In my experience, it's best to hold the glaze firing for fifteen minutes to about 60° lower than the cut off temperature for a pre-programmed firing. To begin controlled cooling, allow the kiln to cool as

KAREN'S STARSHINE
Cone 6

Custer feldspar	51%
Whiting	13
Gerstley Borate	6
Soda Ash (dissolve in hot water)	4
Strontium Carbonate	4
Lithium Carbonate	1
Titanium Dioxide	4
Silica	21
	100%
Add: Copper Carbonate	5%

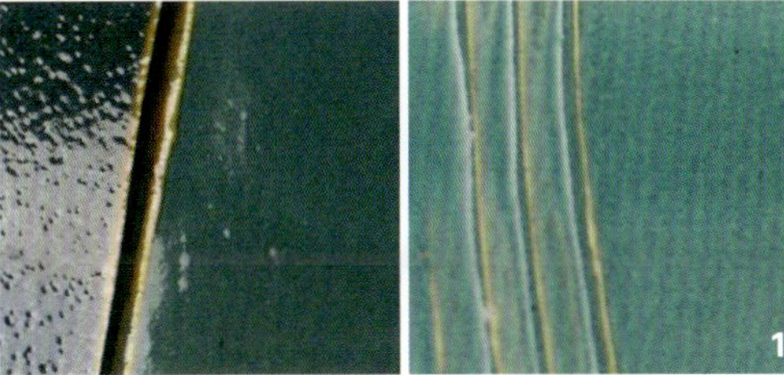

Karen's Starshine. Left: Fired on a medium speed cone 6 program, results are translucent, glossy, pinholed. Right: Fired to the cone 6 program on page 72, results are opaque, glossy, smooth.

DIXIE TEAL
Cone 6

Gerstley Borate	2.9%
Ferro Frit 3124	8.8
Magnesium Carbonate	2.9
Whiting	22.4
Nepheline Syenite	22.7
EPK Kaolin	20.3
Silica	20.0
	100.0%
Add: Copper Carbonate	4.0%
Cobalt Carbonate	3.0%

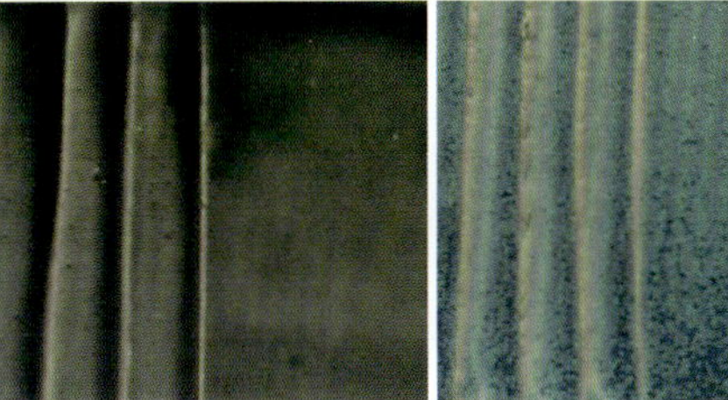

Dixie Teal. Left: Fired on a medium speed cone 6 program, resulting in a glossier, darker color. Right: Fired to the cone 6 program on page 72, resulting in a lighter, speckled glaze.

FROST
Cone 6

Ferro Frit 3134	20.0%
Nepheline Syenite	30.0
Whiting	10.0
Talc	17.0
EPK Kaolin	13.0
Silica	10.0
	100.0%
Add: Zircopax	10.0%
Rutile	3.0%
Cobalt Carbonate	0.5%
Copper Carbonate	1.0%
Bentonite*	3.0%

Frost. Left: Fired on a medium speed cone 6 program, resulting in a glossier, darker color. Right: Fired to the cone 6 program on page 72, resulting in a frostier, satin surface.

JOHN'S TENMOKU
Cone 6

Custer Feldspar	43%
Whiting	21
EPK Kaolin	10
Silica	26
	100%
Add: Red Iron Oxide	16%
Bentonite*	3%

* Weigh the bentonite separately and dry mix it with the other ingredients before adding water.

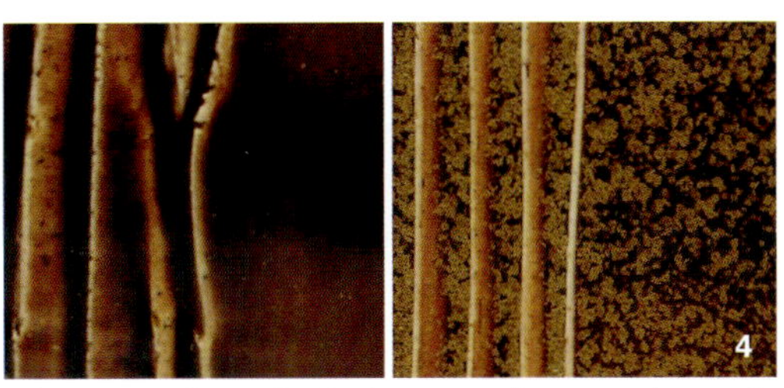

John's Tenmoku. Left: Fired on a medium speed cone 6 program, resulting in a glossier, darker in color. Right: Fired to the cone 6 program on page 72, resulting in gold crystals formed when cooling.

fast as it can for the first 300° so the controlled portion of the firing is taking place about 300° lower than the cut-off temperature. I have experimented with different cooling rates ranging from 125° per hour to 175° per hour depending on the type of glazed surface I desire. To prevent dunting (cooling cracks) in a sculpture firing program, the cooling period isn't done for development of glazes but to minimize fast heat loss around larger work. I recommend a cooling rate of about 200° per hour through quartz inversion (1063°F).

Crystal growth in some glazes can vary depending on the rate of down firing—a fast cool results in a glossy surface, while a slow cool goes matte (figure 2). The crystals creating the satin surface are happening between 1900°F and 1450°F. Some glazes can form small crystals during the soaking period but for the most part, the controlled cooling is allowing the crystalline structure to form. Caution: Make sure that your glazes aren't becoming less stable or less food-safe due to changes in surface texture from crystals forming in the glazes. Perform leach tests on all results.

Controlled Cooling in a Manual Kiln

While controlled cooling is more difficult in a manual kiln, it's not impossible. You can re-engage your kiln sitter, which forces your kiln to remain on despite the cone dropping. This is where things can get a little tricky, so you would want to make sure you set your safety timer as a back-up in case you get interrupted and don't remember to turn off the kiln.

Let the kiln sitter drop and allow the kiln to remain off for 15–20 minutes—the temperature drops rapidly when the kiln first shuts off. After this, use a combination of medium and low switches to create gentle heating as the kiln cools—try 1–2 hours on medium, then 1–2 hours on low so the kiln cools by about 125–175° per hour. This allows extra time for your glazes to develop a crystal structure or for large sculpture to cool slowly. Keep a log of all your changes and results so you can make adjustments to the timing you used to turn switches to medium or low on the down firing.

Down-Firing Kiln Schedules (right)

Because the bisque firing has already changed the clay into ceramic material, temperatures can increase faster through the middle of the glaze firing.

Cone 04 Bisque Firing

This program controls cooling for large sculptural ware and prevents cooling cracks.

- 50° per hour to 150°F—hold 2–6 hours This depends on the size of your work and its dryness
- 150° per hour to 200°F—hold 15 minutes
- 250° per hour to 1000°F—no hold
- 180° per hour to 1150°F—hold 15 minutes
- 300° per hour to 1800°F—no hold
- 108° per hour to 1900°F—hold 5 minutes

On the way down:

- 150° per hour to 1500°F—no hold
- Cool naturally from 1500°F. For large-scale work, cool through quartz inversion (1063°F) at a rate of about 200° per hour, then allow the kiln to cool naturally from 600°F down to room temperature.

Cone 6 Glaze Firing

This program controls cooling for special glaze effects.

- 100° per hour to 220°F—no hold
- 350° per hour to 2000°F—no hold
- 150° per hour to 2185°F—hold 15 minutes (I use 2175°F to a half-bent cone 6 self-supporting cone)

On the way down:

- 500° per hour to 1900°F no hold (I program my kiln for 9999°F to 1900°F so that I don't get an error message if the kiln can't cool at that rate)
- 125–175° per hour to 1450°F—use your glaze results to tell you if this rate should be slower or faster in subsequent firings.
- Allow the kiln to cool naturally from 1450°F down to room temperature.

Expanding a Palette

REPURPOSING GLAZES

by Deanna Ranlett

One man's trash is another man's treasure. That's the sentiment echoed recently in our studio while re-mixing leftover shop glazes together. It's a fairly common practice in large studios to make what's called a "trash glaze" using the remaining bits of various shop glazes to avoid throwing glaze materials down the drain.

While researching online how to safely dispose of glaze materials, I found a number of suggestions from firing the materials inside bisque bowls to a low temperature to sinter them to adding recycled clay then shaping the mixture into bricks or tiles and firing them. Many large studios also utilize hazardous materials bins that are delivered by their local waste management departments. Personally I believe that the best bet is either the latter option or to reuse the materials as trash glazes.

Rescuing Trash Glazes

When making trash glazes, the result is commonly dark gray, dark brown, or dark blue because of the various coloring oxides combining from all of the glazes. One technique is to mix together glazes of a similar nature, for example, mixing leftover clear glazes together, light colors with other light colors, and blues with greens, etc. For our group studio experiment, we chose glazes at random as if you were just cleaning up or retiring some older un-

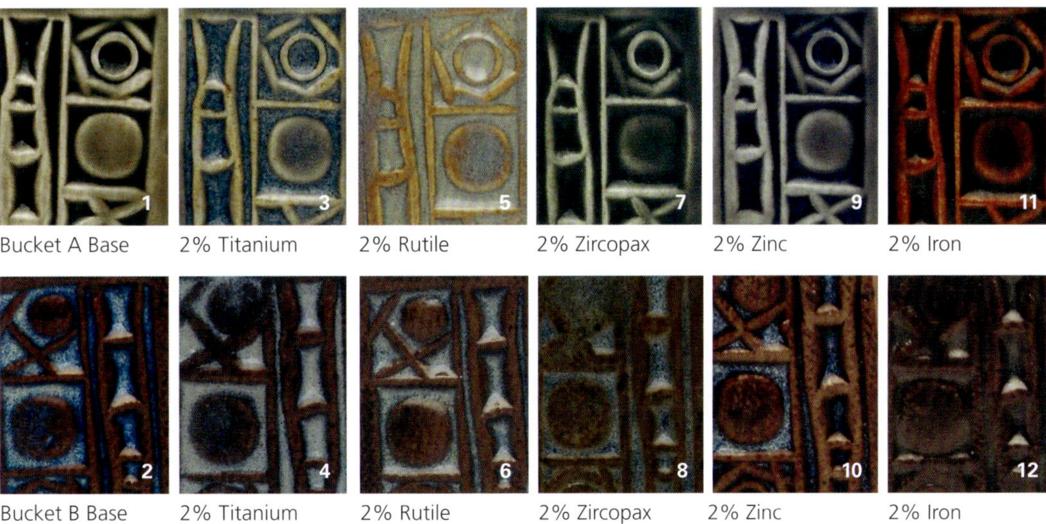

Bucket A Base | 2% Titanium | 2% Rutile | 2% Zircopax | 2% Zinc | 2% Iron

Bucket B Base | 2% Titanium | 2% Rutile | 2% Zircopax | 2% Zinc | 2% Iron

wanted glazes. Often studios are not thrilled with the resulting colors of their studio trash glazes so we decided to also experiment with small additions of modifiers and opacifiers to show some remedies for rescuing a trash glaze. I selected titanium dioxide, rutile, Zircopax, zinc oxide, and iron oxide as additives.

Testing for Food Safety

It's important to test for leaching in the resulting glazes although general consensus says that because of the variety of fluxes present, trash glazes are usually very stable. Performing a basic lemon or vinegar leaching test is the proper thing to do when mixing and firing any new glazes. Allow your fired glazed piece to sit for at least 24 hours with a lemon slice on it or partially submerge it in vinegar to show if color is leaching from your glazes.

Initial Glaze Tests

Bucket A was a mix of five cone-6 glazes: dark green, white, purple, dark blue, and celadon. This group of tests were done on tiles made from Helios porcelain from Highwater Clays, and fired to cone 6. This glaze fired to a translucent gray. Overall, bucket A had more variation among additives (figure 1).

Bucket B was a mix of five cone-6 glazes: dark brown, white, cream, black, and powder blue. This group of tests were done on tiles made from Red Rock stoneware, also from Highwater Clays, and fired to cone 6. The glaze fired to a dark floating blue. Overall, bucket B had less dramatic results among additives (figure 2).

Adding Glaze Modifiers

- *2% titanium dioxide* gave a variegated surface with bright color. In both glazes, the titanium dioxide brought out the cobalt. Bucket A, which initially was a dark gray, came out a soft floating blue that broke green (figure 3). Bucket B, which already appeared as a floating blue had more crystals and a softer color (figure 4).
- *2% rutile* yielded a variegated surface and brightened the color, adding more green hues. It also opacified the glaze a bit more than the titanium dioxide did. The glaze from bucket A resulted in a beautiful soft powder blue (figure 5). Bucket B had almost no change from the original tile with the addition of the rutile (figure 6).
- *2% Zircopax* gave the glazes a boost in brightness. This was expected because Zircopax is an opacifier used to make glazes lighter and whiter. The glaze in bucket A became a brighter, more opaque, and green gray (figure 7). The glaze from bucket B became a softer, more cobalt-hued floating blue and broke less around the textured areas (figure 8).
- *2% zinc oxide* gave the glazes what we called a "starry" quality. The glaze from bucket A became a pale gray with darker blue pools of tiny crystals (figure 9). The bucket B test had a similar starry effect and an even brighter blue where the glaze pooled (figure 10).
- *2% iron oxide* gave the glazes a deeper brown hue as expected. I would view adding iron as a "black out" effect if you aren't happy with the original color of your trash glaze and just want to create a rich deep brown (figures 11–12).

Conclusions

For trash glazes, my approach would be to first add Zircopax to lighten and brighten the color. Our bucket A made a lovely, neutral gray on its own that many studio members wanted to try. Adding titanium dioxide or rutile also made a lot of sense because you're able to produce reduction-like effects with glazes that have variegated, hares-fur type textures on their surfaces. The addition of zinc oxide gave the most interesting variation (although difficult to see in the photos.) It added more flux, which resulted in a nice break on the texture and a star-like effect.

When working with trash glazes, I would suggest making changes in small increments and firing in between to test. Because of the variety of oxides, opacifiers, and ingredients, small changes and additions are all that are needed to make a large impact.

Expanding a Palette

RE-COLORING A CLASSIC

by Deanna Ranlett

In my glaze formulation classes students will often bring in glazes to explore, tinker with, and make their own. Of these recipes, the majority of what I see are the old standards most potters have used at one point. Besides already having the ingredients on hand, using an old favorite often allows a comfort level conducive to experimentation and if you get in a rut, adding a little fun to your palette can be a good way to get those creative ideas flowing.

Also, another benefit of these 'tried and true' recipes is that they have a broad fit range with commercially prepared clay bodies. The recipe I used for testing and experimenting, Falls Creek Shino, has many variations and discussions pertaining to it on the popular Clayart discussion group. Popularity on a chat site doesn't mean you shouldn't test, but it does mean that some common glaze faults aren't present with a recipe that has such widespread recognition. For example, this shino fits every speckled body I've tried, as well as white stoneware and porcelain—I've yet to see any shivering in three years of testing with my students. I would encourage all potters to run acid leaching tests with lemon or vinegar, run a glaze

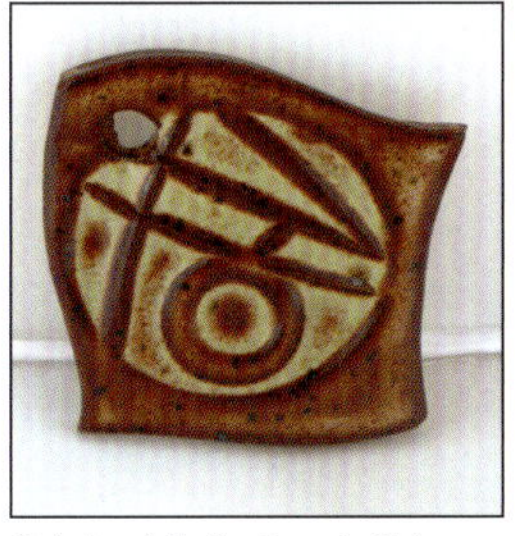
Original Falls Creek Shino

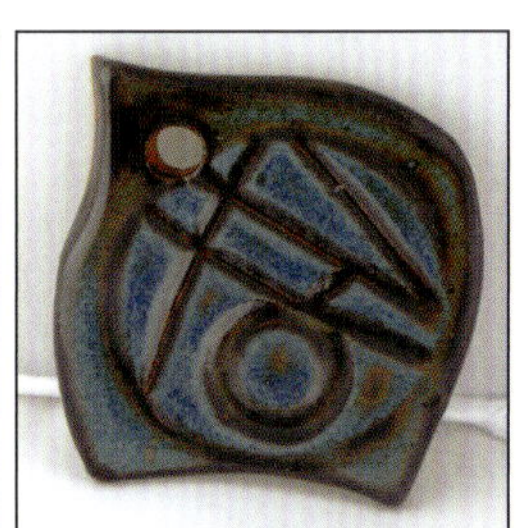
2% cobalt carbonate

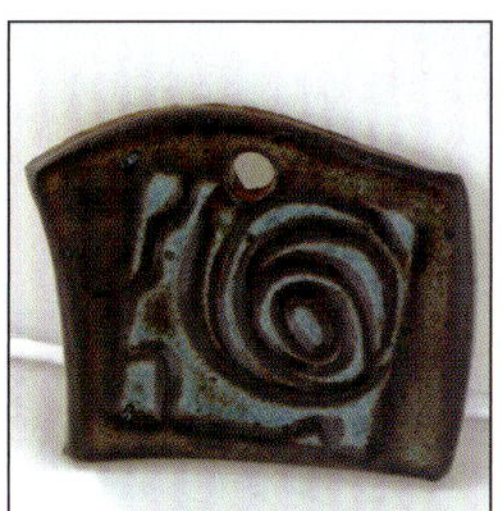
5% Bright Blue stain

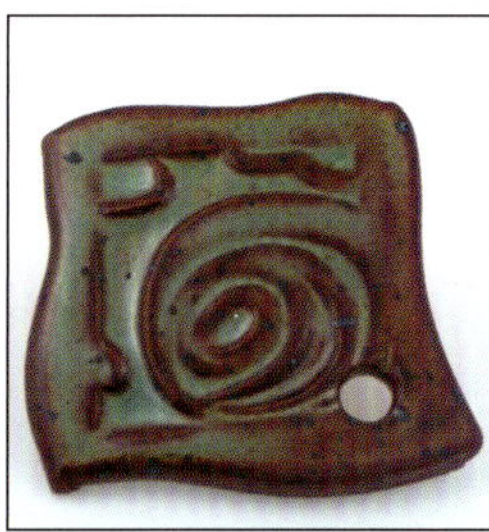
2% copper carbonate

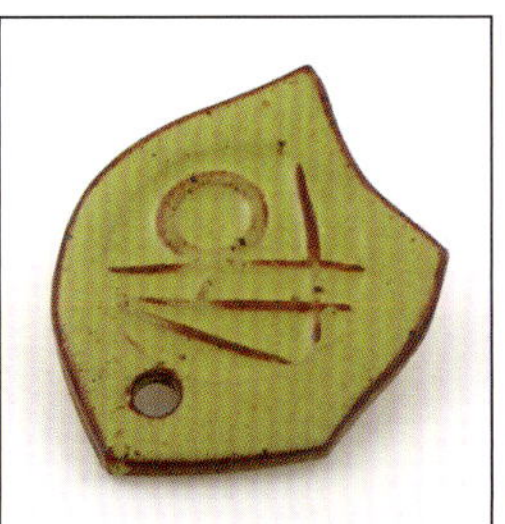
5% 6236 Chartreuse Mason stain

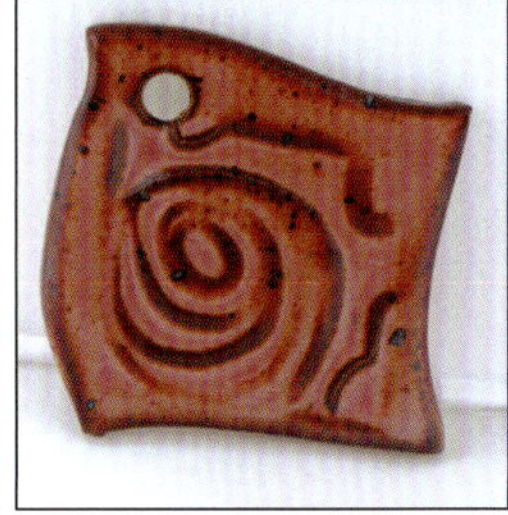
5% 6088 Dark Red Mason stain

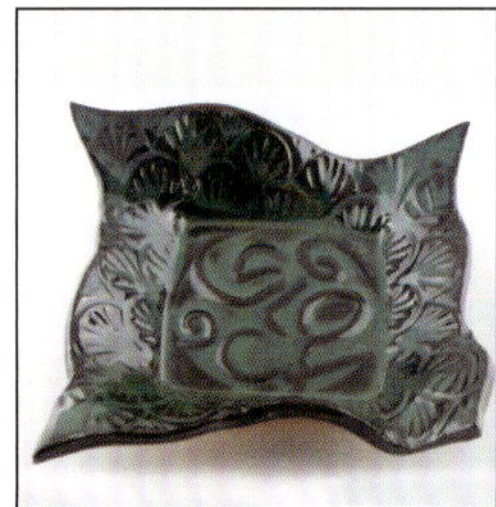
1 coat 2% copper carb over 1 coat 2% cobalt carb

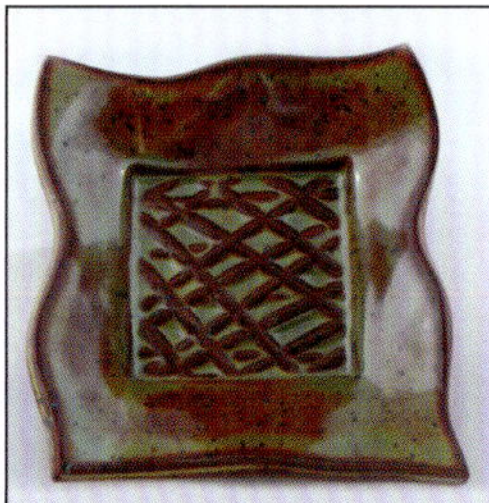
1 coat 5% 6236 Chartreuse MS over 1 coat 2% copper carb

FALLS CREEK SHINO
Cone 6

Gerstley Borate	18.7%
Lithium Carbonate	6.5
Soda Feldspar (Minspar 200)	9.4
Alberta Slip (Albany Slip Substitute)	56.1
Silica	9.3
	100.0%
Add: Superpax (Zircopax)	9.4%
Tin Oxide	4.7%
Blue Shino 1:	
Spectrum 2043 Bright Blue Stain	5.0%
Blue Shino 2:	
Cobalt Carbonate	2.0%
Green Shino:	
Copper Carbonate	2.0%
Chartreuse Shino:	
6236 Chartreuse Stain	5.0%
Pink Shino:	
6088 Dark Red Stain	5.0%

Test tiles made from Highwater Clays' Speckled Brownstone cone 4–6 clay.

in the dishwasher for multiple cycles, and test with freezing and thawing. This is an important step because every potter fires differently and uses glaze in different ways. If you're ever concerned about colorants or glaze ingredients leaching, you can send your piece to a testing lab for extra security. For a small fee, leach tests are run, and you're given a detailed report of the results.

An important first step when exploring a classic recipe is to determine if all the ingredients are still commercially available. For our tests, the traditional Falls Creek Shino recipe called for Albany Slip, which is no longer available, so most potters substitute Alberta Slip.

Colorants are by far the easiest way to experiment with a glaze. In an average base glaze, adding color is the logical next step because colorants can completely change a recipe's appearance. However, if you take a not-so-average base glaze, like the Falls Creek Shino, adding color is unpredictable given the dark base color of the glaze. We tested 2%, 5%, and 10% of stains and 1%, 2%, and 4% of oxides. We found the 'sweet spot' for adding stains to be 5% and 2% for oxides.

In the original recipe, carved lines and texture allow the glaze to pool and collect the pretty cream color leaving the darker brown where the glaze breaks. So, in adding colorants, we were unsure if the background color or the foreground color would change. Opacifiers allow the added colorant to float leaving the darker brown color below almost unchanged. The best analogy I can think of is of a root beer float—but instead of using vanilla ice cream, imagine you'd used a flavored, colored ice cream! The tests maintained the depth and richness of the original glaze as well but allowed for the development of vibrant, opaque colors on top. Also, as a pleasant surprise, the Alberta Slip makes for a glaze that brushes and dips beautifully with virtually no settling in the bucket.

So, when you need a something new in your glaze repertoire, pick up a classic and add some color!

4

Glazes

ATMOSPHERIC EFFECTS FOR ELECTRIC FIRING

by Steven Hill

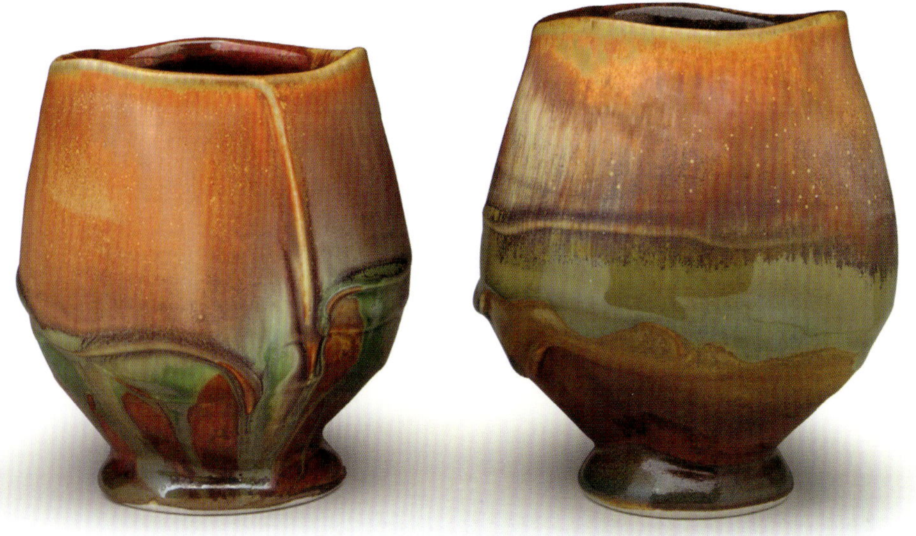

Pair of yunomis, to 4 in. (10 cm) in height. All work shown here is thrown and altered porcelain with applied slip design (either ribbed or slip trailing), multiple sprayed glazes, and single-fired to cone 6 in an electric kiln.

Wood, oil, gas, or electricity—the fuels used for firing have often inspired potters, but seldom do they determine the success of our finished work. All fuels are capable of producing results that range from mediocre to magnificent.

Firing with wood, oil, and gas requires an understanding of the firing process that leads to a relationship with the flame, and potters are also drawn to surfaces that show the "mark of the fire." It happens naturally in salt, soda, and wood firing, but this kind of surface has never been associated with the predictability of electric firing.

It can be a daunting experience for the novice to build and fire a fuel-burning kiln. Compared to their "fire-breathing brethren," electric kilns are safe, affordable, and predictable. Installing and firing an electric kiln is not much more complicated than an electric clothes dryer. Because of this, many feel like they make the choice out of necessity, but the typical cone 6 electric-fired pot, with its shiny and rather flat glazes, leaves many potters wanting more. Firing to cone 10 opens up some possibilities, but many electrics are limited to cone 6.

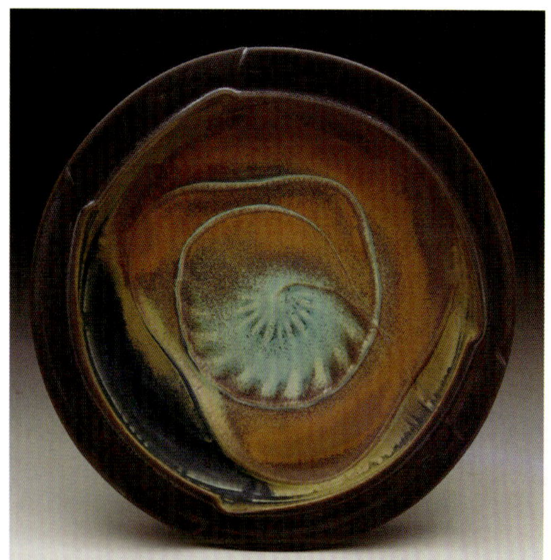

Platter, 16 in. (41 cm) in diameter.

I have learned that kiln atmosphere has less impact on the surface of my pottery than I once thought. This is based on my techniques of layering multiple glazes. I want to help potters who are seeking the soft, textured, and varied surfaces traditionally associated with reduction and atmospheric firings to achieve those surfaces regardless of the firing process. After a little rethinking and adjusting of firing cycles and glazing techniques, you just might be able to free yourself of the alleged limitations of electric firing.

Firing

Fuel-burning kilns tend to be much larger than electric kilns. Because of their size, they usually have a slower heat rise, a soak at the top temperature, and slower cooling cycles. If you want similar results from an electric kiln, especially when firing to cone 6, one of the most important things you can do is emulate the heating and the cooling cycles of larger kilns. This means slowing the temperature gain to about 100°F (38°C) an hour during the last several hours of the firing, soaking the kiln at the top temperature, and then down-firing to slow the cooling cycle. Electric kilns are built with thinner insulation and legs (to allow for air circulation), and they cool very quickly, especially at higher temperatures. If you're seeking buttery, matte surfaces but have trouble achieving them in the electric kiln, it's most likely due to fast cooling. Matte surfaces are usually caused by microcrystal growth during cooling, and, if the cooling cycle is too steep, there isn't enough time for crystals to develop. In extreme cases, I've even seen matte glazes go glossy and transparent.

I came to electric firing with a basic understanding of the significance of the cooling cycle but had my eyes further opened after reading *The Many Faces of Iron* by Dr. Carol Marians (see page 37). Marians describes a controlled experiment in which one application method, one clay body, one forming process, one firing cycle, and seven different cooling cycles were applied to one cone 6 iron saturate glaze. Amazingly, the results looked like seven different glazes. This started me on what will likely become a lifelong experiment with cooling cycles. Currently I am cooling the kiln naturally from the top temperature down to 1700°F (927°C), down-firing for five hours between 1700° and 1500°(816°C), and cooling naturally. I am achieving some of the best microcrystalline formations I have ever had!

I fired cone 10 gas reduction for 38 years, but, when I began electric firing, I knew it was time to drop my firing temperature to preserve elements and electricity. My first experiments were at cone 8, but, to make the final transition to cone 6, I needed to reformulate glazes. With the help of my science/art-major assistant, Mike Stumbras, and Digitalfire's glaze calculation program Insight, I was able to make the transition rather smoothly.

Glazing

In electric firing—and especially at cone 6 it's natural to achieve flat, solid colors that look more paint-like than glazes in reduction firing. If you're seeking a softer effect with more variation and atmospheric qualities, it's up to you to achieve it through glaze application. Remember, the atmosphere is static in an electric kiln, and it's not going to happen naturally!

Throughout my career, there have been occasional "Ah-ha!" moments, backed up with lots of hard work. The latest revelation came through a conversation with Pete Pinnell, in which he helped me understand how I made the transition from gas reduction to electric oxidation as easily as I did. According to Pete, "In reduction firing, glazes can stratify into layers during the course of the firing. Longer firings and slower cooling cycles, along with the effects of reduction, can result in the creation of complex structures that can result in a variety of beautiful visual effects. Even seemingly opaque glazes can have enough translucency for one layer to subtly affect the next, creating variation and softness in surface color. In oxidation, shorter firing cycles, faster cooling, and an oxidizing atmosphere can result in less layering, simpler structures and less interesting visual qualities." It just so happens I have been spraying multiple, undulating layers of contrasting glaze on my pieces for most of my career in an effort to achieve a more atmospheric look. In effect, my sprayed layers are accomplishing what happens naturally in reduction firing, and these layers give my surfaces the softness and variation commonly associated with reduction firing.

Cone 6 Single Firing Schedule

SEGMENT	RAMP	END POINT	HOLD
1	200°F / hour	220°F	1–3 hours, depending on the wetness and/or thickness of the work.
2	100°F/ hour	500°F	0
3	400-500°F / hour	2100°F	0
4	100°F/ hour	2160–2190°F	60 Minutes—this temperature is about cone 5, with an hour soak cone 6 should fall. Not all kilns are calibrated the same, some adjustment may be necessary.
5	9999°F/ hour On L&L Kilns you should program it for 4000/ hour.	1700°F	0
6	50°F/ hour	1600°F	45–60 Minutes
7	50°F/ hour	1500°F	No hold, Kiln OFF!

This firing schedule is based on computerized electric kilns. Remember, temperatures are controlled by thermocouples, which are not very accurate devices. Your kiln could be calibrated differently than mine, so you should always use guide cones.

Nothing is static with my firing schedules, however, so it will most likely change in the future. One thing is certain: there is no sense in extending the firing beyond what is necessary for desired results, as this is wasteful of electricity.

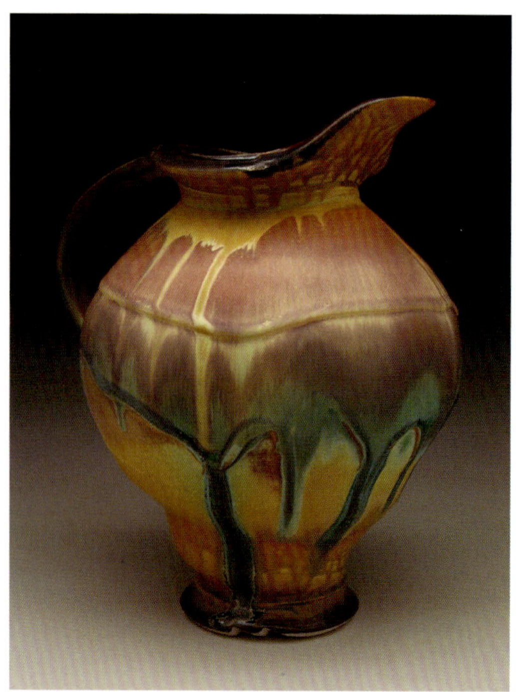

Melon Pitcher, 13 in. in height.

If you apply thin coats of two or more contrasting glazes, they will intermingle as they melt, but the layers never mix thoroughly. The result shows up as soft and subtle surface variation. You can apply multiple layers by any number of methods—dipping, pouring, brushing, splattering, sponging, etc.—but spraying gives you the opportunity to subtly modulate the thickness of each layer, varying glaze surface and color in a way that has the potential to look natural and organic.

A totally separate issue in the oxidation vs. reduction debate is color development. Some coloring oxides change color when fired in reduction. The most dramatic of these is copper, which changes from green to red. So, although the oxidation-fired pots look just like they would in reduction, that they have all of the subtleness and variation that they once had when fired in reduction and that many of them show no appreciable difference.

Certainly, not all glazes create inspired surfaces when layered. There are enormous benefits from experimenting with many different types of glazes. Layering similar glazes creates subtle variations, while using highly contrasting glazes can lead to more drama. If you alternate matte and glossy glazes in layers, it encourages surfaces to break. If you layer light and dark colors, you get variation in both color and value. Geoffrey Wheeler uses stains to color glazes, and often colors both matte and transparent glazes similarly. When spraying these two glazes, he blends a matte glaze gradually into the transparent one, creating a surface that's uniform in color and gradually breaks from matte to glossy.

Most of my pots have four to eight glazes applied in overlapping layers, and my biggest challenge is making everything look cohesive. Some glazes are sprayed with techniques that isolate one from the other others, like theblack or white glazes I apply on the rim of a bowl or the rim, handle, and foot of a pitcher, but most are layered and blended. My intention is for the whole pot to look as if it's one rich and varied surface, much like agate, marble, or layers of metamorphic rock. I want my glazes to ebb and flow (but not run too much!) with color and surface texture gently emphasizing changes in the form. I work with microcrystalline glazes, which can resemble a snowstorm or falling leaves, and use ash-like glazes to encourage streaking, leaving vivid traces of interaction as they melt. Most of my glaze combinations are rather unstable to work with, but, at their best, they have an amazing ability to allure and captivate. One thing is certain: They are never boringly predictable—

just as unstable people are often more captivating, enticing, and provocative than those we regard as "pillars of the community."

If you think about the flame, ash, salt, or soda responsible for the soft surface variations we characterize as "atmospheric effects," the common denominator is that they travel through the kiln via the kiln's draft. When you spray glazes, the spray has the potential to wrap around the piece and move past it in much the same way as the draft moves past a pot in a fuel-burning kiln. Spraying layers of overlapping glazes gives you the ability to create surfaces that naturally flow across a piece, softly highlighting its form. As sublime as this can be at its best, insensitive use of a spray gun can lead to surfaces characterized by obvious spray patterns and blotchy color. With experience, however, spraying glazes has the potential to integrate seamlessly with the form.

Think about how clumsy and uncoordinated your hands felt when you first attempted to throw on the potters' wheel, and compare your experience to how naturally and intuitively a seasoned potter's hands move across the form, applying pressure just where it's needed. The results achieved as a beginning sprayer are not too dissimilar, but, fortunately, the learning curve is much quicker when learning to spray than it's for throwing!

Spraying has the potential to be every bit as painterly as decorating with brush in hand. As with any painting, you will benefit from both a clear vision of what you're trying to create and the flexibility to let the process lead you in directions you never imagined.

The journey into spraying as my main method of glazing began more than 35 years ago. For most of that time, my goal was simply to create atmospheric surfaces on pottery fired in a gas reduction kiln. When I made the transition to electric firing, I was lucky—I had already laid the groundwork for success.

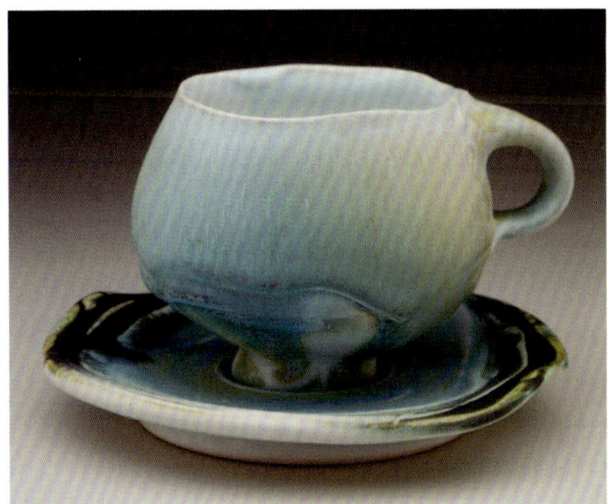

Mug and saucer, 4½ in. (12 cm) in height.

Recipes

I both formulate and collect glazes from other sources, but I am constantly experimenting with new combinations. The base glaze that underlies many of the surfaces and encourages crystal formation on my pots is Strontium Crystal Magic, which began as a Tom Coleman glaze, Yellow Crystal Matte. Through an extended series of experiments and the shift from barium to strontium, it ended up far enough afield to warrant renaming. It is rather dull by itself, but it brings glazes layered over it to life.

Strontium Crystal Magic Warm loves iron-saturated glazes sprayed over it for rich earth tones. Strontium Crystal Magic Cool can develop icy colors with cobalt or copper glazes sprayed over it. Shiny transparent glazes can break from matt to glossy depending on the thickness used. I have never sprayed a workable cone 6 glaze over Strontium Crystal Magic that didn't show some potential.

APRICOT
Cone 6

Ingredient	%
Lithium Carbonate	5.3 %
Whiting	19.9
Talc	3.1
Ferro Frit 3124	6.4
Custer Feldspar	44.0
EPK Kaolin	10.7
Silica	10.7
	100.0 %
Add: Rutile	7.0 %
Bentonite	3.0 %

JEN'S JUICY FRUIT (WITH IRON)
Cone 6

Ingredient	%
Lithium Carbonate	8.2 %
Soda Ash	9.1
Whiting	10.0
Ferro Frit 3124	8.2
Nepheline Syenite	44.5
EPK Kaolin	9.1
Silica	10.9
	100.0 %
Add: High Purity Red Iron Oxide	7.3 %
Bentonite	2.0 %

RED ORANGE
Cone 6

Ingredient	%
Bone Ash	12.1 %
Lithium Carbonate	4.2
Talc	13.8
Ferro Frit 3124	7.5
Kona F4 Feldspar	36.7
EPK Kaolin	12.9
Silica	12.8
	100.0 %
Add: High Purity Red Iron Oxide	9.0 %
Bentonite	2.0 %

STRONTIUM CRYSTAL MAGIC WARM
Cone 6

Ingredient	%
Lithium Carbonate	4.6 %
Strontiun Carbonate	12.6
Whiting	17.2
Ferro Frit 3124	4.6
Custer Feldspar	46.0
EPK Kaolin	15.0
	100.0 %
Add: Titanium Dioxide	12.0 %
Yellow Iron Oxide	2.5 %
Bentonite	2.0 %

Combine with iron-saturated glazes for rich earth tones.

STRONTIUM CRYSTAL MAGIC COOL
Cone 6

Ingredient	%
Lithium Carbonate	4.6 %
Strontiun Carbonate	12.6
Whiting	17.2
Ferro Frit 3124	4.6
Custer Feldspar	46.0
EPK Kaolin	15.0
	100.0 %
Add: Titanium Dioxide	12.0 %
Bentonite	2.0 %

Combine with glazes containing either copper or cobalt to develop icy colors.

FROST BLACK—SATIN MATTE
Cone 6

Ingredient	%
Whiting	22.7 %
Zinc Oxide	9.1
Nepheline Syenite	31.8
OM4 Ball Clay	13.6
Silica	22.7
	100.0 %
Add: Black Iron Oxide	4.3 %
Cobalt Oxide	3.0 %
Black Copper Oxide	1.8 %
Manganese Dioxidde	1.8 %
Bentonite	2.0 %

SATIN WHITE #6
Cone 6

Ingredient	%
Talc	14.1 %
Whiting	10.0
Zinc Oxide	2.7
Ferro Frit 3124	12.2
Nepheline Syenite	27.5
EPK Kaolin	13.7
Silica	19.8
	100.0 %
Add: Zircopax	10.0 %
Bentonite	2.0 %

HANNAH'S FAKE ASH
Cone 6

Ingredient	%
Strontium Carbonate	10.1 %
Whiting	29.0
Ferro Frit 3195	4.8
Redart Clay	56.1
	100.0 %
Add: Red Iron Oxide	3.3 %
Yellow Iron Oxide	2.8 %
Bentonite	1.0 %

SH COPPER ASH
Cone 6

Dolomite	2.8 %
Whiting	32.5
Ferro Frit 3124	14.9
Alberta Slip	19.1
EPK Kaolin	24.7
Silica	6.0
	100.0
Add: Copper Carbonate	5.6 %
Bentonite	2.0 %

WATER COLOR GREEN
Cone 6

Lithium Carbonate	4.1 %
Strontium Carbonate	7.7
Whiting	16.4
Ferro Frit 3124	5.1
Custer Feldspar	49.2
Silica	17.4
	100.0 %
Add: Copper Carbonate	8.0 %
Bentonite	2.0 %

Glaze Spraying Tips

- Work with the same general glaze consistency for spraying as you do for dipping.
- Any glaze is suitable for spraying as long as you use an appropriate spray gun. If the glaze is particularly coarse, such as a chunky ash glaze, you can use a gun made for spraying textured ceilings.
- Use guns with an air adjustment, but no gauge, and set the line pressure for 50 or 60 lbs. While spraying, adjust each gun down while watching the spray pattern. If you have too little air pressure the glaze will splatter. If it atomizes well, but is not too forceful of a spray, your gun is adjusted properly.
- Gravity HVLP (high volume, low pressure) guns with stainless steel inner parts work well with glazes. They're available in both full size and detail guns. If you're aiming for broad coverage, use a full size gun, but if you're highlighting small areas use a detail gun.
- Always test the gun by spraying into the side of the booth before you spray the pot. This is to make sure the gun is adjusted and not clogged. Then spray towards the area on the pot you want to glaze. Experienced sprayers often want to start spraying off the piece and move across it, this is fine as long as you are going for general coverage, but it doesn't give you enough control to highlight specific details.

  The most important spraying technique to know is feathering. This can be generally defined as applying the glaze sensitively and it can be accomplished with three different methods:

  1. Spray short, overlapping, wispy strokes either back and forth or up and down. Use this technique to highlight details and on smaller pieces.
  2. Hold the trigger down, keep the gun moving in a circular motion, and apply overlapping strokes, while slowly rotating the piece on a banding wheel. This gives you faster coverage, but less control over details.
  3. For even application on symmetrical pots with no appendages, hold the trigger down as you spin the pot on a banding wheel, slowly making your way either up or down the side. This works well for evenly applying one glaze or blending horizontal bands of color.
- One of the challenges of spraying is to know when enough glaze has been applied. Watch for the sprayed glaze turning to liquid on the surface and you will be close. There is no substitute for the intuition gained through repeated practice.
- I always use an underlying base glaze and think of glazes layered over it as modifiers. The base establishes the general character and also helps ensure that the final result is more cohesive. The modifiers are used to enliven the surface and introduce color and/or texture change.
- You don't want the total glaze thickness to be much thicker than when dipping or pouring. You might want to layer four glazes, but you should never apply four full layers of glaze. One of the advantages of spraying is you have the ability to apply anything from a dusting to a full coat. If you're layering, spray less of each glaze. The only way to make effective decisions about blending and thickness is through experimentation.

Glazes

CELADON IMITATION

by John Britt

CHUN CLEAR
Cone 6

Whiting	14.0 %
Zinc Oxide	12.0
F-4 Feldspar or Minspar 200	38.0
Kentucky Ball Clay	6.0
Silica	30.0
	100.0 %
Add: Barium Carbonate (optional)	0.75 %
Stains	2–3.0 %
Or: Cobalt Carbonate	0.1 %

Celadon glazes are some of the most popular glazes in ceramics. In particular, transparent blue celadons have a very delicate, beautiful color that shows carving very nicely. But celadons can range from blue to blue-green to gray-blue to gray-green to green to amber, and even to white. They often have distinctive crackle patterns that are sought after but can also be craze-free.

Celadons originated in China thousands of years ago and were meant to mimic jade. The Lung-chuan (Longquan) satin green celadons were important Chinese exports for over 500 years. The term "celadon" is a French word thought to have derived from a character in a French play who wore gray-green ribbons over his cloak. However, there are several competing theories of its origin.

Technically, celadons are feldspathic transparent high-fire glazes that are colored with iron and fired in reduction. This differentiates them from transparent copper greens known as Oribe, but both glaze names denote a type of ware as well as a color of glaze. Celadons were thought to have been made from the local clay body and ash, but as the glaze traveled to Korea and Japan, potters began using porcelain stone (a naturally occurring decomposed feldspathic rock).

Purists would say that a cone 6 celadon is impossible, since, by definition, it is high fired, but if we take a more practical approach and widen our definition of celadon to a transparent blue-green glaze, then we can include cone 6 celadons in oxidation.

Grolleg porcelain white stoneware dark stoneware

Chun Clear with 2% Turquoise Mason Stain 6393

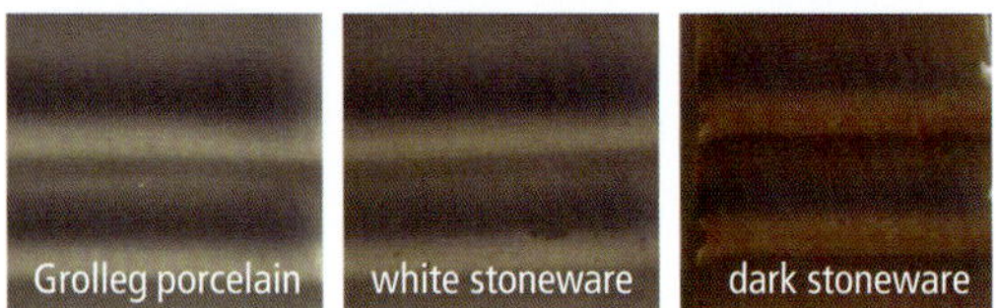

Chun Clear with 2% Cadet Blue Mason Stain 6302

Using Stains to Imitate a Celadon

Using stains in a cone 6 base allows you to fire in oxidation in an electric kiln. Zinc oxide in oxidation makes a wonderful cone 6 flux and can produce some nice colors with both oxides and stains. Many stain manufacturers recommend using 8% stain, but that makes the glaze flat and uninteresting to me, so I use very small amounts (1–3%) to keep the color delicate and transparent.

Clay Body Considerations

Clay body must be considered when making cone 6 celadons. If you want a blue/green celadon, there are many cone 6 porcelains that will work, as well as light and dark stonewares. Different clay bodies have different CTEs (coefficients of thermal expansion) and that will affect the crazing or the crackle pattern. Also, expansion and contraction is affected by firing temperature, and mid-range firing (cone 5–7) spans a large temperature range (2167– 2262°F) so maintaining consistent firings is essential.

Glazes

SNOWFLAKE CRACKLE

by John Britt

I only had a brief glimpse of this glaze some fifteen years ago in a museum gift shop. It was on a little sake set in a traditional Japanese wooden box. It was glazed with the most beautiful crackle glaze—not the usual crackle glaze that is common in raku. It had a conchoidal fracture, with the crazes layered on themselves like a stack of books that had slid over.

Only later did I find out that this glaze was called Snowflake Crackle; actually, it has many names (Snowflake Crackle, Fish Scale Crackle, Ice Crackle, Ice-like Crazing, and Tortoise Shell Crackle), which is generally a sign of how much people like something.

Regardless of what you call it, it's a crazed glaze that is applied so thick that the fractures run not just vertically but horizontally. These crackle patterns can be large or small, and they are distinct hexagonal shapes. When they are large, it is easy to see why it is sometimes called tortoise shell crackle.

Crazing

It is often said that, if you don't like it, you call it crazing; if you like it, you call it crackle. Crazing is often thought of as a glaze defect, but as Nigel Wood describes in his book *Chinese Glazes: Their Origins, Chemistry, and Recreation*, the Song dynasty potters are thought to be the first to treat crazing as a decorative effect. Commonly called Guan (Kuan) Crackle, the Ru, Guan and Ge ware were all beautiful examples of crazing as a decorative technique. In a specifically beautiful type called "iron wire and golden threads," or "golden floss and iron threads," the larger cracks, or primary cracks, were stained black while the pots were still hot. The smaller, secondary cracks developed over months or years as the delayed crazing occurred, leaving them brown.

Almost everything (except rubber and ice) will expand when heated and contract when cooled. When a clay body and a glaze are fired on a pot,

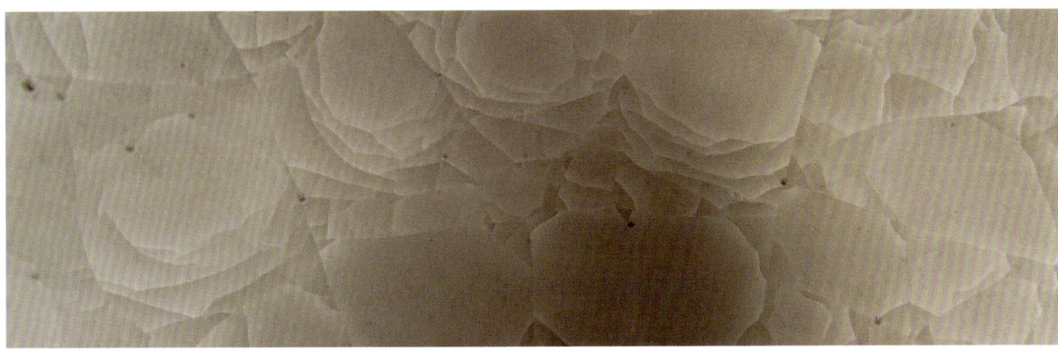

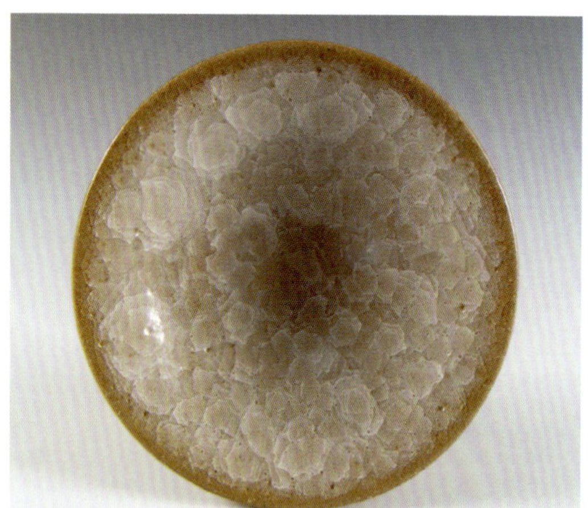

Snowflake Bowl, 5 in. (13 cm) in diameter, wheel-thrown Brownstone Clay, with Snow Flake Crackle Glaze #8.

they fuse together. As they cool, if the glaze contracts more than the clay body, it cracks or crazes. If the opposite occurs and the clay body contracts more than the glaze, the result is shivering, where the glaze actually pops off the pot. But if there is just the right amount of compression between a clay body and a glaze, it adds strength to the piece.

Crazing is usually thought of as a glaze defect because a crazed piece can be approximately 75% weaker than its uncrazed counterpart. It is also thought that the craze lines can harbor bacteria and viruses. For these reasons, dinnerware suppliers like to provide uncrazed ware.

Snowflake crackle is the most extreme kind of crazing, where the glaze is applied so thick and the fit with the body is just right so that the crackles appear to lay on top of one other. The glaze can be twice as thick as the body, just like during the Song dynasty. According to Wood, to get the glaze thick enough, Song Dynasty potters often bisque fired pieces between glaze coats.

A crazing pattern is always the result of the relationship/marriage between the expansion and subsequent contraction (governed by the coefficient of thermal expansion, or CTE) of a clay body and a glaze. By knowing a little about the CTE of oxides, you can easily control the crackle pattern in glazes to create any range of crazing from very small to very large crackles. Since a glaze is a mixture of oxides with a variety of CTEs, knowing that sodium oxide has a high CTE and magnesium oxide has a low CTE allows you to control the overall CTE of the glaze by adding one or the other.

As a glass, silica has a low CTE (it is amorphous), but as a crystal, it has a high CTE. So adding silica to a glaze can lower its CTE, because the silica melts to its glassy state. However, adding silica to the clay body (where it remains a crystal) can increase its CTE. It's important to keep the firing cone consistent as heating the piece a cone higher results in melting more of the silica in the body to glass, thus lowering its CTE. Similarly, firing to a lower cone melts less of the silica in the body giving it a higher CTE. The time and temperature of the firing is extremely important to the CTE of the clay body and thus to the crazing pattern.

Testing

Since seeing this glaze in the museum store, I tried many potential recipes with only moderate success. Since I couldn't get anyone to share their recipe with me, and I had no understanding of the principles of how to achieve this effect, I postponed my search, but in the back of my mind I remembered this beautiful glaze.

Fast forward about fifteen years to a workshop I was giving last year. I had assigned a student a series of tests to improve a magnesium crawling (reticulated) glaze that she was working on in cone 6 oxidation:

I had her make up the glaze (above) without the magnesium carbonate and then add it back in 5% increments up to 40%. She then dipped tiles of stoneware, dark stoneware, and porcelain. Fortunately, one of the clay bodies she was using was a very dark low-fire Redart body that she liked to fire to cone 6 (it is rated from cone 05–6). When the tiles came out of the firing, my eye went im-

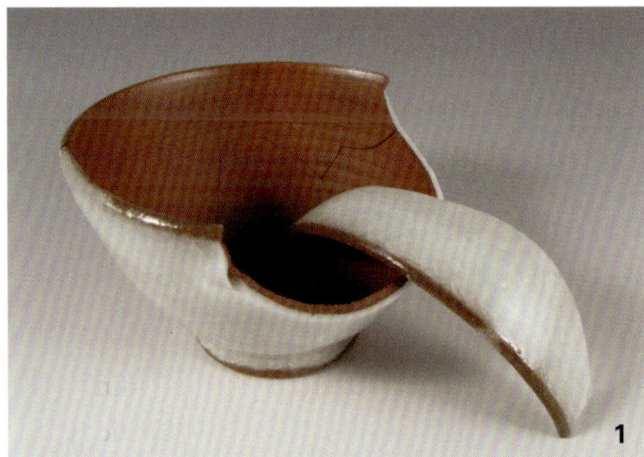

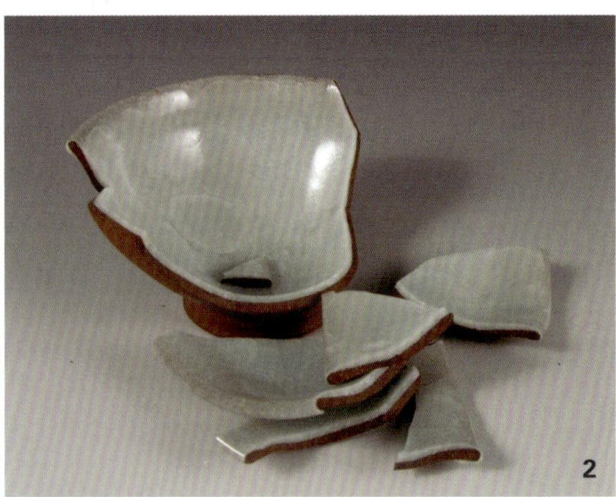

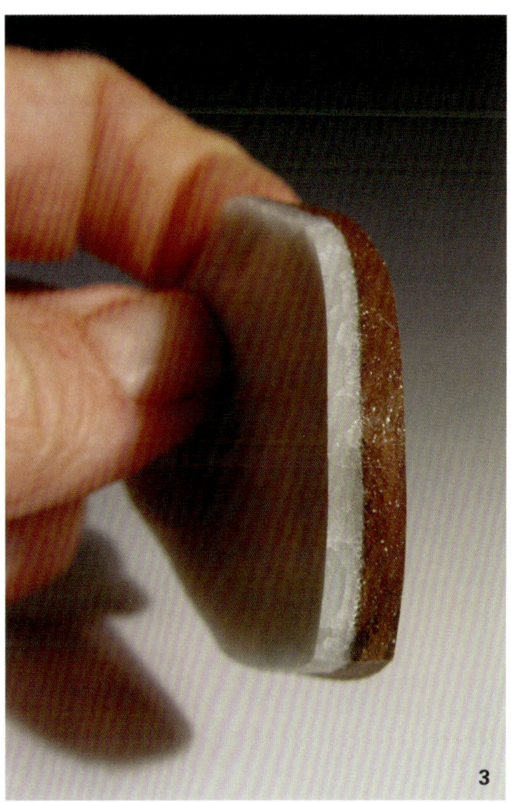

mediately to the 5% magnesium carbonate test on the dark body; it was Snowflake Crackle!

When I returned home, I tried the glaze on a variety of store-bought cone 6 clays. The best, in terms of CTE, were Highwater's Earthen Red and Brownstone at cone 6, and Orangestone at cone 10. There very well may be others that work, but these were the best of those I tested.

Since potters today generally buy premixed clay bodies rather than making their own, changes in CTE are usually made to the glaze rather than the clay body. This glaze crawled a bit, so I decided to remove the magnesium carbonate (because it has such a high shrinkage) and substituted talc.

While I was analyzing the glaze in the glaze calculation software program Insight (www.digitalfire.com), I decided to look at the CTE numbers, which were around 8.59 (Insight CTE). I then constructed about four more glazes with similar CTEs, between 8.59 and 8.70. I came up with several nice glazes this way, but I also tested the original recipe with a simple progression of Ferro frit 3124, just to see if it would melt a bit more. The result was a nice transparent Snowflake Crackle with 8% frit (Snowflake Crackle #8).

Color

The first thing I noticed when I did color tests with the usual colorants and opacifiers (copper carbonate, red iron oxide, chrome oxide, stains, Zircopax Plus, etc.) was that, as the color improved, the crazing ceased. This was because all oxides have expansion/contraction rates and adding them changed the CTE of the glaze enough to stop the crackle effect. I ran more tests with very low levels of colorants (under 1%), which kept the crazing yet still produced a nice color.

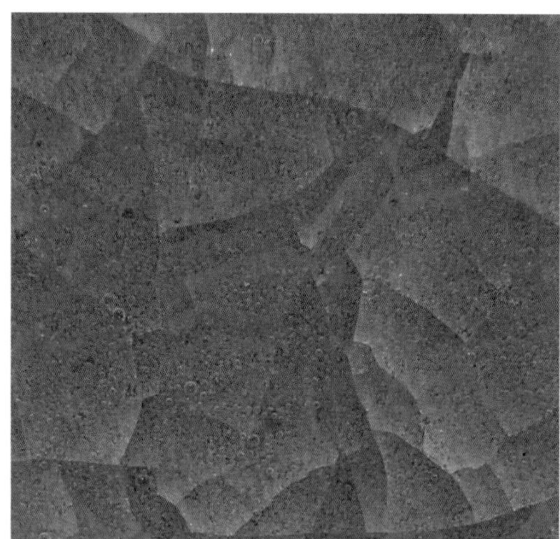

Test tile of Snowflake Crackle #4 with 0.2% copper carbonate on Brownstone clay, fired to cone 6 in an electric kiln.

Mixing and Application Notes

These glazes contain high amounts of nepheline syenite, which is partially soluble, so the glaze slop can easily deflocculate affecting application thickness. Adding Epsom salts corrects the problem. Mix to a specific gravity of approximately 155–160.

These glazes must be applied thick, between an eighth and a quarter of an inch (3–6 mm).

Snowflake crackle is not limited to cone 6; that is just the first temperature where I discovered it. In the cone 10 versions, watch for the flocculating effect of bone ash. You may need to add a deflocculant (sodium silicate), otherwise the glazes can flake off before you get the pots into the kiln. If they don't flake off, they usually crawl badly during the firing. Be sure to wait a couple of days after firing for the crazing to finish forming enough to see it (this is called delayed crazing.) One load came out and I thought they were unsuccessful, with no crazing. I went away for a long weekend and, to my surprise, when I came back they were all crazed nicely with the snowflake crackle effect.

These glazes are not recommended for functional work as you can often feel the crazing patterns with your hand.

Glazing only one side of a bowl, either inside only or outside only, will cause the bowl to shatter from unequal tension.

After the pots are fired, the glaze sometimes thins on the rim and you can see the brown clay body. This is called "brown mouth" or "purple rim and iron foot" (the glazed rim will reoxidize differently from the unglazed foot).

The crackle works best on the inside of bowls as the concave interior accentuates the crackle effect.

ORIGINAL SNOWFLAKE CRACKLE
Cone 6–7

Magnesium Carbonate	4.3 %
Nepheline Syenite	89.4
OM-4 Ball Clay	6.4
	100.0 %
Add: Bentonite	2.0 %

SNOWFLAKE CRACKLE #8
Cone 6–7

Magnesium Carbonate	3.9 %
Ferro Frit 3124	7.4
Nepheline Syenite	82.8
OM-4 Ball Clay	5.9
	100.0 %
Add: Bentonite	2.0 %
Turquoise: Copper Carbonate	0.2 %
White: Superpax	0.5 %
Blue: Cobalt Carbonate	0.07 %
Yellow: Degussa Stain 239416	0.5 %
Rust: Red Iron Oxide	0.5 %

SNOWFLAKE CRACKLE #4
Cone 6–7

Talc	7.9 %
Ferro Frit 3124	5.8
Nepheline Syenite	86.3
	100.0 %
Add: Bentonite	2.0 %
Turquoise: Copper Carbonate	0.2 %

SDSU CRAWL/BEADS
Cone 6

Magnesium Carbonate	25 %
Nepheline Syenite	70
OM-4 Ball Clay	5
	100 %

Note: This is not a Snowflake Crackle glaze.

CRYSTALLINE GLAZES

by William Schran

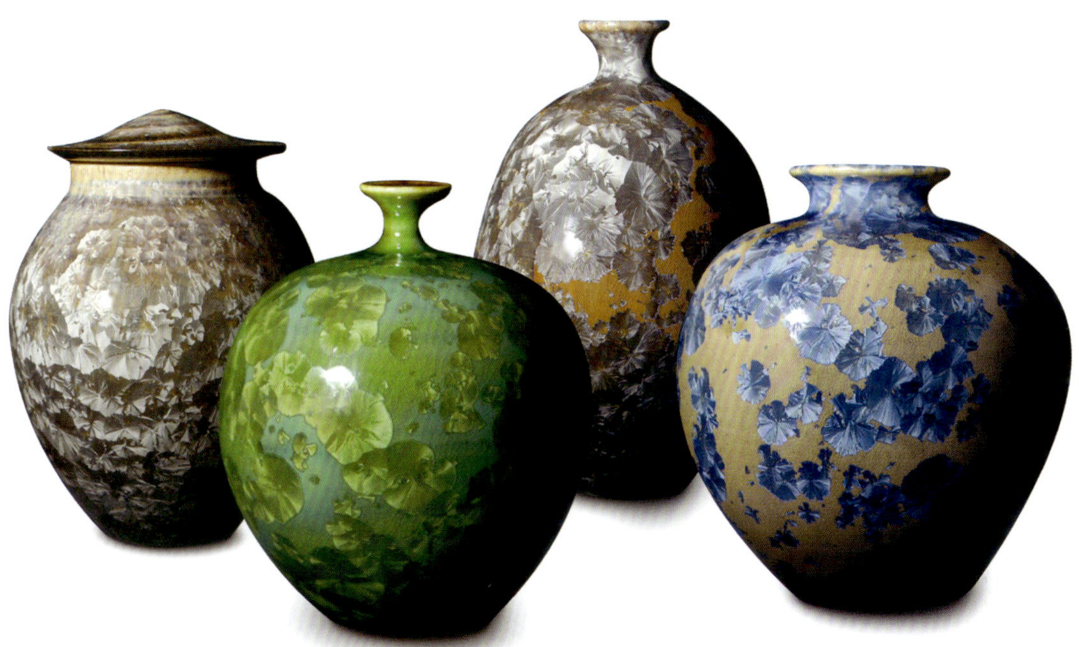

Four vessels, to 8 inches in height, thrown B-Mix clay. Glazes are as follows (left to right): Fa's Cone 6 Base glaze revised with 3% manganese dioxide and .5% cobalt carbonate; MFE (Dan Turnidge Revised) glaze with 3% manganese dioxide and 1% cobalt carbonate; Fa's Cone 6 Base (Revised) glaze with 3% manganese dioxide and .5% cobalt carbonate; MFE (Dan Turnidge Revised) glaze with 3% manganese dioxide and 1% cobalt carbonate.

My fascination with macrocrystalline glazes began as a graduate student. While visiting a local exhibition of an individual's collection, I discovered two small porcelain bottles by Herbert Sanders. The glazes appeared to have blue colored snowflakes frozen on a transparent sky of orange. From that initial encounter, macrocrystalline glazing has become a process that I've revisited many times over the years.

Sanders had published *Glazes for Special Effects* in 1974, which contained recipes for crystalline glazes. In 1976, I began experimenting with several recipes listed in the book, but since it was difficult to fire our electric kilns to the required cone 9–10 temperature range, I had little success. An article by David Snair in *Ceramics Monthly* provided additional glaze recipes and techniques for preparing the pots for firing. Though all the recipes were for cone 9, a comment in the article stated that firing to cone 6 would also produce crystals. I had some limited success with these glazes, but that comment stuck in my head.

Fast forward to 1994. Discussions of glazes with a group of my students lead to a question about crystalline glazes. This one question resulted in a semester-long series of glaze tests that resulted in few successes. It was the problem I had encountered years before, our electric kilns only reached cone 9–10 with much difficulty. The lack of success producing crystals by my students only strengthened my resolve to find a solution. It was then, that I recalled the Snair article and the comment about cone 6.

With additional information gathered through Internet searches and interlibrary loans, I discovered some artists experimenting with crystalline glazes at lower temperatures. Since we conducted our glaze firings to cone 6 at school, I decided to target this temperature for my testing. My initial experiments involved firing cone 10 glaze recipes only to cone 6. These tests resulted in finding that crystalline glazes could be produced in this lower temperature range by simply introducing additional fluxes. The flux that produced the best results was lithium carbonate. Other materials that would function as a powerful flux were either soluble or contained additional silica and alumina, which are not desirable in crystalline glazes.

All of my experiments with crystalline glaze firings, up until fall 2006, have been done in a manually operated electric kiln. The kiln has infinite controls, so with careful monitoring, I was able to control the firing schedule fairly accurately. A digital pyrometer is an essential tool to closely track temperature changes, especially during long holding cycles. Acquisition of my first kiln with a programmable controller has allowed for more complicated, repeatable firing schedules. The ability to be able to alter temperature ramp speeds and specific temperature hold times have opened up new avenues of experimentation. I have also found that, for both types of kilns, a direct vent system is important for rapid cooling cycles and maintaining an oxidizing atmosphere.

Crystalline Technique

Crystalline glazes produce the best results when applied to a smooth white clay body. Many artisans work with a porcelain clay body. Porcelain comes with its own set of issues and I have found a cone 10 porcelaneous stoneware clay—B-Mix or Bee-Mix—that works very well with my glazes. I chose to use a cone 10 clay to reduce the amount of alumina that might be picked up by the glaze.

A normal glaze has a mix of silica/flux/alumina in a ratio that provides a glassy surface and remains in place when melted on a vertical surface. A crystalline glaze contains little or no alumina, which would inhibit crystal growth. The glaze is comprised of silica, flux and a saturation of zinc oxide. This highly fluxed mix of materials leads to a very fluid glaze and steps must be taken to avoid destroying kiln shelves or the kiln.

Catch Basins and Pedestals

Every pot must have its own catch plate/basin to contain the glaze that runs off the pot (figure 1). The catch plate need not be made from the same clay as the pot. The plate can be wheel-thrown or handbuilt. Each pot must also have some type of pedestal device to facilitate removal of the pot after firing. Some potters use insulating firebrick to create the pedestal. The brick must be at least a 2600K-type and coated with kiln wash. Another technique involves throwing the pedestal from the same clay body as the pot. After bisque firing, the pedestal is attached to the pot with a mix of white glue, which holds the pedestal in place before firing, and kaolin, which acts as a separating agent after firing. Striking with a sharp chisel or heating with a small torch just below the joint with the pot

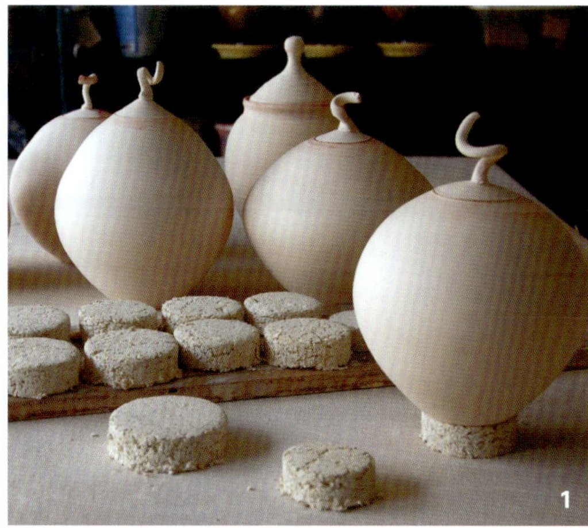

Crystalline glazes run off the pot so you need to raise the piece on a pedestal that sits in a catch basin. These are made of insulated firebrick.

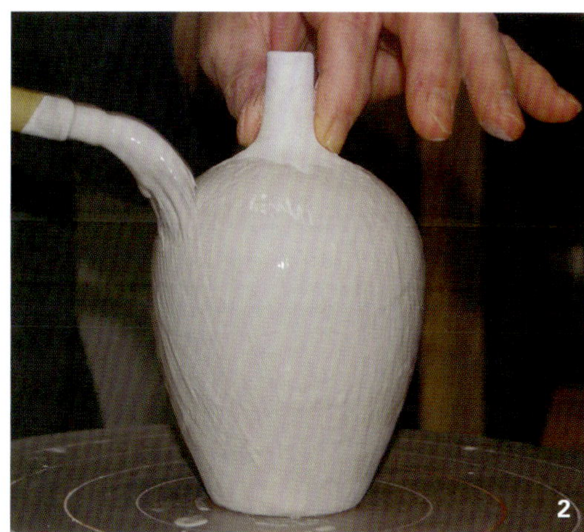

Apply three to four coats of glaze. If you are brushing, be sure to brush each layer in a different direction.

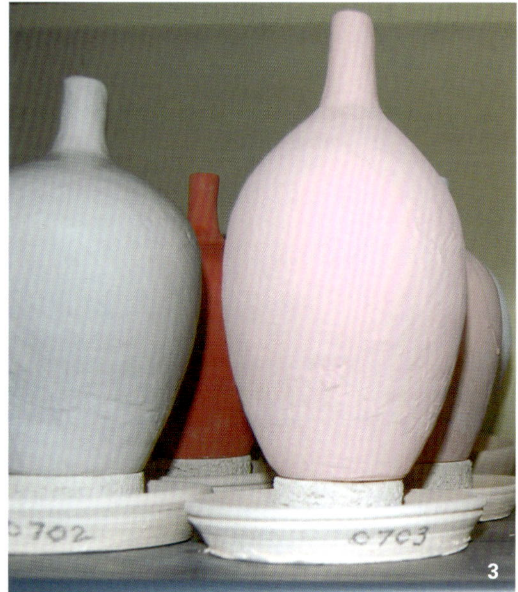

Each glazed pot is positioned on a pedestal that is placed in a catch basin and is now ready to load.

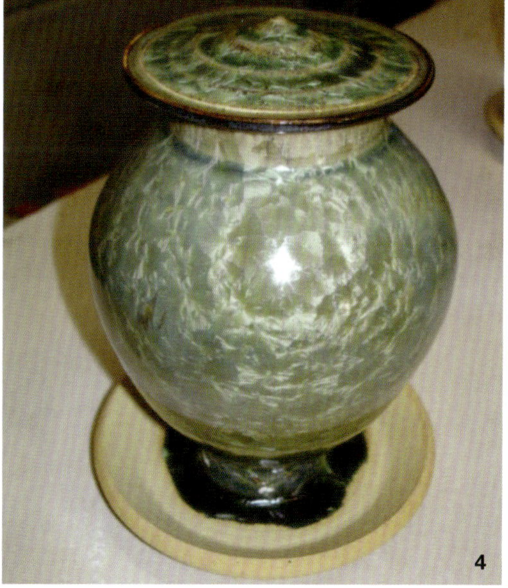

After the firing, the fluid glaze will have run down over the pedestal and into the catch basin.

removes the pedestal. After encountering a number of problems with each of these methods, such as pots falling over or broken foot rings, I sought another solution. Ellie Blair, a fellow crystalline artist, provided this process to me—the pedestals are a mix of equal parts by volume: alumina, kaolin and sawdust. Add just enough water to bind the materials and form the mix into ¾-inch thick "biscuits" cut to the foot diameter of the bisque fired pot using round cookie cutters. I've found this material to stand up well to the melting glaze and soft enough to be easily knocked off with a chisel. Any remaining pedestal is easily ground away from the pot.

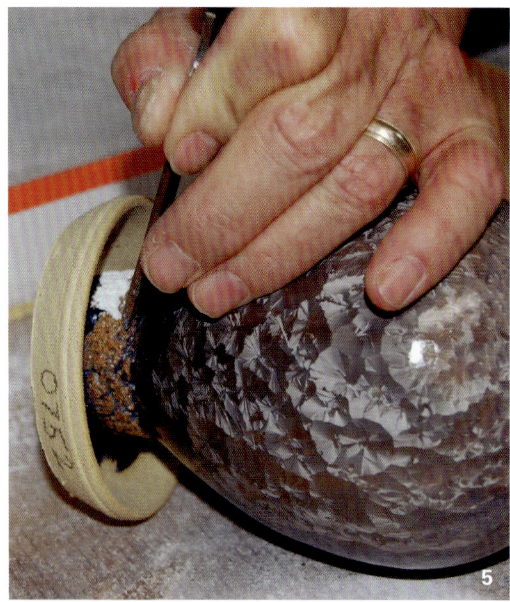

Remove the pedestal and catch basin by tapping with a small chisel along the line where the pedestal joins the pot.

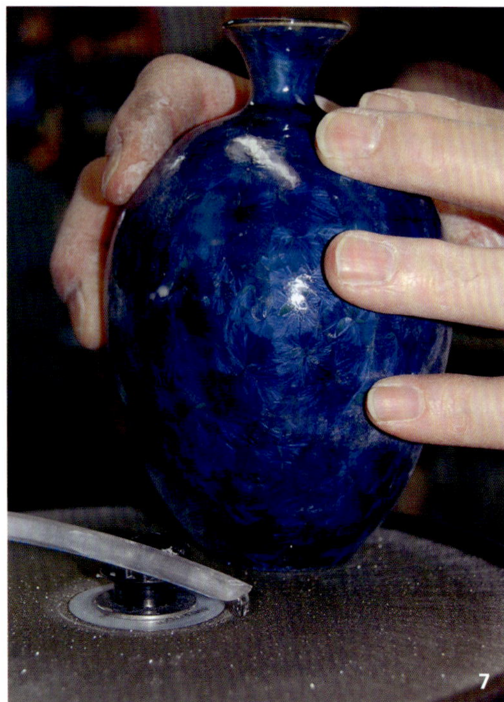

Smooth the bottom of the foot with 100 and 260 grit disks.

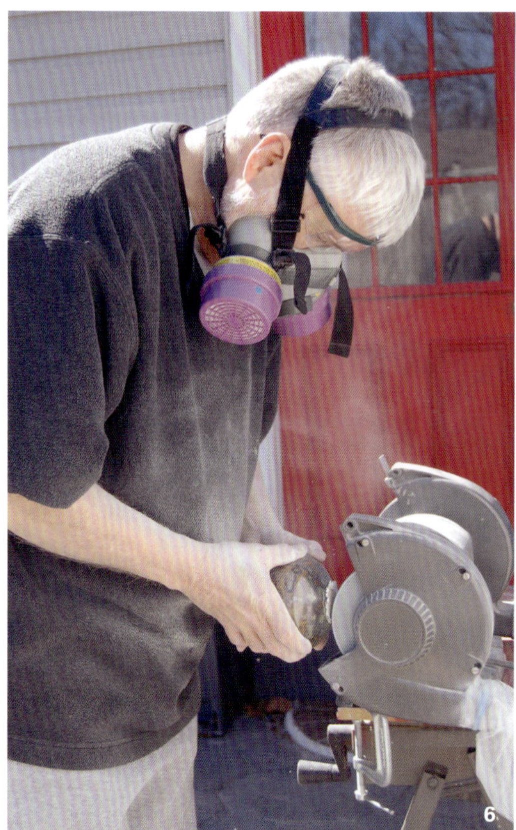

Grind off excess material and from the bottom using a bench grinder fitted with a silicon carbide grinding wheel.

WARNING
Proper eye and respiratory protection must be worn during this process. Do all grinding outside the studio, if possible.

Glaze Application

Crystalline glazes may be applied like most other glaze, but I apply them by brush (figure 2). Most of the time I mix a few hundred grams at a time, which is sufficient to glaze two or three small pots. Since the crystalline glaze contains no added clay to keep it in suspension, you don't want to add just water to wet the glaze. To wet the glaze, I use a CMC gum solution by adding about two heaping tablespoons of CMC powder to one quart of hot water. I let the powder soak into the water for at least 24 hours. The soaked gum is then stirred, resulting in a thin honey consistency. I add this to the dry glaze, stir and pass through 40 mesh, then 80 mesh sieves. The wetted glaze should have the consistency of thick honey.

Apply the glaze fairly thick. I apply one coat by brush horizontally around the pot. When that dries, I apply a second coat vertically, then a third coat in a diagonal direction to the upper 2/3 of the pot. Sometimes I'll apply a fourth coat to the top.

On the interior of vase/bottle forms and on the exterior of bowls, I use a cone 6 stoneware glaze. I selected a glaze that fits my clay body to create a watertight seal. With a crystalline glaze on just the interiors of bowls, I don't have be concerned with pedestals or catch plates.

Firing

Pots, with their pedestals and catch plates are loosely loaded in the kiln (figure 3). In my 4 cubic-foot-kiln, I will have at the most a dozen pots. Avoid using too much kiln furniture. It takes more energy and time to heat and cool kiln furniture than it does the pots. Always use witness cones in every firing. Even if you fire with a programmable kiln and don't look at the cones during the firing, they will be the best record of the firing. Keep meticulous notes of every firing. Keep a logbook of your firings and cross-reference each glaze to its firing. Fara Shimbo and Jon Singer gave the best advice during a presentation at the Lattice Structures Crystalline Glaze Symposium in fall 2005: When you're testing, change only one thing at a time. If you alter the glaze in any way, change only one amount or material at a time. Do not change anything else. If you alter the firing schedule, do not change the glaze until you see what change the firing has made.

Should the pot come out of the firing with few or no crystals, give it another chance. If the glaze has not filled the catch plate, simply apply another coat of the same glaze or a different glaze and fire it again. Should the catch plate be filled with glaze, remove the pot from the pedestal, grind the foot even and create another pedestal and catch plate. I have refired some pots up to five times before I achieved results that were to my satisfaction.

Cleanup

After the firing, knock the pedestal loose with a small chisel or screwdriver. Strike the pedestal material, not the joint between the pots and pedestal (figure 5). I use a bench grinder fitted with a silicon carbide grinding wheel to remove any remaining pedestal material and glaze (figure 6). I do all of my grinding outside and I always wear proper eye and respiratory protection. After coarse grinding, I use a portable flat lap fitted with diamond disks to even out and smooth the foot (figure 7). Silicon carbide disks and diamond disks with self adhesive backing can be attached to plastic bats and used on the wheel to grind and smooth pot bottoms. Squirting or spraying with water while grinding will help keep down the dust.

Firing Schedule

Use one of the following firing schedules for cone 6 crystalline glazes. You will need to experiment to determine the best firing schedule for your kiln. The ability of the kiln to respond to rapid heating and cooling ramps is a critical factor in successful crystalline glazes. Kilns should be loaded loose, using as little kiln furniture as possible. Older, well-used elements may not be able to keep up with programmed demands of the kiln. I've found heavy duty elements begin to be unable to keep up with the programmed firing schedule after about forty crystalline firings.

Firing Schedule for Programmable Kilns

Note: My kiln uses an "S" type platinum thermocouple with the thermocouple offset turned off. Each kiln may indicate a different temperature when cone 6 bends over. Use witness cones and closely monitor them until the correct peak temperature is determined.

- Increase temperature 350°F per hour to 700°F
- Increase temperature 750°F per hour to 2000°F
- Increase temperature 150°F per hour to 2210°F (this puts cone 6 over, cone 7 at 1 o'clock position)
- Hold at 2210°F for 10 minutes
- Cool down 750°F per hour to 2000°F, hold for 1 hour
- Cool down 750°F per hour to 1900°F, hold for 3 hours
- Kiln off, vent off, total firing 9–9½ hours

Higher holding temperatures results in fewer but larger crystals with more ground (areas without crystals) exposed.

Firing Schedule for Manual Kilns with Infinite Control

- Low: ½ hour
- Medium: ½ hour
- High: cone 6 over
- Turn off kiln, cool to holding temperature (1850°F–1880°F)
- Turn on kiln to a medium setting and monitor closely.
- Try to maintain the holding temperature for 3–4 hours.

Each section of the kiln may need to have a different setting to maintain a constant temperature. For my kiln, a setting of #3 on the top and middle section, and "M" setting on the bottom section provided a fairly consistent reading.

MFE (DAN TURNIDGE REVISED)
Cone 6

Ferro Frit 3110	50.0 %
Silica (325 mesh)	22.5
Zinc Oxide	22.5
	95.0 %
Add: Lithium Carbonate	1–5.0 %

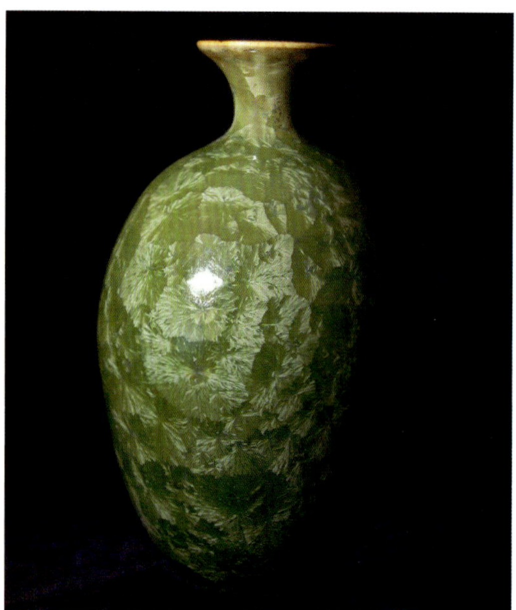

Bottle, 7 inches in height, thrown B-Mix clay, with Fa's #5 (Revised) glaze with additions of 4% manganese dioxide and 1% cobalt carbonate.

FA'S BASE (REVISED)
Cone 6

Zinc Oxide	25.0 %
Dolomite	5.0
Ferro Frit 3110	51.0
Silica (325 mesh)	19.0
	100.0 %
Add: Lithium Carbonate	2–4.0 %

FA'S #5 (REVISED)
Cone 6

Zinc Oxide	27.0 %
Talc	5.0
Ferro Frit 3110	50.0
Spodumene	4.0
Silica (325 mesh)	14.0
	100.0 %
Add: Titanium Dioxide	2.0 %

Colorants

Add colorants individually or in combination:

Add: Cobalt Carbonate	0.25–3.0 %
Copper Carbonate	0.5–6.0 %
Manganese Dioxide	0.5–3.0 %
Iron Oxide	0.5–3.0 %
Rutile	0.5–3.0 %
Nickel Oxide	0.25–3.0 %

LINER GLAZES

by Deanna Ranlett

What is a liner glaze? Why do you need one? A liner glaze is used on the inside of functional pottery to prevent exposure of the user to glaze ingredients that are prone to leaching. In theory it doesn't contain any toxic ingredients such as barium, lead, or heavy metals. It also shouldn't craze. It's a potter's responsibility to put a safely glazed pot into the world that can be used repeatedly with any food without causing harm.

Food-Safe Tests

It's important to test liner glazes to ensure that the glaze inside is a good functional choice and won't fade or etch over time due to exposure to acids commonly found in food or drink (e.g., coffee, lemon, orange, tomato) or bases (e.g., dishwasher soap).

A liner glaze should not contain heavy metals such as manganese, copper, or cobalt, which are prone to leaching. This isn't to say that you can't have colored glazes that pass leach tests—some liner glazes can be colored with small amounts of commercial stains or rutile to create a soft color. If the colored glazes pass the leaching test, you can use them as liners.

Every potter should test for acid leaching in their glazes either with a lemon slice (very acidic and acts quickly) left on the glaze-fired surface overnight or by soaking it in vinegar for 1–2 days. If you see any change in gloss level or color, your glaze is not acid safe and should not be used as a liner glaze. You should also test for deterioration to the glaze through repeated base exposure. Dishwasher detergent is a common base and, over time, it can cause the glaze to wear down. This test takes additional time, normally requiring the pot to remain in the dishwasher for 30 or more cycles to create any possible change in the glaze.

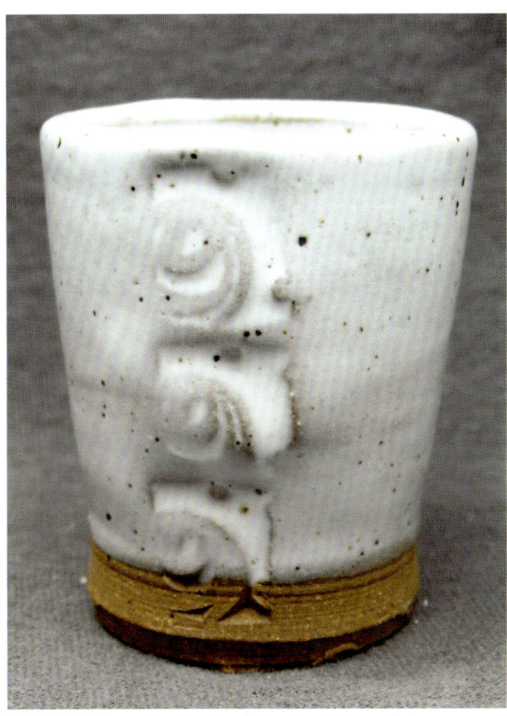

Richard Zakin's mid-range liner recipe on Highwater Clay's Speckled Brownstone clay. This clay body contains light speckles, which gives a good indication of the liner glaze's overall coverage.

Liner Considerations

Beyond leaching concerns, liner glazes can be beneficial in many ways. For example, using a white or clear liner glaze saves money on dry glaze materials because you won't be including the more expensive oxides and colorants.

Consider glazing the inside and outside of the pot in different colors and on different days. We recently had a workshop where a potter described how much improvement he had seen in his glazing because the clay had dried thoroughly between applications and had therefore accepted the glaze in a smoother, thicker application than when he glazed it all at once.

A white liner glaze highlights what is in the mug—sometimes when I drink tea in a dark mug it appears a bit murky and a nice white or soft colored glaze sets it off better. We tested only clear or white glazes for that reason.

ZAKIN'S BUTTER SATIN
Cone 6

Custer Feldspar	36 %
Ferro Frit 3124	20
Talc	16
Wollastonite	8
EPK Kaolin	20
	100 %
Add: Zircopax	5 %
Titanium Dioxide	3 %

Add 3% rutile instead of the titanium dioxide for a buttery hue. This glaze has a nice semi-gloss finish with beautiful feel and great coverage.

G-19 SHINY CLEAR
Cone 6

Wollastonite	30 %
Ferro Frit 3195	30
EPK Kaolin	20
Silica	20
	100 %

Wayne Bates' color friendly base, produces shiny versions of most of the Mason stain colors. Can be used as a liner glaze, unlikely to produce leaching.

PV BASE BLACK LINER GLAZE
Cone 6

Gerstley Borate	30 %
Whiting	10
PV Clay	15
Custer Feldspar	35
Silica	10
	100 %
Add: Mason 6600	6 %

BRICK RED LINER GLAZE
Cone 6

Gerstley Borate	20.3 %
Custer Feldspar	13.8
Ferro Frit 3134	14.2
Spodumene	10.5
EPK Kaolin	16.2
Silica	25.0
	100.0 %
Add: Zinc Oxide	4.8 %
Chrome Oxide	1.1 %
Cobalt Carbonate	3.1 %
Copper carbonate	1.1 %
Red Iron Oxide	5.2 %
Bentonite	2.0 %

SATIN MATTE

by Sherman Hall

This is a magnesium/calcium matte glaze that I use because of how it feels in the hand. For that reason, it's great for functional ware (and my leach tests have come back clean). However, it does not make the best liner glaze, since the surface is not quite smooth enough to keep flatware quiet.

base, no colorant	5% MS 4200	5% MS 4250
1% cobalt oxide	1% chrome oxide 1% cobalt oxide	5% MS 6373
5% MS 6265	5% MS 6304	5% MS 6129
3% copper carbonate	5% red iron oxide	5% MS 6600

SHERMAN'S SATIN MATTE
Cone 6

Dolomite	10 %
Talc	15
Nepheline Syenite	35
Ferro Frit 3124	10
EPK Kaolin	15
Silica	15
	100 %

Tangerine
Add: Mason Stain 4200 . . . . 5 %

Yellow
Add: Mason Stain 4250 . . . . 5 %

Blue
Add: Cobalt Oxide . . . . 0.5–2 %

Blue Green
Add: Chrome Oxide . . . . 1 %
Cobalt Oxide . . . . 1 %

Turquoise Blue
Add: Mason Stain 6373 . . . . 5 %

Light Green
Add: Mason Stain 6265 . . . . 5 %

Lavender
Add: Mason Stain 6304 . . . . 5 %

Ochre
Add: Mason Stain 6129 . . . . 5%

Dark Green
Add: Copper Carbonate . . . . 3 %

Medium Brown
Add: Red Iron Oxide . . . . 5 %

Charcoal Gray
Add: Mason Stain 6600 . . . . 5 %

The magnesium in this glaze can cause cobalt to lean toward the purple side of blue. You can see this even in the Turquoise Blue (MS 6373) stain. Iron will pretty much stay brown rather than warming up to red/orange, even though there is a fair amount of calcium in this glaze.

Glazes

BRISTOL GLAZES

by Cheryl Pannabecker

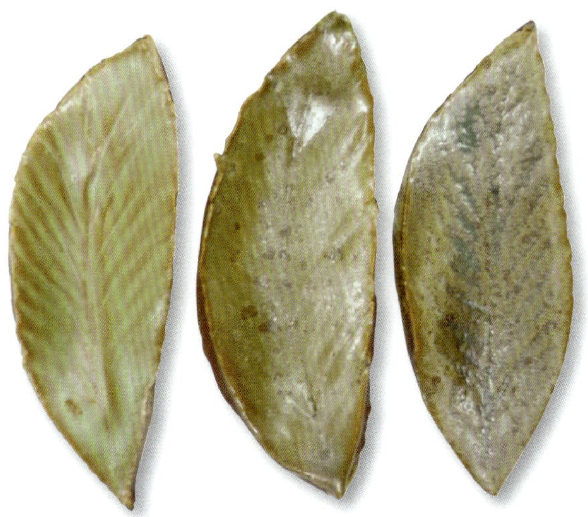

Bristol glazes were developed when the 19th century British ceramics industry moved away from using lead as its principal fluxing agent and started using zinc oxide instead. It remained the chief flux until its role was usurped by another industry advance—fritted leads. These newer glazes were easier to apply and less temperamental than the Bristol glazes.

Although the variations in surface qualities in Bristol glazes were unsuitable for industry, in the individual potter's studio they can create beautiful effects. Glaze application, thickness and thinness, its layering, the clay body, and the forms to which the Bristol glazes are applied as well as the timing and temperature of the kiln all contribute to a variety of results, earning these zinc oxide glazes their place as a mercurial glaze set.

In his 1971 book, *Glaze Projects*, Richard Behrens (1896–1977) explains that Bristol glazes work well for potters because of their capacity for mottling and patterning. In more contemporary glazes, we rely on zinc oxide's characteristic microcrystalline development to produce opacity in a cone 4–6 glaze. This same quality can give Bristol glazes a patterned or mottled surface. In the cone 6 glazes, it's most noticeable when colorants have been added to the glaze. The cone 4 glaze I tested flowed quite a bit and had visible patterning and mottling.

Exploring the Base Glaze

As application was initially difficult, I substituted calcined zinc oxide, which made applying the glazes easier and more successful. Brushability was a challenge with the Bristol glaze bases. Bristol IX was the most difficult, but I found adding some laundry starch to the glaze allowed an easier application.

I tested the cone 6 glazes at both cone 6 and at cone 4 on red and white stoneware, and the cone 4 glaze was tested only at cone 4. The glazes generally worked well at both temperatures, though some pinholing and pitting occurred on tests with the red stoneware body, and Bristol IX blistered and shivered off the red stoneware.

At first, I used both fast and slow glaze firing schedules when testing the glazes at cone 6 to see

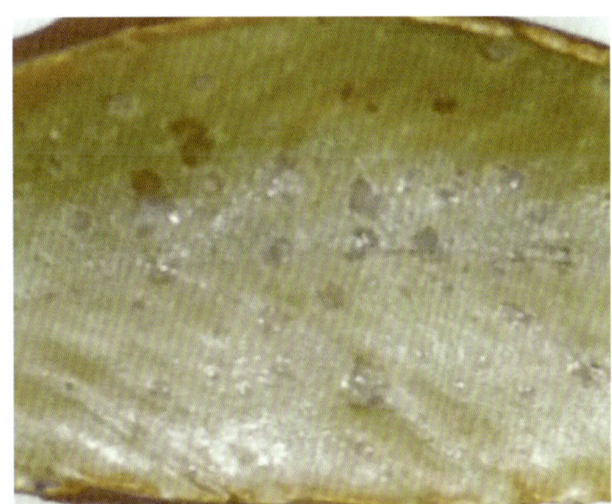
Red stoneware with Shadow Green Glaze under Bristol X with 3% copper carbonate, fired to cone 6.

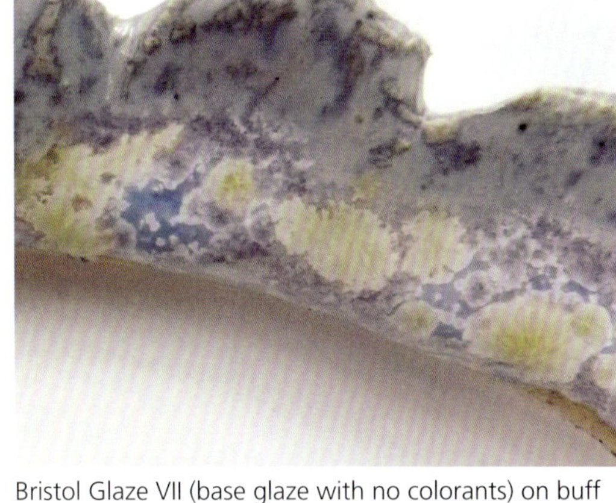
Bristol Glaze VII (base glaze with no colorants) on buff clay, fired to cone 4.

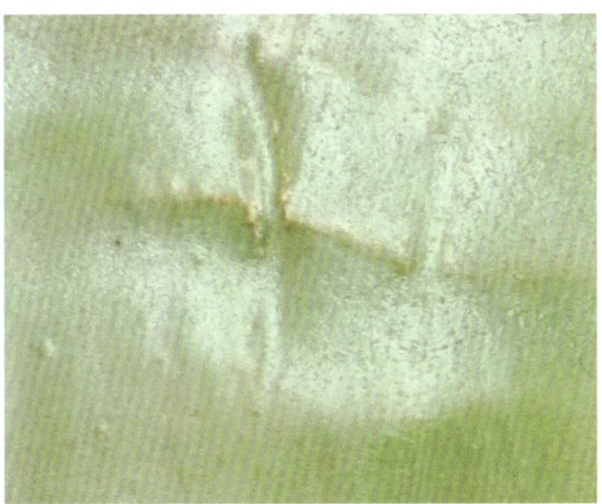
One coat Shadow Green Glaze on buff clay fired to cone 4.

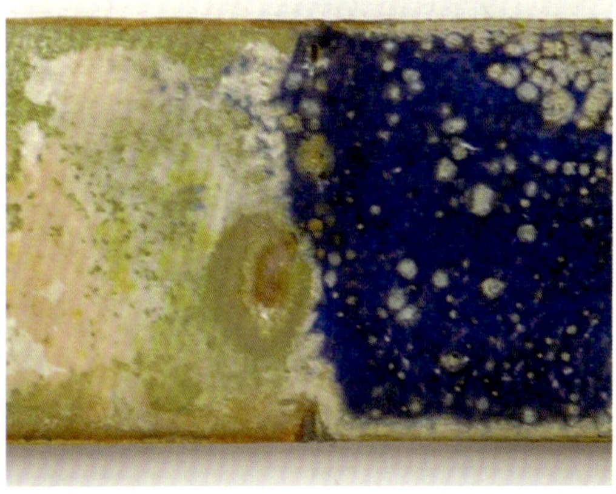
Left: Bristol VII over Bristol X with .5% cobalt carb. Right: Bristol IX with 1.5% chromium oxide over Bristol VII. Fired to cone 4.

how they would respond. The first was a rapid firing, with no soak at the end, and the second was a crystalline-type firing schedule with a rapid 100° drop at the end of the firing followed by a three hour soak. I also did a fast cone 4 firing with a 30 minute soak at the end. I noted no significant difference in either firing, and settled on a fast firing with a 30 minute soak for the rest of my testing. This limited the amount of pinholing on the red clay. Use a clay body free of iron oxide if pinholing and other glaze defects are a consistent problem [pinholing can also be caused by a fast bisque].

Adding Color

Next, I moved on to experiment with colorants. Behrens had a Shadow Green Glaze elsewhere in the handbook that made a lovely green and happened to be Bristol VII with 1.5% green chromium oxide added, so I started there. This addition also works well in the other glaze bases.

I experimented with iron oxide, rutile, milled ilmenite, copper carbonate, and cobalt carbonate. Iron oxide made a glaze that was too muddy, but I found that small amounts of rutile (3%), and copper carbonate (less than 2%) worked the best. The rutile glaze was tan with significant mottling. When more than 2% copper carbonate was used, Bristols VIII and IX turned black. Bristol X was the only glaze base that allowed a nice copper green to develop, with additions of copper carbonate up to 3%. (Bristol X is the only one of these four glazes that Behrens described as bright and clear.) The addition of ilmenite or titanium encouraged a mottled surface. Cobalt carbonate produced an even, straightforward cobalt blue color, but when layered with other glazes, the coloration became dynamic.

All of the glazes were very fluid, particularly when layered together. Keep the glaze at least a half inch from the bottom of the piece, and when in doubt, use a firing slab. Glaze effects will also depend on how tightly packed the kiln is and the general mass and thickness of the ceramic pieces.

BRISTOL GLAZE VII
Cone 4

Lithium Carbonate	10.0 %
Whiting	4.6
Zinc Oxide	22.0
EPK Kaolin	17.7
Silica	38.3
Titanium Dioxide	7.4
	100.0 %

For Shadow Green Glaze, add 1.5% green chrome oxide.

BRISTOL GAZE VIII
Cone 6

Lithium Carbonate	4.5 %
Zinc Oxide	12.0
Nepheline Syenite	40.5
EPK Kaolin	7.8
Silica	35.2
	100.0 %

BRISTOL GLAZE IX
Cone 6

Lithium Carbonate	8.7 %
Zinc Oxide	9.3
Nepheline Syenite	25.9
Calcined Kaolin	9.7
EPK Kaolin	11.3
Silica	35.1
	100.0 %

BRISTOL GLAZE X
Cone 6

Lithium Carbonate	3.2 %
Zinc Oxide	6.9
Ferro Frit 3269 (Pemco Frit 25)	27.3
Calcined Kaolin	7.6
EPK Kaolin	9.3
Silica	45.7
	100.0 %

Notes: I used calcined zinc—as recommended in *Glaze Projects*—and Ferro Frit 3269 to replace Pemco Frit 25. Glazes were tested on Standard Ceramic Clay bodies (Brooklyn Red and Buff Clay), bisqued to cone 05.

LICHEN GLAZES

by Deanna Ranlett

There's a wide range of lichen glaze recipes available with sub-categories such as crawls, crackles, and crazing glazes—some result in a dry, crackled surface; others a glossy, pearly effect; and some a snowflake pattern. We chose a lichen glaze recipe that gives a glossy surface but still maintains a distinct separation while staying adhered to the pot. We wanted a recipe that didn't need a special or altered firing cycle and could be fired in the kiln alongside other cone 6 work.

We tested several reticulated cone 6 glaze recipes then experimented further by layering them with other translucent base glazes. We layered the lichen glazes both on top of and underneath the base glazes (two different Chun recipes with different stains added for color). The samples with the lichen glazes underneath the base glazes were not so exciting, but the samples with the lichen glazes applied over the base glazes were very striking. The lichen glaze adds a shimmering quality to the glaze underneath when applied in a single coat, two coats give a delicate crackled surface, and three coats give more separation between crackles and a larger crawl pattern. Up close, there is an almost silvery or pearlescent effect that is very lovely.

Our favorite samples resulted from using the more subtle glazes (light green and applying them over textured tiles. This layering technique is useful for creating a visual texture on a solid surface and also for creating a crackle-like effect where you might not normally use a crackle. The results using the lichen glaze on top of the base glaze were equally beautiful over areas with and without texture. Combining the more subtle glazes (light greens and blues) by applying them over textured tiles allowed the lichen glaze to break over the raised parts of the texture and rest in the recesses, giving it a lovely, lace-like effect.

Application Notes

Lichen glaze recipes include a large percentage of magnesium carbonate and the resulting mixed consistency is very fluffy, similar to frosting. The glaze is thick but brushes on thin and smooth. Do not mix this glaze too thin; when it's mixed properly, the result is an almost non-existent crackle pattern when you apply the first coat. When you apply the second and third coats, you can start to see the patterning appear. Take care when handling the pieces because the glaze the has already begun to crackle and can easily be chipped off of the surface before you get it into the kiln.

Different application methods of lichen glazes result in different surfaces. It helps to brush them because it's easier to control the effect of the glaze. If applying over another glaze, first dip the piece into the base glaze, let it dry, then brush the lichen glaze on top. The resulting crackle effect and the size of cracks varies based on the direction of the brush stroke. The base glazes below work for both brushing and dipping. Add a small amount of CMC or Veegum-T to aid in their brushability.

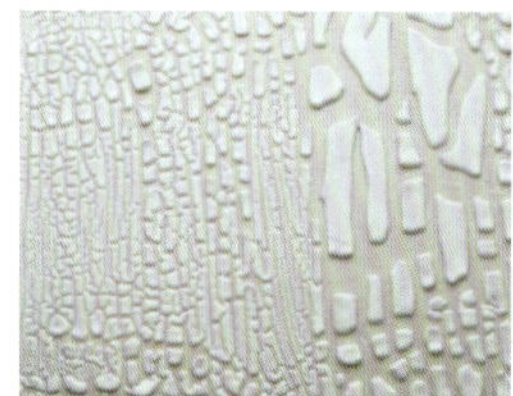
Lichen Glaze alone

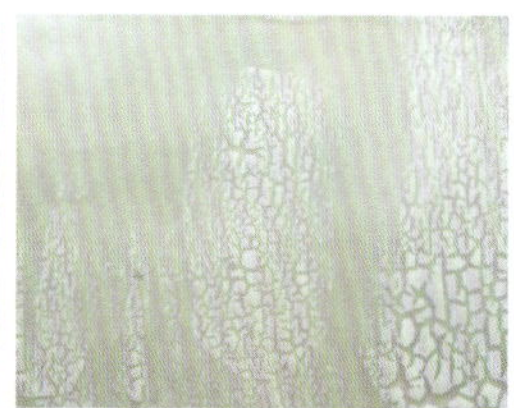
Chun 1 + 2% Spectrum 2086 Bright Green stain under Lichen

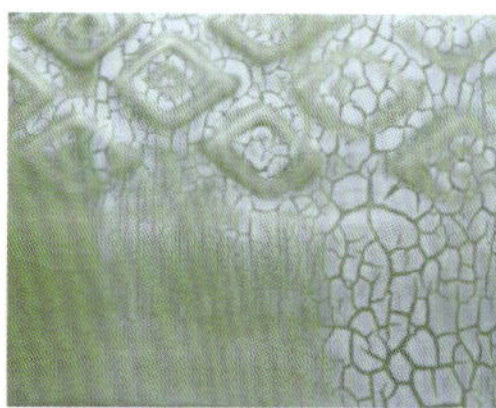
Chun 1 + 3% Spectrum 2086 Bright Green stain under Lichen

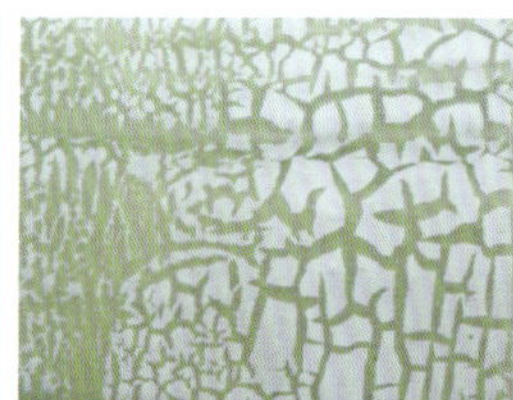
Chun 2 + 3% Spectrum 2086 Bright Green stain under Lichen

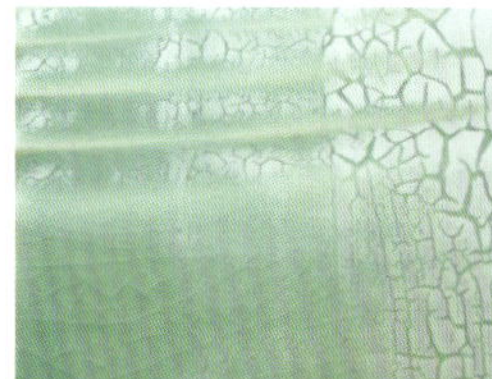
Chun 1 + 3% Spectrum 2032 Bermuda stain under Lichen

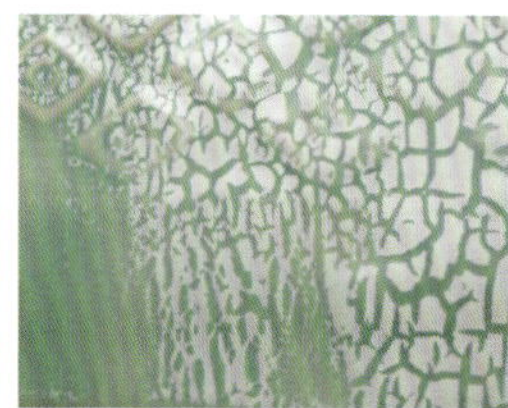
Chun 2 + 3% Spectrum's 2032 Bermuda Stain under Lichen

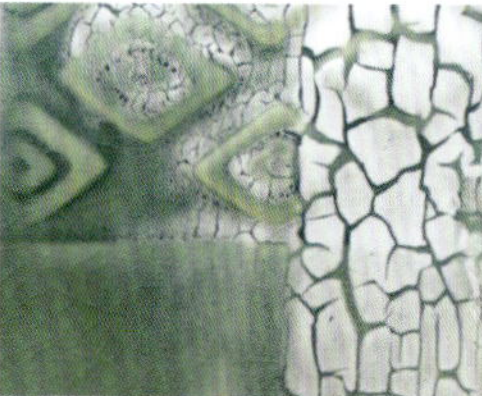
Chun 1 + 2% Mason 6266 Peacock stain under Lichen

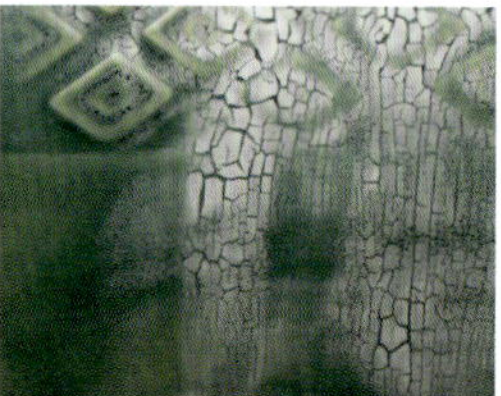
Chun 1 + 2% Mason 6266 Peacock stain under Lichen

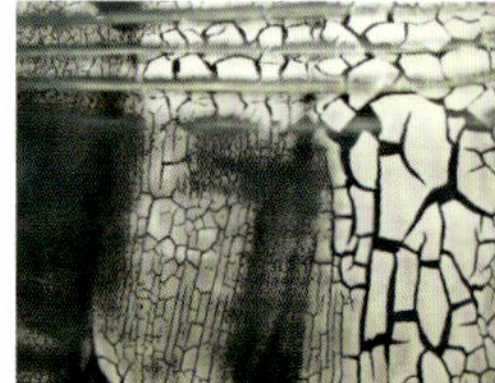
Chun 1 + 3% Mason 6591 Gun Metal stain under Lichen

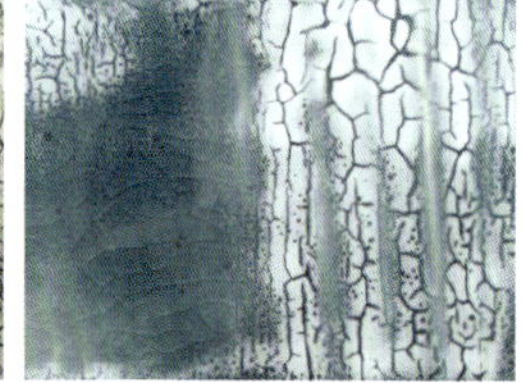
Chun 1 + 2% Mason 6591 Gun Metal stain under Lichen

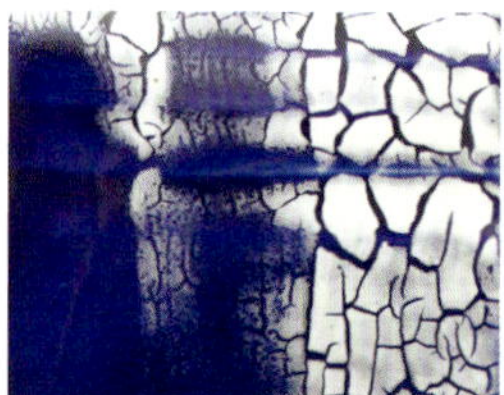
Chun 1 + 2% Cobalt Carbonate under Lichen

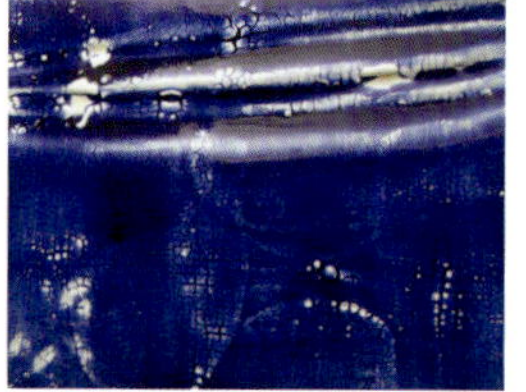
Lichen under Chun 1 + 2% Cobalt Carbonate

Each tile is brushed left to right with 1, 2, and 3 coats of lichen glaze on top of 2–3 brushed coats of base glaze, excepted where noted.

LICHEN GLAZE
Cone 6

Ingredient	%
Magnesium Carbonate	25 %
Nepheline Syenite	70
OM4 Ball Clay	5
	100 %
Add: Zircopax	5 %

CHUN 1 BASE GLAZE
Cone 6

Ingredient	%
Soda Feldspar	50 %
Wollastonite	20
Gerstley Borate	10
EPK Kaolin	10
Silica	10
	100 %

CHUN 2 BASE GLAZE
Cone 6

Ingredient	%
Soda Feldspar	38 %
Whiting	14
Zinc Oxide	12
OM4 Ball Clay	6
Silica	30
	100 %

A WOOD-FIRED LOOK

by Richard Busch

Like most people who take up pottery, I was limited at the beginning of my career to firing my pots to cone 6 in an electric kiln. This was at the local community center where I lived in northern Virginia. I say limited, but for the first year or so it didn't seem like a limitation. Just learning to center, make simple forms and digest a lot of basic information about the pottery process was enough to keep my focus pretty narrow. But it wasn't too long before I began to notice the differences between oxidation- and reduction-fired pottery.

A few years later, I took a wood-firing workshop with McKenzie Smith at Baltimore Clayworks. Out of that kiln—which we fired to cone 10 in

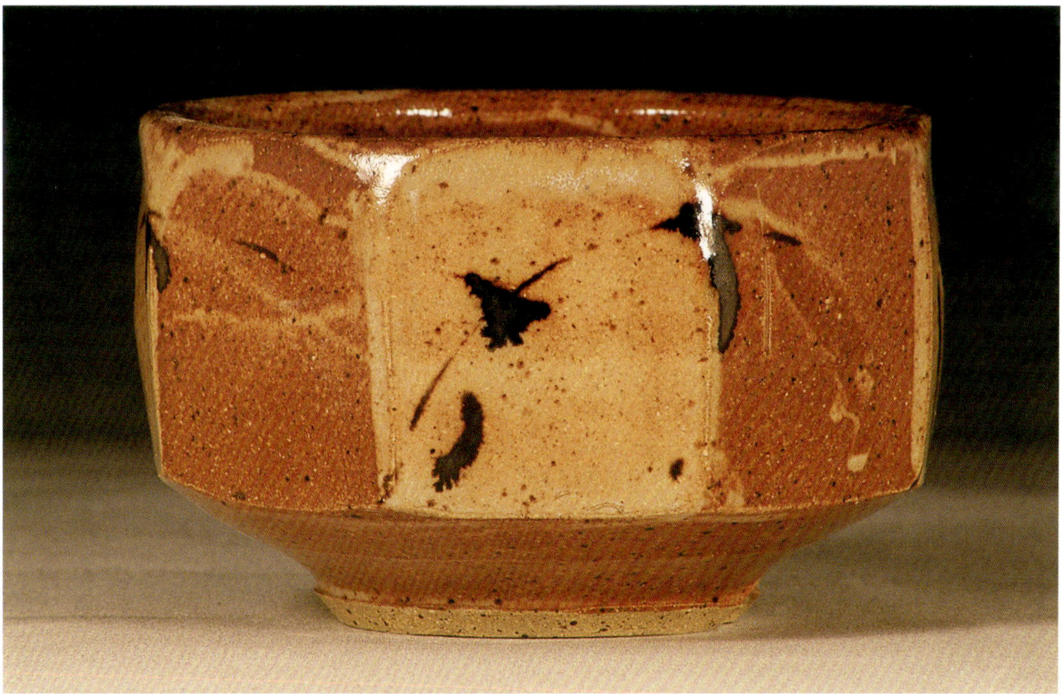

Bowl, 2½ inches in height, thrown and faceted stone-ware, with brushed stain and layered glazes, fired to cone 6.

about 14 hours, throwing in some salt around cone 8—came some of the warmest, toastiest, most wonderfully earthy and handsome pots I'd ever seen. It was inspiring. It changed my outlook. I was hooked on the whole idea. But then, not seeing any possibility of doing wood/salt myself on a regular basis, I grew frustrated.

If, as they say, necessity is the mother of invention, I would suggest that frustration can also be that mother. At least it was for me. Out of that sense of frustration came the desire to develop a cone 6 oxidation glaze that would yield the wood/salt-fired look that had become something of an obsession.

So I started playing around with glaze recipes and, after awhile, came up with something that filled the bill—until I finally built the salt kiln I'd been planing for a long time.

Not only did my ersatz wood/salt-glazing technique keep me happy for years of electric-kiln firing, it also fooled a lot of people, including some pretty experienced potters—at least at first glance. Of course, when they picked up a pot and looked at the bottom, they could see that the unglazed clay body had not been reduced. Nevertheless, the illusion was good enough for me. And over the years, I've had a number of people ask me for the recipe, which I've always been happy to give.

The recipe is actually a combination of two glazes that I mix in different proportions, depending on the result I want. One of them is called White Satin Matt, and the other is the one is called Nutmeg.

Most of the time, I mix the two glazes together in a ratio of two-thirds Nutmeg to one-third White Satin Matt. This gives me a light toasty color. For a darker, more quintessential wood-fired appearance, I decrease the proportion of White Satin Matt to about one-quarter or less.

On many of these pots, I also added some black brushwork. An oxide stain was applied with a long, thin brush made from deer bristles. This recipe was passed along to me by my former teacher, mentor and good friend, Sybil West.

To enhance the look of the black brushmarks, I first applied a fairly thick—roughly the consistency of heavy cream—swash of White Satin Matt over the main glaze combo, using a wide brush. This lightened the area behind the black, and made the brushwork really pop out.

I also discovered that I could alter the surface texture by varying the kiln temperature. Pots fired to about cone 5 tended to produce a drier surface, while those fired to cone 7, or even a little higher, came out with a shinier, more salted appearance.

I would encourage anyone who wants a wood/salt look from cone 6 oxidation firings to experiment a bit with kiln temperatures and with layered glazes. With a few tweaks here and there to adjust for your own kiln and firing techniques, you'll likely find a combination of color and texture that suits your taste to perfection. And who knows, you might even wind up fooling your friends in to thinking you're actually firing with wood and salt—at least at first glance.

WHITE SATIN MATT GLAZE
Cone 6

Gerstley Borate	31.6 %
Talc	14.0
Kona F-4 Feldspar	19.8
EPK Kaolin	5.0
Silica	29.6
	100.0 %
Add: Zircopax	5.1 %
Bentonite	2.0 %

NUTMEG GLAZE
Cone 6

Dolomite	23.3 %
Spodumene	23.3
Ferro Frit 3134	6.8
Kentucky OM 4 Ball Clay	23.3
Silica	23.3
	100.0 %
Add: Red Iron Oxide	1.1 %
Yellow Ocher	3.2 %
Tin Oxide	4.9 %
Bentonite	2.0 %

SYBIL'S BLACK STAIN

Black Copper Oxide	24 %
Cobalt Oxide	2
Manganese Dioxide	49
Nickel Oxide	5
Red Iron Oxide	20
	100 %

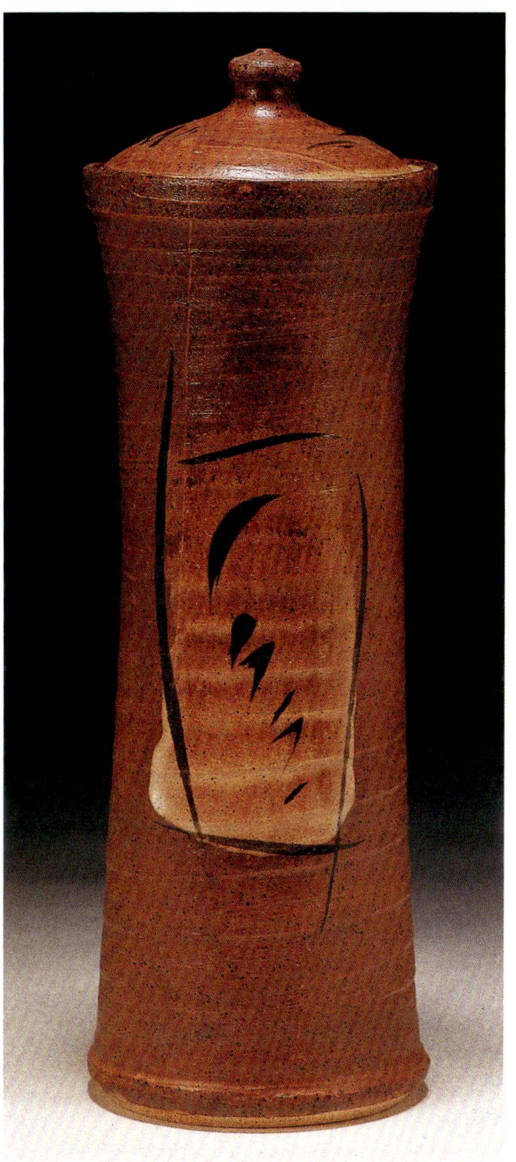

Spaghetti Jar, 11¾ inches in height, stoneware, with stain and glazes, fired to cone 6.

NUTMEG REMIX

by Deanna Ranlett

Richard Busch explored the wood-fired aesthetic at cone 6 electric (see p. 103). Getting that toasty, warm, orange effect can be a challenge in an electric kiln, and many glazes are just too flat to resemble atmospheric fired surfaces. Richard's Nutmeg glaze is popular in many studios, and one of my students was excited by this recipe although it was a little dark, so I suggested the following changes:

Replace OM4 ball clay with EPK kaolin. At first this glaze was too matte. The lower iron and titanium content of EPK resulted in a brighter glaze with more crystallization. Adding Redart to this blend allowed us to reduce the red iron oxide to 0.5% instead of the original 1.1%. We named the resulting glaze Nutmeg Revision with EPK Kaolin.

Replace a portion of OM4 ball clay with Redart. We decided to do this to see if we could still get a richly colored glaze while using less red iron oxide. We also thought that if we used less iron we could use less tin oxide. Since Redart would also be a source of iron, we assumed that some of that rich rust color would still be present if we dropped the red iron oxide. We know Redart is in a lot of shino glazes and wood-fired slip recipes and thought it might be just the ticket. We ended up dropping the iron altogether to make a glaze that looked like Richard's original two glazes combined. We named this glaze Creamy Nutmeg.

Remove the tin oxide, all the colorants, and retest as a base glaze. For the Rosemary Float (green) glaze variation we experimented with the OM4 ball clay revision as a base glaze. The result was a nice translucent base with an interesting float-like effect on the surface. So we decided to start testing colorants. Many colorants had beautiful results including the green. The floating quality of this glaze isn't as intense as many floating glazes and isn't as runny. Due to the color and floating speckles, we called this glaze Rosemary Float.

Application of Nutmeg can be tricky—too thick and you don't get the breaking effect you want, too thin and the glaze can be dry. We found no issues with at least two coats of glaze fired to cone 6. Dipping and brushing small forms was easy with all the glazes but, if you're applying solely by brush, add a brushing medium.

Firing Schedule

- 100°F per hour to 200°F then hold for 1 hour to dry the work
- 350°F per hour to 2000°F (no hold)
- 150°F per hour to 2185°F (15 minute hold) (test the kiln for accuracy to a true cone 6 and adjust this temperature if necessary)
- 9999°F per hour to 1900°F (no hold)
- 150°F per hour to 1500°F (no hold)

NUTMEG
Cone 6

Dolomite	23.3 %
Spodumene	23.3
Ferro Frit 3134	6.8
OM4 Ball Clay	23.3
Silica	23.3
	100.0 %
Add: Red Iron Oxide	1.1 %
Yellow Ochre	3.2 %
Tin Oxide	4.9 %
Bentonite	2.0 %

NUTMEG REVISION WITH KAOLIN
Cone 6

Dolomite	23.0 %
Spodumene	23.0
Ferro Frit 3134	7.7
Redart	13.3
EPK Kaolin	9.7
Silica	23.3
	100.0 %
Add: Red Iron Oxide	0.5 %
Yellow Ochre	3.2 %
Tin Oxide	4.9 %
Bentonite	2.0 %

This Nutmeg glaze version has a nice break of cream coming from the tin and the color was very rich using both iron and Redart.

CREAMY NUTMEG
Cone 6

Dolomite	23.0 %
Spodumene	23.0
Ferro Frit 3134	7.7
OM4 Ball Clay	10.0
Redart	13.0
Silica	23.3
	100.0 %
Add: Yellow Ochre	2.0 %
Tin Oxide	4.0 %
Red Iron Oxide	0.5 %

A creamier version of the original Nutmeg Glaze with no added iron.

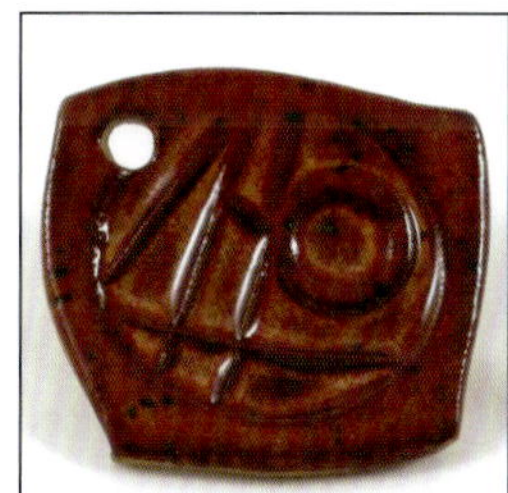
Nutmeg

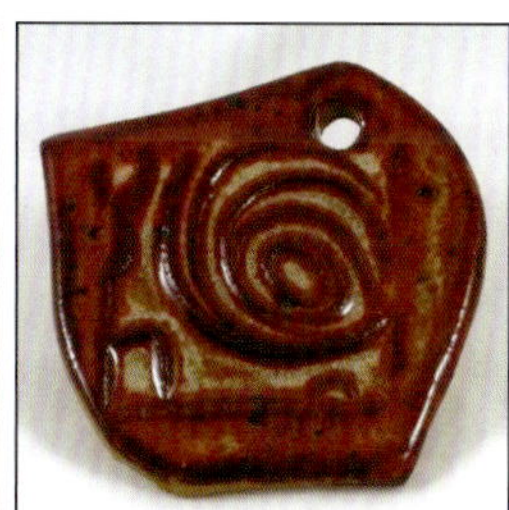
Nutmeg Revision with EPK

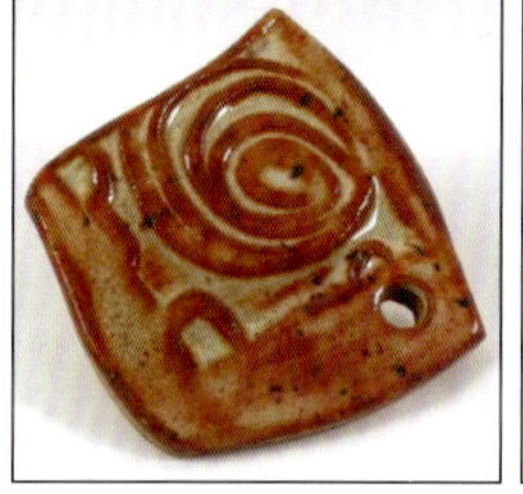
Creamy Nutmeg

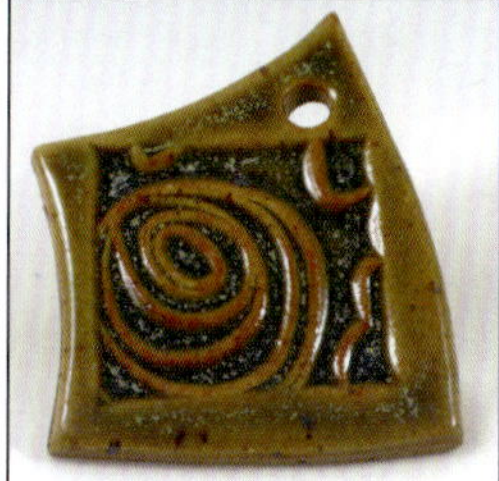
Rosemary Float

Test tiles have three brushed coats over Highwater Clay's Speckled Brownstone clay body and are electric-kiln fired according to a schedule adapted from www.masteringglazes.com.

ROSEMARY FLOAT
Cone 6

Dolomite	23.0 %
Spodumene	23.0
Ferro Frit 3134	7.7
OM4 Ball Clay	10.0
Redart	13.0
Silica	23.3
	100.0 %
Add: Yellow Ochre	1.0 %
Copper Carbonate	3.0 %

For more crystallization

Add: Rutile	1.0 %

For a Midnight Blue version

Add: Yellow Ochre	1.0 %
Cobalt Carbonate	1.0 %
Copper Carbonate	1.0 %

Glazes

WOOD-ASH GLAZING

by Harry Spring

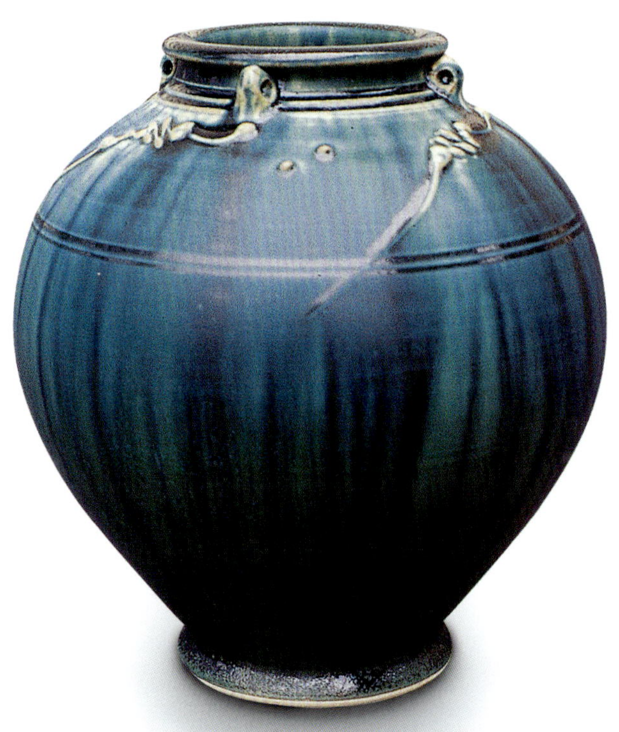

Round vase, 9 inches in height, white stoneware, with slip trailing, blue Wood Ash Glaze over Green Dragon Matt Glaze, fired to cone 6 in oxidation.

High firing in a gas kiln for many years has a downside—you can come to depend upon the kiln to give you the wonderful, serendipitous effects that are part of the magic of reduction. Of course, wonderful glazes can also be achieved without reducing the kiln's atmosphere. Several years ago, I was forced to use an electric kiln as my only firing source for my line of production stoneware. Since then, I have not only come to "put up" with electric firing and the challenges of a static kiln atmosphere, but also to appreciate the convenience of electronically controlled kilns and the challenge of discovering ways of developing interesting and even exciting glaze effects.

I use a commercial white stoneware (Miller 65) that's durable and totally vitrified at cone 6. Available through Laguna Clay Company, it's good for throwing small- to medium-sized pieces, weighing 1 to 10 pounds.

I wanted more interesting surfaces so I tried carving patterns into the clay to create places where the glaze could flow and pool. I also learned from a friend in California to take the slurry from my throwing bucket, run it through a 60- to 80-mesh sieve and apply it with an ear syringe for slip trailing.

Next, I tried overlapping two and three glazes to create some movement on the surface. This worked wonderfully, but caused some irregularities where the glaze saturated the bisqueware, and some running onto the kiln shelves when the glaze application was too thick. I found I could control the application thickness more easily and avoid running by spraying the second and third coats of glaze.

I also use wood ash in and over my cone 6 glazes to create visual interest with good results. I was fortunate to find a recipe that does not require washing the ash before adding it to the glaze. Of course, this makes the glaze caustic, but I wear surgical gloves when I glaze, so it's not a problem.

I have found that this recipe works best if it is dipped or sprayed over another glaze; alone, it is a little too dry to the touch. I like using Wood Ash Glaze over a matt glaze rather than a gloss glaze.

To prepare the wood ash, screen the dry ash (any wood will do) through a 60- to 80-mesh sieve and add it to the glaze batch.

Another way to get interesting effects is to simply sieve wood ash over a damp, newly glazed surface. I do this over a trash barrel. (Remember: ash is caustic, so always wear a mask.)

For the most dramatic effects, do both. Sieve the dry wood ash over the rim and shoulder of a pot that has just been sprayed with Wood Ash Glaze over a dipped or sprayed base glaze.

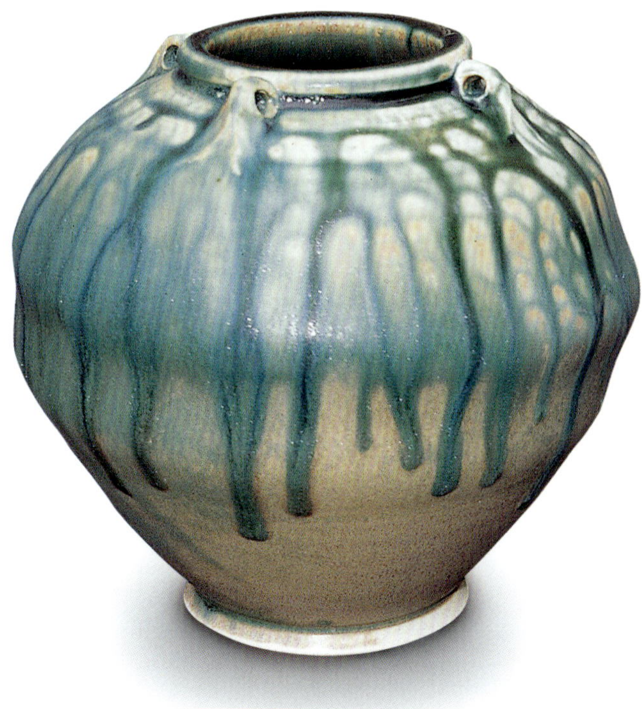

GREEN DRAGON MATT GLAZE
Cone 6

Whiting	17.7 %
Zinc Oxide	8.0
Cornwall Stone	22.0
Soda Feldspar	44.1
Bentonite	3.2
EPK Kaolin	5.0
	100.0 %
Add: Titanium Dioxide	4.0 %
Copper Carbonate	4.3 %

FRASCA WOOD ASH GLAZE
Cone 6

Whiting	11.4 %
Wood Ash (unwashed)	54.6
Potash Feldspar	11.3
Ball Clay	11.3
Silica	11.4
	100.0 %
Green	
Add: Copper Carbonate	4.0 %
Blue	
Add: Cobalt Carbonate	2.0 %

Wood ash contains a good deal of calcium, as well as potassium, phosphorus, magnesium and sodium—all rather active fluxes in a glaze—so I limit the application of Wood Ash Glaze to the top one-fourth of the pot.

Glazes

PURPLE GLAZES

by Deanna Ranlett

Purple is a non-spectral color, meaning that it isn't included in the rainbow as conceived by viewing from a prism on a sun-filled rainy day, but it should definitely be in your glaze palette! To me, purple says extravagant, special, and definitely unusual—think royalty or even better, Prince, (or should I say the artist formally known as...)

You can get purple in a glaze in a variety of ways:

- *Chrome plus tin.* You can get a raspberry hue by mixing chrome oxide and tin oxide. These formulas have been published and featured prominently for oxidation red or burgundy at cone 6—typically 5% tin oxide and 0.2% chrome oxide.
- *Cobalt.* Add .25% cobalt oxide incrementally, up 1% to increase the purple hue from lavender to eggplant.
- *Manganese.* Our studio limits manganese usage so we don't use it to make our purples, but a lot of recipes using manganese as a colorant are available.
- *Barium.* Barium is classified as toxic and we don't use barium in our studio, but there are some amazing barium purple recipes available for use on sculptures. These glazes aren't food safe.

Commercial stains. These colorants provide an opportunity to use a product formulated to give consistent color results.

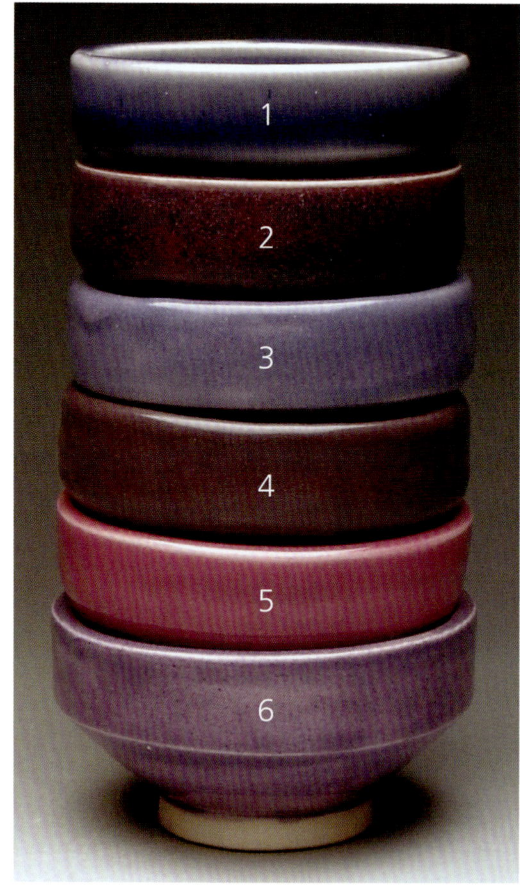

Stacked bowls with cone 6 test glazes. **1** George Bowes Base with 3% MS #6319 Lavender + 3% MS #6385 Pansy Purple. **2** George Bowes Base with 5% MS #6088 Dark Red + 5% MS #6363 Sky Blue. **3** Sherman's Satin Matte with 5% MS #6319 Lavender. **4** Sherman's Satin Matte with 5% MS #6374 Turquoise + 5% MS #6088 Dark Red. **5** Amy's Base with 6% MS #6304 Chrome Tin Violet. **6** Amy's Base with 6% MS #6304 Chrome Tin Violet + .25% cobalt carbonate.

Working With Stains

For our focus here, we used primarily stains to highlight their vast possibilities in both low- and high-fire recipes. Stains come in a lot of color varieties and are available from many different manufacturers—including Mason Color Works, Inc. (www.masoncolor.com) and US Pigment (www.uspigment.com). Most pottery suppliers carry commercial stains.

Stains have ingredients such as chrome oxide, cobalt carbonate, and tin oxide that have been fired and ground to make a consistently colored pigment that is easy to use. It's sometimes possible to mix stains to get a new color, but not all stains are compatible in this way, so testing is required.

We discovered through our testing that you can successfully mix red and blue stains to make a purple of your very own. You can use a stain containing cobalt such as Mason stain #6363 Sky Blue, or you can use smaller amounts of cobalt carbonate—a milder form of cobalt oxide. For a red stain, try Mason stain #6088 Dark Red. You can vary amounts to make the purple hues cooler (blue) or warmer (red.) You can also use any number of a variety of chrome-tin-violet stains like Mason stain #6304, which is a purple with a more reddish hue.

Tips When Using Stains

- Start small, experiment, and take good notes.
- Use a gram scale capable of mixing small measurements. Check your scale's calibration by measuring the weight of a nickel—it should weigh 5 grams.
- Sieve your glaze and don't mix them too thin. The stains can, and will end up on the bottom of your container if you do.
- Visit the manufacturer's website to make sure you're using stains and colorants that are compatible with your glaze ingredients. You need to pay attention to the calcium and zinc content in your recipe when using stains because they can have a negative impact/effect on the colorant. Each manufacturer will provide you with that information. To get that color, you may need to experiment with different base glazes.
- Some stains are more refractory (have a higher-melting point due to their composition) than others and you may need to make changes in your base glaze to compensate for this.
- Some stains might require the addition of an opacifier such as Zircopax to create the color and intensity you desire.

Future Testing

Based on the success I had mixing stains, I would recommend tests blending a variety of red and blue stains in incremental amounts. I also suggest mixing red stain with cobalt carbonate in incremental amounts. Layering purple glazes with each other could be fun too. The Sherman Matte Glaze has a beautiful buttery surface and layering it with a glossier version like George Bowes or Amy's Base could have some lovely results.

AMY'S BASE
Cone 6

Wollastonite	10.0 %
Ferro Frit 3134	25.0
Soda Feldspar	15.0
EPK Kaolin	25.0
Silica	25.0
	100.0 %
Add: Zircopax	2.5 %

Dips and pours more successfully than it brushes.

SHERMAN'S SATIN MATTE
Cone 6

Dolomite	10 %
Talc	15
Ferro Frit 3124	10
Nepheline Syenite	35
EPK Kaolin	15
Silica	15
	100 %

Brushes and dips well.

GEORGE BOWES BASE GLAZE
Cone 6

Gerstley Borate	18 %
Whiting	16
Custer Feldspar	40
EPK Kaolin	10
Silica	16
	100 %

5

Recipes
LANA WILSON

by Annie Chrieztberg

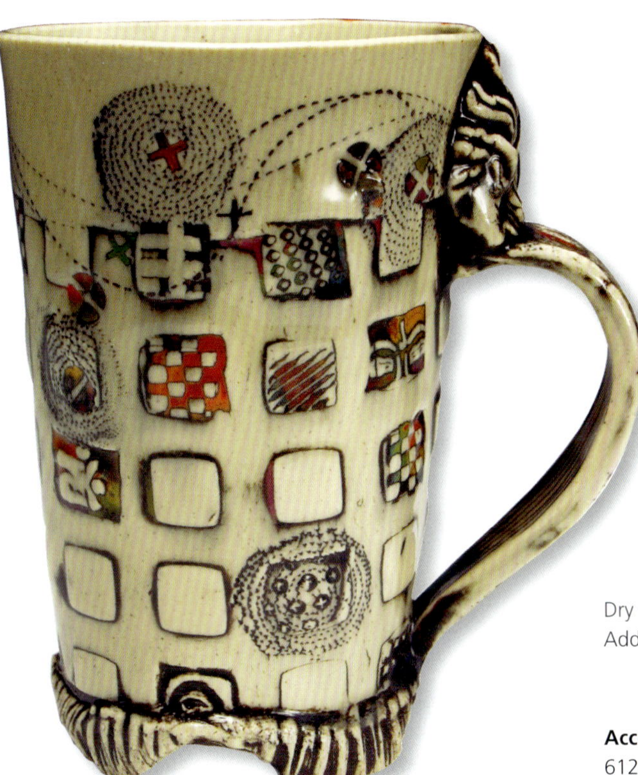

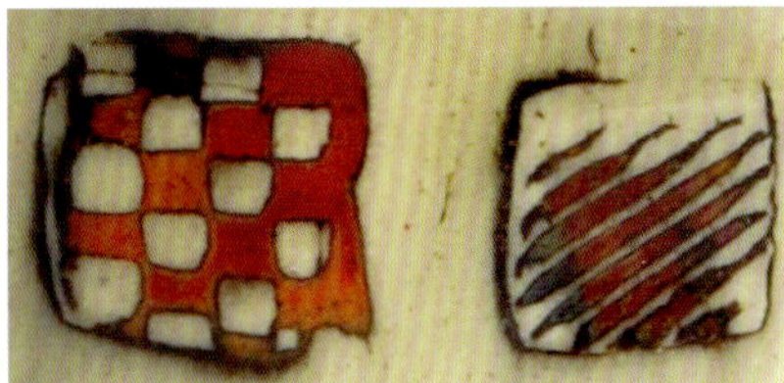

Texture and isolated areas of bright color make Lana Wilson's work really pop.

KATE THE YOUNGER CLEAR GLAZE
Cone 6

Wollastonite	10 %
Ferro Frit 3195	70
EPK Kaolin	8
Silica	12
	100 %
Add: Bentonite	2 %

From Richard Burkett. Use over colored slips. Shiny, resistant to crazing, cool slowly.

BASE COAT OR WASH COLORS
Cone 6

Dry Clay Body	100 %
Add: 6600 Best Black	10 %
6339 Royal Blue	5–10 %
6069 Dark Coral	35 %

Accent Slips

6129 Golden Ambrosia	30 %
6485 Titanium Yellow	20 %
6024 Orange	30 %
6236 Chartreuse	50 %
6027 Tangerine	15 %
6211 Pea Green	50 %
6288 Turquoise	50 %
6242 Bermuda	10 %
6069 Dark Coral	35 %
6122 Cedar	25 %
6304 Violet	60 %
K5997 Cherry Red*	30 %
27496 Persimmon Red (Cerdec)*	30 %

*Inclusion pigments

Lana Wilson's work is mostly black and white with bits of vibrant color splashed about. She gleaned this current surface treatment from two artists, Denise Smith of Ann Arbor, Michigan, and Claudia Reese, a potter from Texas.

To prepare the slip, Lana takes 100 grams of small pieces of bone dry clay and adds 10–50 grams of a stain. The percentages of stains varies according to the intensity of color she is trying to achieve.

The clay Lana uses is Half & Half from Laguna, formulated for firing at cone 5, though she fires it to cone 6. This clay body is half porcelain and half white stoneware. It's not as white as porcelain, but it does isn't as finicky as porcelain, and works well with Lana's making methods. If you're buying clay from the East Coast, she suggests a clay body called Little Loafers from Highwater Clays.

Brush on black slip or one of the base colors (figure 1) then sponge it off, leaving slip in the crevices (figure 2). Then, using colored slips dab on bits of color here and there (figure 3). Remove some of that with steel wool (figure 4). "I can't use water for this step or it will muddy the colors," Lana explains.

There are two groups of colored slips. The first group Lana uses for the base coat that she washes off, leaving color in all the recesses. The accent slips are more intense and removed with steel wool. All stains are Mason stains except for 27496 Persimmon Red, which is from Cerdec. Add the stains and bone dry clay to water and allow to sit for 30–60 minutes so it will mix easier. Stain-bearing slips applied to surfaces that come into contact with food need to be covered with a food-safe clear glaze.

Recipes

MARY BARRINGER

by Leigh Taylor Mickelson

WHITE SLIP BASE
Cone 6

Ferro Frit 3124	10 %
Nepheline Syenite	15
Ball Clay	25
EPK Kaolin	25
Silica	25
	100 %

Black

Add: Black Stain	10 %
Red Iron Oxide	8 %

Blue-Black

Add: Black Stain	10 %
Cobalt Carbonate	2 %

Gray-Green

Add: Chrome	3 %
Copper Carbonate	3 %

Light Green

Add: Copper Carbonate	5 %

Strong Green

Add: Chrome	6 %

Blue-Green

Add: Chrome	3 %
Cobalt Carbonate	1.5 %

Teal

Add: Copper Carbonate	3 %
Teal Stain	6 %

Medium Blue

Add: Cobalt Carbonate	1 %
Rutile	3 %

Cream

Add: Rutile	5 %

Yellow

Add: Yellow Stain	10 %

Pink

Add: Pink Stain	10 %

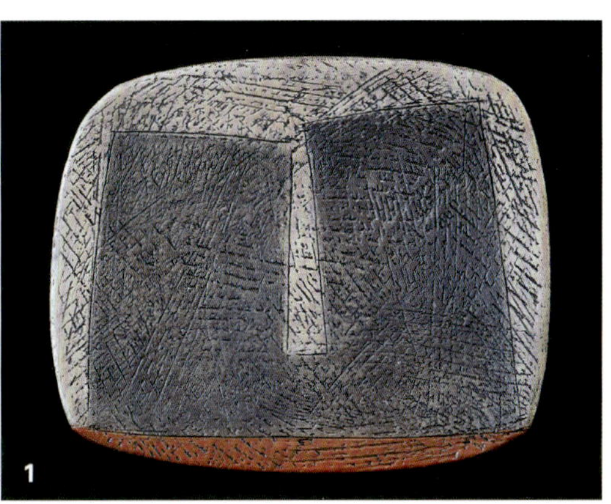

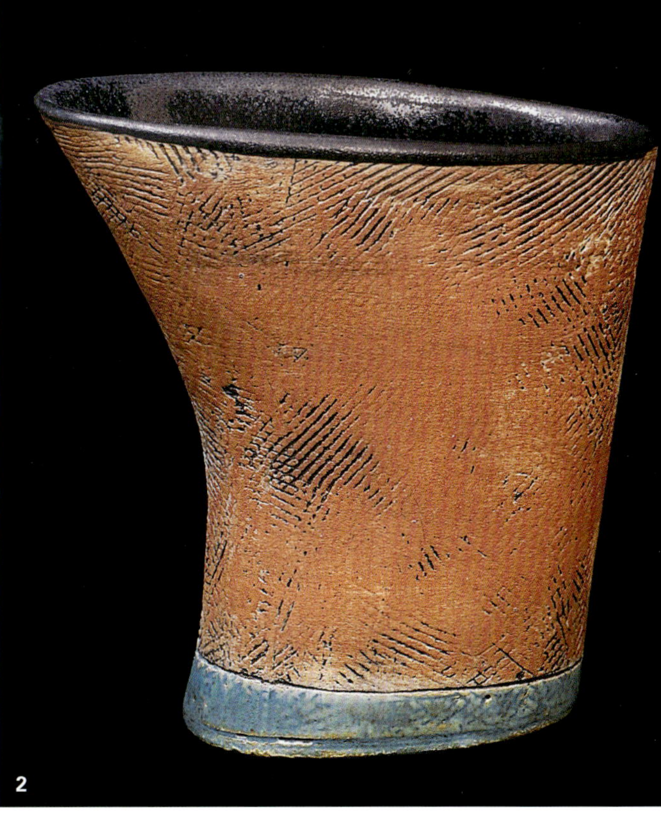

1 Rectangular platter, 13 inches in length, slab-built and incised stoneware, with multiple slips, fired to cone 6.
2 Creamer, 4¼ inches in height, slab-built stoneware, with multiple slips, fired to cone 6.

GLASSY SLIP
Cone 6

Ingredient	%
Gerstley Borate	5 %
Lithium Carbonate	80
Bentonite	15
	100 %

RC SLIP
Cone 6

Ingredient	%
Whiting	30 %
Kona F-4 Feldspar	20
Cedar Heights Redart	40
Silica	10
	100 %

REDART SLIP
Cone 6

Ingredient	%
Lithium Carbonate	10 %
Spodumene	10
Cedar Heights Redart	80
	100 %
Add: Red Iron Oxide	2 %

VITREOUS BLACK SLIP
Cone 6

Ingredient	%
Borax	10.0 %
Nepheline Syenite	23.0
Kaolin	22.0
Ball Clay	23.0
Silica	22.0
	100.0 %
Add: Cobalt Oxide	1.0 %
Copper Oxide	4.5 %
Red Iron Oxide	4.5 %

STEVENSON VITREOUS ENGOBE
Cone 6

Ingredient	%
Whiting	3 %
Feldspar	8
Ferro Frit 3124	45
Ball Clay	10
Kaolin	12
Silica	12
Tin Oxide	10
	100 %

DENSE WHITE ENGOBE
Cone 6

Ingredient	%
Ferro Frit 3110	10 %
Nepheline Syenite	20
Ball Clay	30
Zircopax	40
	100 %
Add: Bentonite	2 %
Macaloid	1 %

ASH ENGOBE
Cone 6

Ingredient	%
Talc	15.0 %
Wood Ash (unwashed)	20.0
Cornwall Stone	25.0
Ferro Frit 3124	15.0
Ball Clay	25.0
	100.0 %

White/tan

Ingredient	%
Add: Tin Oxide	7.5 %

Pink/brown

Ingredient	%
Add: Nickel Oxide	1.5 %
Pink Stain	8.0 %

BURLINGTON BASE GLAZE
Cone 6

Lithium Carbonate	2.0 %
Strontium Carbonate	5.4
Whiting	12.2
Soda Feldspar	20.4
Albany Slip	22.4
Ball Clay	25.4
Zircopax	12.2
	100.0 %

Color variations are possible with oxide, carbonate and/or stain additions.

BURLINGTON BASE GLAZE
Cone 6

Lithium Carbonate	2.0 %
Strontium Carbonate	5.4
Whiting	12.2
Soda Feldspar	20.4
Albany Slip	22.4
Ball Clay	25.4
Zircopax	12.2
	100.0 %

Color variations are possible with oxide, carbonate and/or stain additions.

SINGLE-FIRE ASH GLAZE
Cone 6

Wood Ash	19 %
Potash Feldspar	25
Kaolin	12
Red Clay	13
Silica	31
	100 %
Add: Cobalt Carbonate	1–5 %
Red Iron Oxide	15 %

SUPER-DRY MATT GLAZE
Cone 6

Gerstley Borate	5 %
Lithium Carbonate	6
Strontium Carbonate	15
Nepheline Syenite	60
Calcined Clay	8
Silica	6
	100 %

Color variations are possible with oxide, carbonate and/or stain additions.

METALLIC BLACK GLAZE
Cone 6

Gerstley Borate	11 %
Whiting	5
Feldspar	79
Kaolin	5
	100 %
Add: Cobalt Oxide	2 %
Copper Carbonate	4 %
Manganese Dioxide	4 %

SHEEN-O GLAZE
Cone 6

Soda Ash	2.9 %
Gerstley Borate	4.9
Spodumene	22.8
Nepheline Syenite	54.5
Ball Clay	14.9
	100.0 %
Add: Chrome	0.5 %

YELLOW OXIDE GLAZE
Cone 6

Lithium Carbonate	4.5 %
Zinc Oxide	18.5
Ferro Frit 3110	28.0
Kaolin	31.5
Silica	17.5
	100.0 %
Add: Tin Oxide	4.5 %
Copper Carbonate	0.5 %
Iron Oxide	4.5 %
Yellow Ocher	0.5 %

Recipes

HOBART COWLES BLUE & GREEN GLAZES

by Lili Krakowski

These Hobart Cowles blue and green glazes were tested on a buff clay body at cone 5. It is possible that texture and maturity will vary on different clays and at different temperatures (cone 4 to cone 6). The type of kiln and firing cycle also may affect the outcome. In addition, you may wish to test these recipes with other colorants, or without colorants (for whites).

PEA GREEN GLAZE

Cone 5

Dolomite	21.7 %
Custer Feldspar	26.1
Ferro Frit 3134	13.0
Kaolin	17.4
Silica	21.7
	100.0 %
Add: Copper Oxide	2.5 %
Rutile	2.0 %

A pea green recipe with gold runs.

PALE GREEN GLAZE

Cone 5

Cryolite	5.8 %
Dolomite	17.0
Strontium Carbonate	9.1
Kaolin	22.7
Silica	45.5
	100.0 %
Add: Tin Oxide	4.9 %
Zinc Oxide	13.6 %
Copper Carbonate	1.3 %

MOTTLED PEA GREEN GLAZE

Cone 5

Fluorspar	5.4 %
Talc	9.5
Custer Feldspar	28.3
Ferro Frit 3134	14.2
Kaolin	18.9
Silica	23.6
	100.0 %
Add: Tin Oxide	7.6 %
Copper Oxide	2.5 %
Vanadium Pentoxide	5.0 %

COPPER GREEN MATT GLAZE

Cone 5

Ingredient	%
Barium Carbonate	24.4 %
Dolomite	12.2
Petalite	12.2
Cornwall Stone	12.2
Nepheline Syenite	12.2
Kaolin	12.2
Silica	14.6
	100.0 %
Add: Tin Oxide	4.9 %
Copper Carbonate	3.5 %

DULL BLUE-GREEN GLAZE

Cone 5

Ingredient	%
Dolomite	12.6 %
Lithium Carbonate	3.2
Whiting	3.8
Nepheline Syenite	3.2
Ferro Frit 3134	26.7
Kaolin	21.5
Silica	29.0
	100.0 %
Add: Copper Carbonate	4.0 %

The base recipe is good with other colorants too.

LAVENDER-BLUE SATIN GLAZE

Cone 5

Ingredient	%
Dolomite	11.8 %
Lithium Carbonate	3.4
Whiting	3.4
Ferro Frit 3134	24.4
Kaolin	17.6
Silica	39.5
	100.0 %
Add: Cobalt Carbonate	1.0 %

DARK NAVY BLUE GLAZE

Cone 5

Ingredient	%
Dolomite	12.4 %
Gerstley Borate	27.6
Magnesium Carbonate	11.1
Kaolin	16.9
Silica	32.0
	100.0 %
Add: Cobalt Carbonate	2.5 %

ULTRAMARINE GLOSS GLAZE

Cone 5

Ingredient	%
Wood Ash	41.7 %
Petalite	58.3
	100.0 %
Add: Tin Oxide	3.0 %
Cobalt Carbonate	1.0 %

FLUID BLUE-GREEN GLAZE

Cone 5

Ingredient	%
Lithium Carbonate	4.5 %
Nepheline Syenite	4.5
Frit 3134 (Ferro)	50.0
Kaolin	36.5
Silica	4.5
	100.0 %
Add: Tin Oxide	7.3 %
Copper Oxide	3.0 %

Without the copper, this recipe yields a handsome white glaze.

Recipes

PAT ANTONICK'S ANTIQUE WEATHERED LOOK

by Pamela Collins

Pat Antonick was always interested in industrial objects. History has always fascinated her as well, so when she came upon fully-embossed Michigan and Ohio license plates, her creative wheels started turning. One of the results o`f that find was a series of pieces called "Ohio Sesquicentennial Vases with Amphora Handles," the largest of which includes the entire license plate.

Nature and leaves are a prominent theme in Antonick's works. "The Weller Company, here in Ohio, did very beautiful pottery in the early 1900s," she said, "and they used a lot of leaves on their pieces. That really inspired me." As an example, large, ridged leaves snake up and across the base in "Acme Green Leaves." Faux screws "hold" the sides together, while the ubiquitous brand Acme announces itself on the handle.

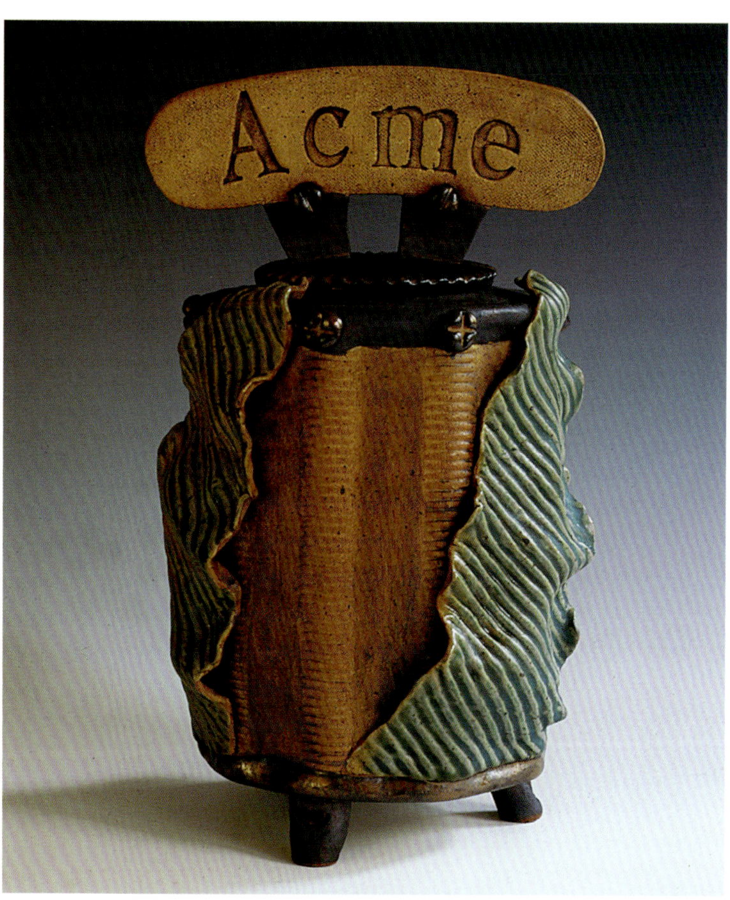

Acme Green Leaves, 10 inches in height, with glazes, iron oxide and stain, fired to cone 7 in oxidation.

GOLD METALLIC GLAZE

Cone 6–7

Manganese Dioxide	39.0 %
Ball Clay	4.3
Cedar Heights Redart	52.4
Silica	4.3
	100.0 %
Add: Black Copper Oxide	4.3 %
Cobalt Oxide	2.7 %

GREEN WOLLASTONITE GLAZE

Cone 6–7

Barium Carbonate	15.6 %
Gerstley Borate	10.4
Wollastonite	15.6
Nepheline Syenite	39.7
Kaolin	10.4
Silica	8.3
	100.0 %
Add: Black Copper Oxide	3.1%
Bentonite	2.1 %

BLACK SLIP

Black Iron Oxide	17.6 %
Ferro Frit 3134	35.3
C&C Ball Clay	47.1
	100.0 %
Add: Black Stain	17.6 %

Apply to leather-hard or bisqued surfaces.

Recipes

STUDIO GLAZES

by Jeff Dietrich

Developing glazes is an ongoing process requiring careful experimentation and the ability to tolerate failure. Guidelines and theories presented by Richard Zakin provided me with the understanding necessary to begin. Armed with a pile of notes, including the capabilities of various materials, I have worked out a useful series of cone 6 oxidation glazes.

VIRGINVILLE WHITE GLAZE

Cone 6

Gerstley Borate	16.7 %
Spodumene	11.1
Potash Feldspar	61.1
Goldart Clay	8.9
Ball Clay	2.2
	100.0 %
Add: Zircopax	11.1 %

A strongly opaque glaze well suited for functional pottery.

KLINESVILLE GOLD

Cone 6

Magnesium Carbonate	4.5 %
Whiting	20.2
Wollastonite	5.6
Nepheline Syenite	56.2
Cedar Heights Redart Clay	13.5
	100.0 %
Add: Red Iron Oxide	6.7 %
Zircopax	12.4 %

A golden glaze that adds warmth.

DIETRICH VALLEY GLAZE

Cone 6

Gerstley Borate	10.9 %
Magnesium Carbonate	13.0
Wollastonite	5.4
Nepheline Syenite	59.8
Goldart Clay	10.9
	100.0 %
Add: Zircopax	8.7 %

The wollastonite contributes to the glossy surface. Zircopax adds a fine, tight texture.

Light Green

Add: Copper Carbonate	2.2 %

Lavender

Add: Cobalt Carbonate	2.2 %

Blue Gray

Add: Cobalt Oxide	1.1 %
Rutile	2.2 %

STONY RUN STRONTIUM GLAZE

Cone 6

Dolomite	8 %
Spodumene	5
Strontium Carbonate	25
Potash Feldspar	50
Kaolin	12
	100 %

A rich, soft, slightly waxy surface that imitates the patina of oxidized metal.

Turquoise

Add: Copper Carbonate	2 %

Midnight Blue

Add: Cobalt Carbonate	1 %
Chrome Oxide	1 %

Tan

Add: Rutile	6 %

Recipes

COLLEGE STUDIO GLAZES

by Jan Rider

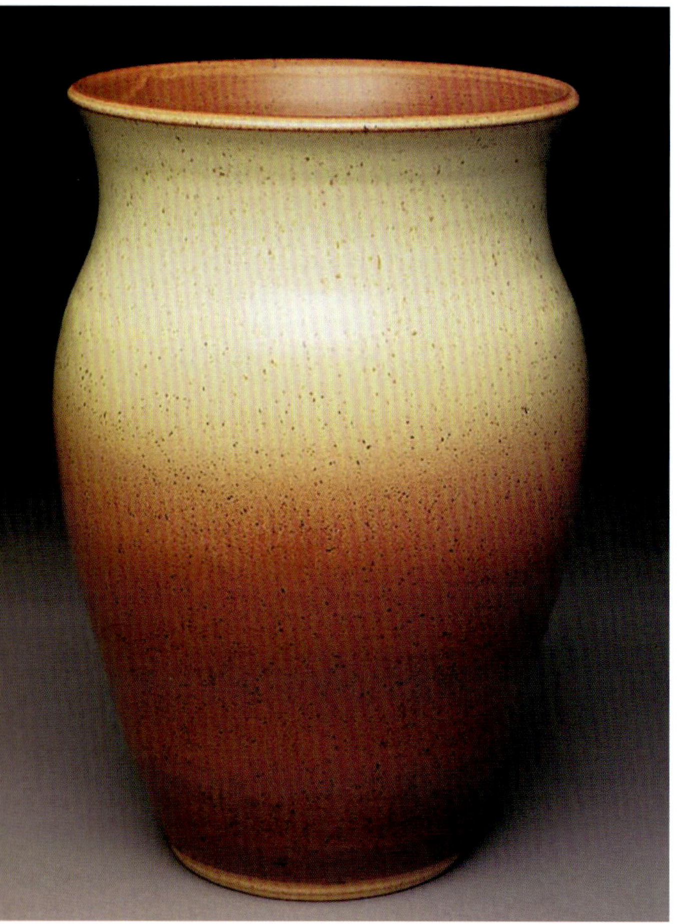

Vessel, 9 inches (23 centimeters) in height, wheel-thrown stoneware with Eggshell Glaze and Nutmeg Glaze (see page 105), fired to Cone 6, by Richard Danek, Carrboro, North Carolina.

WANAMAKER MATT GLAZE

Cone 6

Dolomite	24.7 %
Spodumene	11.2
Nepheline Syenite	50.6
Ball Clay	13.5
	100.0 %
Add: Zircopax	12.4 %

A soft, flat matt glaze.

WANAMAKER SATIN GLAZE

Cone 6

Dolomite	19.3 %
Spodumene	12.1
Nepheline Syenite	54.2
Ball Clay	14.5
	100.0 %
Add: Titanium Dioxide	2.4 %
Zinc Oxide	4.8 %

A finely textured satin glaze.

WANAMAKER STEELY GREEN GLAZE

Cone 6

Dolomite	21.2 %
Spodumene	11.8
Nepheline Syenite	52.9
Ball Clay	14.1
	100.0 %
Add: Copper Carbonate	1.2%
Zinc Oxide	4.7%
Zircopax	12.9%

A beautiful steely matt that breaks with a shiny crystal-line structure in recesses.

WHITE SATIN MATT GLAZE
Cone 6

Ingredient	%
Gerstley Borate	32 %
Talc	14
Kona F-4 Feldspar	20
EPK Kaolin	5
Silica	29
	100%
Add: Zircopax	5 %
Bentonite	2 %

RON ROY BLACK
Cone 6

Ingredient	%
Talc	3 %
Whiting	6
Kona F-4 Feldspar	21
Ferro Frit 3134	26
EPK Kaolin	17
Silica	27
	100 %
Add: Cobalt Carbonate	1 %
Red Iron Oxide	9 %

VAL'S TURQUOISE
Cone 6

Ingredient	%
Dolomite	4 %
Gerstley Borate	22
Whiting	11
Custer Feldspar	36
Silica	27
	100 %
Add: Copper Carbonate	3 %
Bentonite	1 %

RITA SCHIAVONE'S PERIWINKLE
Cone 6

Ingredient	%
Gerstley Borate	32 %
Talc	14
Kona F-4 Feldspar	20
EPK Kaolin	4
Silica	30
	100 %
Add: Cobalt Oxide	1 %
Rutile	2 %

EGGSHELL GLAZE
Cone 6

Ingredient	%
Whiting	9.5 %
Zinc Oxide	5.5
Ferro Frit 3124	44.5
Custer Feldspar	20.0
Bentonite	7.5
EPK Kaolin	5.0
Silica	8.0
	100.0 %
Add: Tin Oxide	9.0 %
Red Iron Oxide	3.0 %

Recipes

WHITE GLAZES

by Dwain Naragon

The following white glazes are tried-and-true recipes for Cone 5 oxidation. They have been tested on porcelain, red stoneware and buff stoneware bodies. All work well on porcelain; most work well on stoneware. Color response is good for all, though some are bright while others are more subdued. Most of these recipes were developed in my studio; the rest are altered versions of base glazes from other sources.

CONRAD G184 ALTERED BASE GLAZE

Cone 5

Dolomite	6.3 %
Gerstley Borate	13.5
Whiting	8.3
Kona F-4 Feldspar	47.9
Kaolin	3.1
Silica	20.9
	100.0 %

Gloss white

Add: Zircopax	10.4 %

Matte white

Add: Magnesium Carbonate	2.1 %
Zircopax	10.4 %

Antique Matte White

Add: Magnesium Carbonate	2.1 %
Zircopax	10.4 %
Barnard Slip	1.6 %

SPODUMENE WHITE GLAZE
Cone 5

Colemanite	12.7 %
Dolomite	21.8
Spodumene	27.3
Potash Feldspar	19.1
Kaolin	8.2
Silica	10.9
	100.0 %
Add: Zircopax	4.5 %

For a matt glaze, decrease the amount of colemanite.

N2 SATIN WHITE GLAZE
Cone 5

Dolomite	3.2 %
Whiting	4.3
Wollastonite	19.2
Kona F-4 Feldspar	44.7
Ball Clay	14.9
Kaolin	3.2
Silica	10.5
	100.0 %
Add: Zircopax	10.6 %

NARAGON WHITE GLAZE
Cone 5

Colemanite	25.8 %
Dolomite	4.0
Whiting	5.9
Kona F-4 Feldspar	31.7
Kaolin	7.9
Silica	24.7
	100.0 %
Add: Zircopax	11.9 %

N2/NT41/HGB WAXY WHITE GLAZE
Cone 5

Colemanite	5.5 %
Dolomite	8.8
Talc	3.3
Wollastonite	15.4
Kona F-4 Feldspar	41.7
Ball Clay	7.7
Kaolin	7.7
Silica	9.9
	100.0 %
Add: Zinc Oxide	0.6 %
Zircopax	11.0 %

NT33 WHITE GLAZE
Cone 5

Barium Carbonate	9.7 %
Dolomite	4.3
Whiting	17.2
Potash Feldspar	35.5
Ball Clay	11.8
Silica	21.5
	100.0 %
Add: Zinc Oxide	7.5 %
Zircopax	12.9 %

Recipes

FROM HIGH-FIRE TO MID-RANGE

by Jayne Shatz

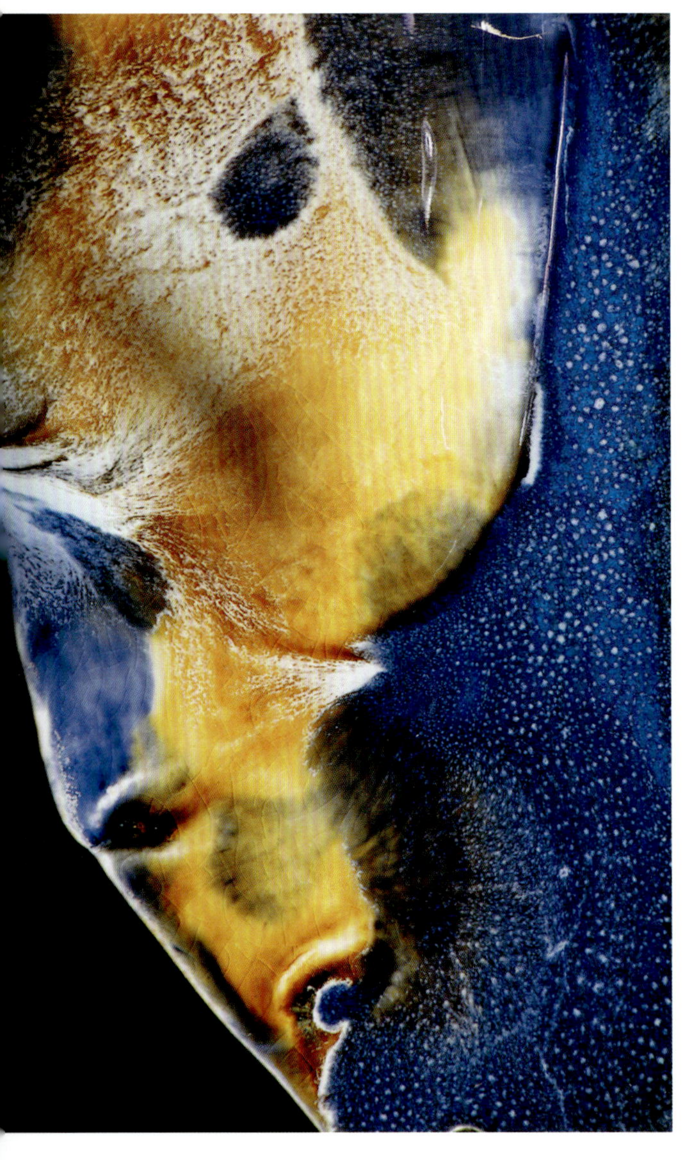

After firing with gas at cone 10 reduction for many years, I bought an electric kiln and switched over from reduction to oxidation and began working at cone 6 in oxidation.

A reduction clay body develops its toasty warm color when the oxygen entering the kiln is reduced by closing down the kiln's dampers. This reduction of oxygen and increase in carbon creates the autumnal colors of reduction stoneware. I developed a cone 6 clay body that was rich in iron and would develop into a toasty warm color in oxidation.

Then I began bringing down the melting temperatures of my glazes to cone 6. I delved further into chemistry, learning the various effects oxides produced in an oxidizing atmosphere. Very slowly, and with many glaze tests, I began to obtain the colors I was seeking. My first success was to duplicate an iron saturated glaze from my college days, Ketchup Red. I then continued down my palette of glazes. This process took two years. Developing a cone 6 palette was an enormous struggle, but I learned a great deal about clay and glazes.

Porcelain with Clear Base Glaze, Blue Matt, Costello Carbonate and Rutile Matt glazes.

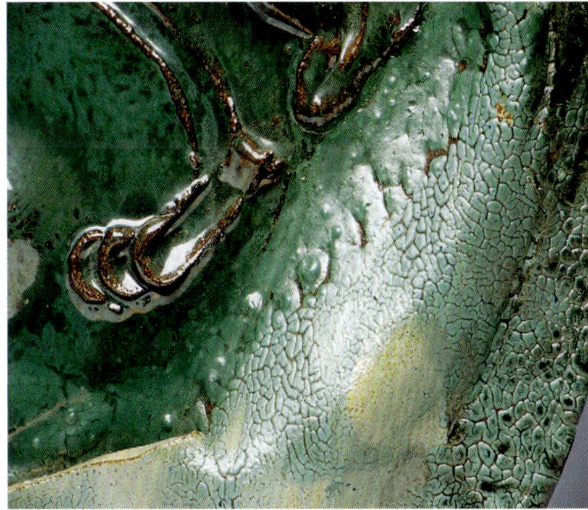
Stoneware with Matt Black, Costello Carbonate and Alligator Green glazes.

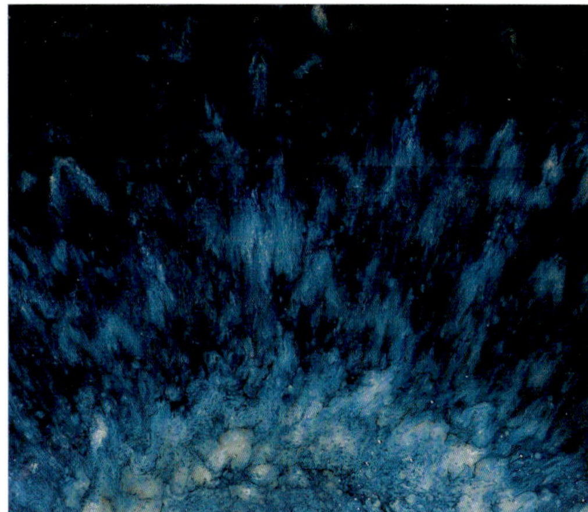
Stoneware with Glossy Black over Blue Matt glaze.

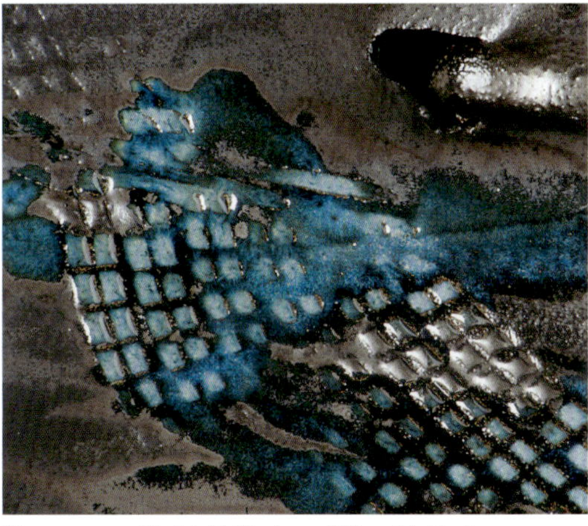
Stoneware with Matt Black and Blue Matt glazes.

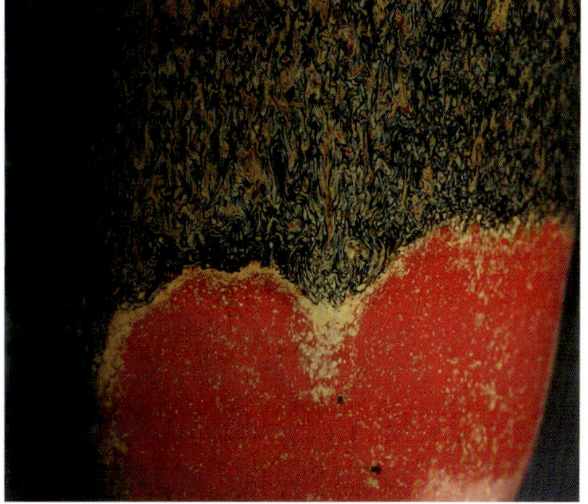
Stoneware with Ketchup Red under Glossy Black to create a hare's fur pattern.

COSTELLO CARBONATE

Cone 6

Barium Carbonate	6.0 %
Gerstley Borate	20.0
Whiting	2.0
Custer Feldspar	45.0
Tennessee Ball Clay	2.0
Silica	25.0
	100.0 %
Add: Copper Carbonate	6.0 %

This is beautiful when used with Rutile Matt as a decorative addition.

BLUE MATT

Cone 6

Dolomite	7.2 %
Gerstley Borate	11.3
Talc	13.9
Nepheline Syenite	39.1
EPK Kaolin	9.5
Silica	19.0
	100.0 %
Add: Cobalt Carbonate	1.0 %
Cobalt Oxide	1.0 %
Rutile	6.0 %

ALLIGATOR GREEN
Cone 6

Barium Carbonate	7.6 %
Gerstley Borate	18.5
Talc	6.5
Whiting	2.1
Custer Feldspar	41.3
Silica	24.0
	100.0 %
Add: Copper Carbonate	6.8 %
Zinc Oxide	8.7 %
Zircopax	86.9 %

RUTILE MATT
Cone 6

Whiting	20.0 %
Nepheline Syenite	56.0
EPK Kaolin	18.0
Silica	6.0
	100.0 %
Add: Rutile	7.0 %
Zinc Oxide	9.0 %

A beautiful, soft, tan matt, this glaze pools creamy white where thick.

MATT BLACK
Cone 6

Barium Carbonate	18.4 %
Gerstley Borate	8.0
Custer Feldspar	36.8
Barnard Clay	18.4
EPK Kaolin	9.2
Silica	9.2
	100.0 %
Add: Cobalt Oxide	2.3 %
Copper Oxide	3.4 %
Iron Oxide	2.3 %
Zinc Oxide	9.2 %

KETCHUP RED
Cone 6

Gerstley Borate	31.0 %
Talc	14.0
Custer Feldspar	20.0
EPK Kaolin	5.0
Silica	30.0
	100.0 %
Add: Spanish Red Iron Oxide	15.0 %

GLOSSY BLACK
Cone 6

Gerstley Borate	10.7 %
Whiting	5.5
Custer Feldspar	78.9
EPK Kaolin	4.9
	100.0 %
Add: Cobalt Oxide	2.1 %
Copper Carbonate	4.1 %
Manganese Dioxide	4.1 %

Rich black with silvery highlights where thick. For hare's fur pattern, layer over Ketchup Red.

CLEAR BASE GLAZE
Cone 6

Barium Carbonate	8.7 %
Gerstley Borate	25.0
Whiting	8.7
Custer Feldspar	38.0
Silica	19.6
	100.0 %
Add: Bentonite	8.7 %

Glossy White

Add: Zircopax	13.0 %

Apple Green Celadon

Add: Copper Carbonate	1.0 %

Jade Green

Add: Copper Carbonate	3.2 %

Recipes

ROLLIE YOUNGER'S INDUSTRIAL LOOK

by Lauren Zolot Younger

Rollie Younger creates his industrial teapots from wheel-thrown and extruded parts with added bridges. The bridges connect the spouts to the teapot body. Welding marks are made at each point of connection, and rivets are applied last. The dark-metal finish of each teapot body is a sprayed Bronze Glaze from Cuesta College, fired to cone 5 in oxidation. The rivets are either painted with bronze enamel or are bronze luster fired to cone 017. To further pique the interest of the viewer, Younger attaches pressure gauges and copper fittings to certain pieces. The gauges are fixed into the crowns with epoxy.

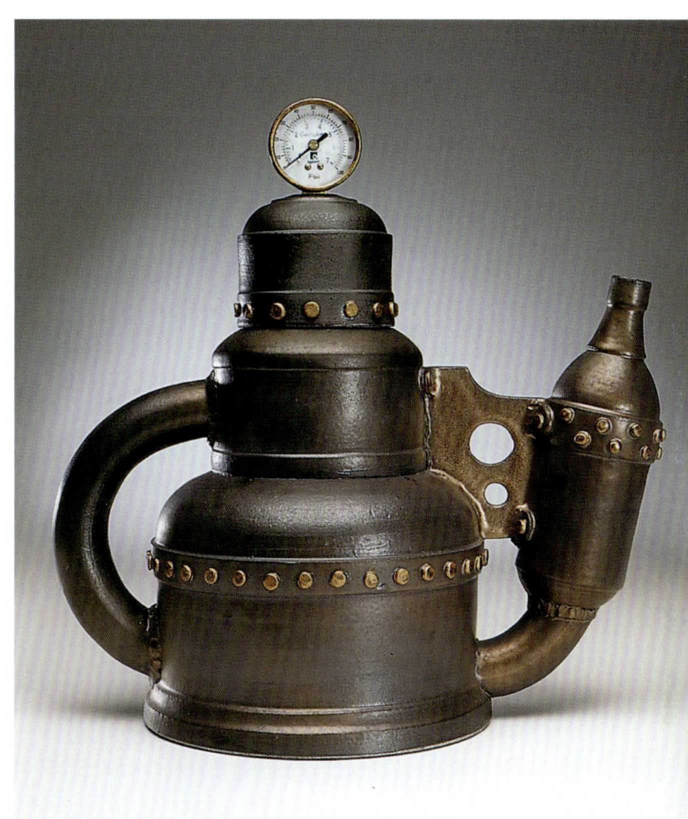

High (pressure) Tea, 14½ inches in height, thrown, extruded and assembled stoneware, with sprayed Bronze Glaze, fired to cone 5–6, with metal gauge.

RED GLAZE

Cone 6

Gerstley Borate	21.0 %
Whiting	20.0
Nepheline Syenite	16.0
EPK Kaolin	11.0
Silica	32.0
	100.0 %
Add: Tin Oxide	5.0 %
Chrome Oxide	0.2 %

A thick application turns this glaze mauve or purple. Best when fired in an electric kiln. Any reduction in the atmosphere turns this glaze pink.

BRONZE GLAZE

Cone 5–6

Manganese Dioxide	39.0 %
Cedar Heights Redart	52.4
Kentucky OM 4 Ball Clay	4.3
Silica	4.3
	100.0 %
Add: Cobalt Carbonate	2.7 %
Copper Oxide	4.3 %

A medium/thin application yields a matt gold. Extreme care should be taken while working with manganese dioxide. A NIOSH-approved respirator with a HEPA (high-efficiency particulate air) filter should be worn, and kilns should be vented to remove all fumes during firing.

Recipes

BLACK GLAZE DECORATION

by Frank Fisher

Nearly every item around my studio or house has the potential to be a glaze applicator. It just takes a little imagination to see the potential, and experimenting is key to discovering new ideas. Here are three glaze application ideas you can try out.

- 1. The direct approach involves dipping an object into glaze (e.g., a sponge roller) and pressing the object against the surface. The shape of the object and the action used to apply the glaze determines the type of mark it leaves. The object can be soft and absorbent like a sponge roller or it can be rigid like a kitchen spatula—any object can leave a unique mark.
- 2. The stencil approach involves applying glaze through or around another object. This mark is based on a positive versus negative image. The cheese cloth acts as a stencil and the roller is the applicator. After applying the glaze through the cloth, a unique grid of squares is created. Other materials with an open weave, for example, lace curtains, can also be used.
- 3. The transfer approach involves selecting a textured object, applying glaze to its raised surface and printing the texture onto the ceramic surface. Any object that has a distinct texture can be used. The glaze is rolled onto the object. The image is transferred by pressing the glazed object against the pot's surface.

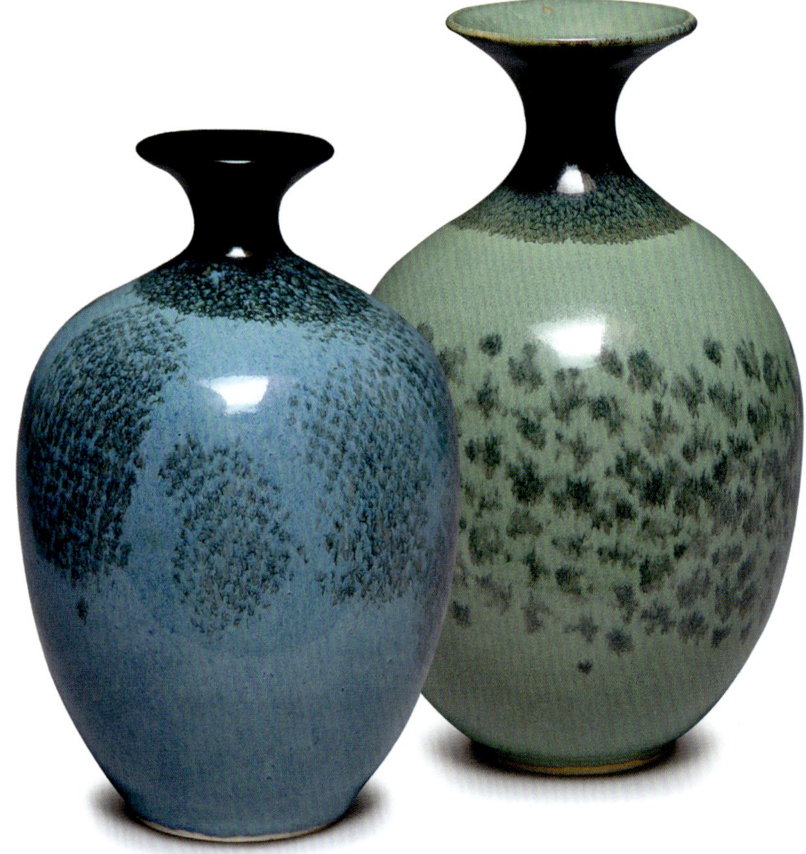

Bottles glazed with Shelly's Blue and Warm Jade Green with Licorice Black decoration.

WARM JADE GREEN
Cone 6

Whiting	16 %
Ferro Frit 3124	9
Talc	9
Custer Feldspar	40
EPK Kaolin	10
Silica	16
	100 %
Add: Copper Carbonate	4 %
Rutile	6 %

LICORICE BLACK
Cone 6

Whiting	4 %
Ferro Frit 3134	26
Custer Feldspar	22
Talc	5
EPK Kaolin	17
Silica	26
	100 %
Add: Cobalt Carbonate	2 %
Red Iron Oxide	9 %

SHELLY'S BLUE
Cone 6

Dolomite	4 %
Whiting	6
Zinc Oxide	4
Custer Feldspar	47
Gillespie Borate	13
EPK Kaolin	3
Silica	23
	100 %
Add: Rutile	2.0 %
Copper Carbonate	1.5 %
Cobalt Carbonate	0.5 %
Bentonite	2.0 %

From Michelle Bonior

Recipes

GLAZES FOR MULTI-FIRED SURFACES

by Geoffrey Wheeler

I reformulated my cone 10 base glazes to mature at cone 6, and got good results. I leave some exterior areas of the pots unglazed during the initial cone 6 firing and apply cone 04 glazes that differ in surface quality and color intensity for the second firing. Multiple firings, using a variety of types of glazes, can come together to build a palette of extraordinary richness and depth. Glazes with chrome sometimes flash onto other surfaces, giving a taste of serendipity in an otherwise controlled atmosphere.

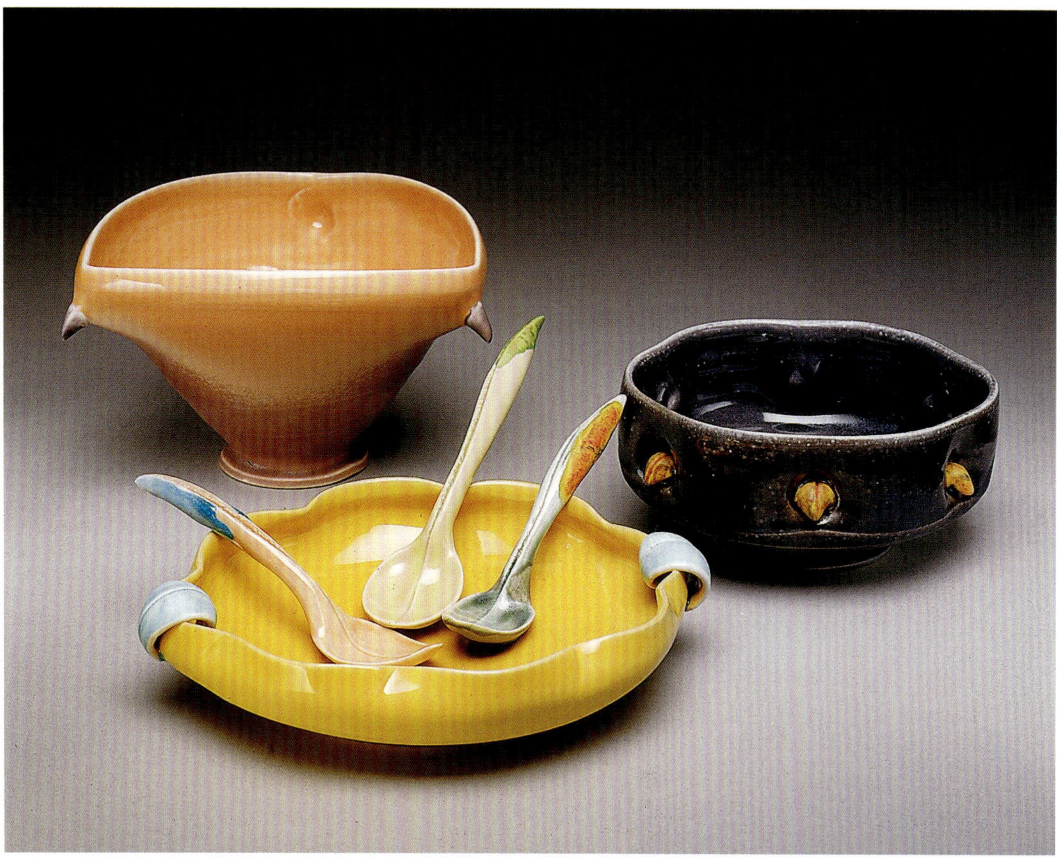

Bowl, 15 inches in diameter, porcelain, with encapsulated-stain glaze, fired to cone 6, then refired to cone 04 electric.

The following glazes are used on pots made from a Grolleg porcelain produced by Standard Ceramics of Pittsburgh.

GLASSY ALKALINE GLAZE

Cone 6

Ingredient	%
Gerstley Borate	1.2 %
Lithium Carbonate	3.4
Strontium Carbonate	9.3
Ferro Frit 3110	21.1
Kona F-4 Feldspar	46.3
Silica	18.7
	100.0 %
Add: Bentonite	3.0 %

This glaze begins to flux at cone 04, but I have used it as high as cone 10. It runs easily at the higher temperatures and tends to craze badly when thick.

Water-Blue

Add: Copper Carbonate	1.0 %

Yellow (A)

Add: Zirconium Yellow Stain	5.0 %

Yellow (B)

Add: Vanadium Yellow Stain	5.0 %

ROB'S/G.A. BLEND GLAZE

Cone 6

Ingredient	%
Gerstley Borate	2.9 %
Lithium Carbonate	1.7
Strontium Carbonate	9.3
Whiting	8.4
Cornwall Stone	34.6
Ferro Frit 3110	10.6
Kona F-4 Feldspar	23.2
Silica	9.3
	100.0 %
Add: Bentonite	3.0 %

A waxy, semitransparent glaze.

Deep blue

Add: Cobalt Carbonate	2.0 %
Manganese Carbonate	4.0 %

Warm pink

Add: Coral Stain	5.0 %
Rutile	3.0 %

Apple Green

Add: Green Stain	5.0 %

MATT "B" GLAZE

Cone 6

Ingredient	%
Lithium Carbonate	2.7 %
Strontium Carbonate	26.5
Nepheline Syenite	57.5
Kentucky OM 4 Ball Clay	6.2
Silica	7.1
	100.0 %
Add: Bentonite	3.0 %

The matt quality of this glaze is easily affected by colorants, so variations have different surface qualities as well as colors.

Dark Green

Add: Copper Carbonate	3.0 %
Nickel Oxide	2.0 %

Orange

Add: Encapsulated Orange Stain	5.0 %
Zirconium Yellow Stain	5.0 %

Maroon

Add: Coral Stain	5.0 %
Manganese Carbonate	3.0 %

I use Degussa encapsulated stains; to be considered food safe, these must be prepared/used in accordance with the manufacturer's instructions.

Recipes

SHUJI IKEDA

by James Irwin

Shuji Ikeda's favorite form is the handbuilt basket. These forms blend a solid architectural stateliness with an intricate texture of coils and strips of clay that have been wrapped, braided and woven, or fashioned into delicate twigs and leaves.

Some of the baskets are glazed with a blue-green matt glaze, which Shuji calls Sei Shya (Blue Rust). Others are sprayed with iron or manganese oxides. Many have no surface treatment, but instead show off the dark, smoke-colored clay body from which they are constructed. In some, the dark body has been combined with a red clay by partial wedging, a traditional Japanese technique known as nerikomi. The degree to which the clays are wedged together results in varying effects when the clay is cut into strips or rolled into coils, then braided or wrapped.

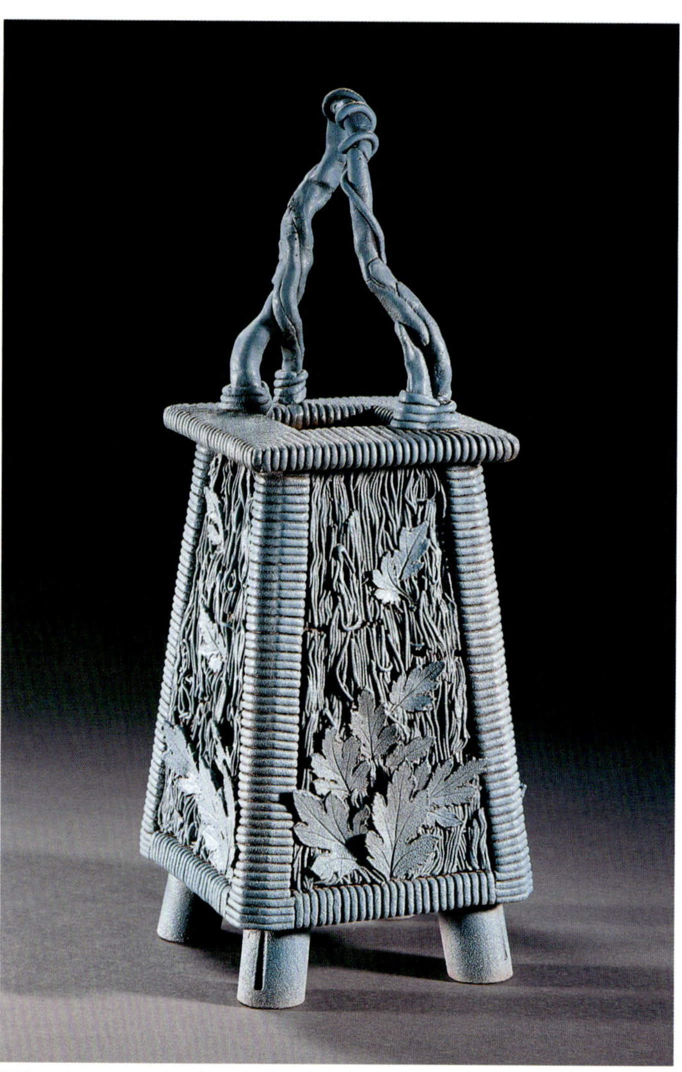

"Mum Leaves Basket," 17 inches in height, slab and coil built, with Blue Rust Glaze, fired to cone 5.

BLUE RUST GLAZE

Cone 4–5

Barium Carbonate	32.5 %
Dolomite	23.3
Custer Feldspar	37.2
EPK Kaolin	7.0
	100.0 %
Add: Copper Carbonate	2.3 %

CLEAR 3B GLAZE

Cone 5

Gerstley Borate	47.5 %
EPK Kaolin	24.2
Silica	28.3
	100.0 %

Recipes

A WHITE BASE FOR DECORATION

by Kelly King

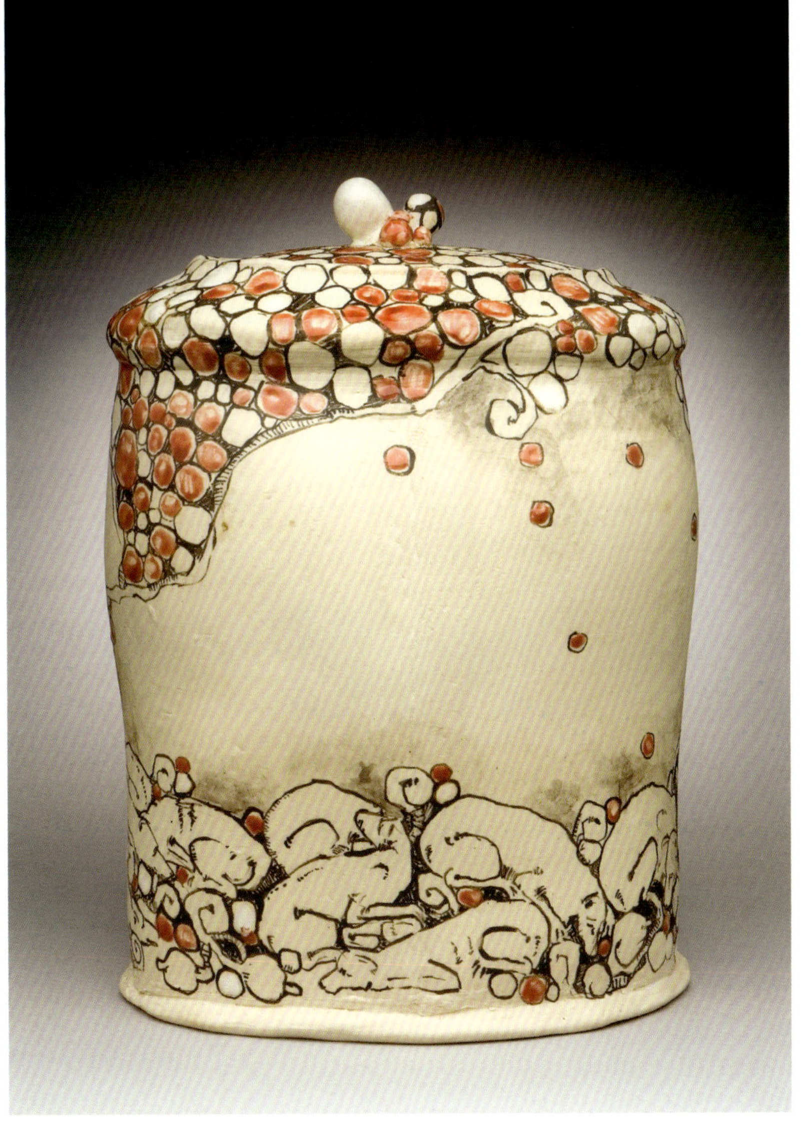

VAL CUSHING SATIN WHITE
Cone 6

Talc	9%
Whiting	16
Ferro Frit 3124	9
Custer Feldspar	40
EPK Kaolin	10
Silica	16
	100%
Add: Bentonite	1%

Nestle, Nuzzle, Run for Cover, 9 inches in height, slab-built cone 10 porcelain, fired to cone 6, Val Cushing Satin White with china paints, by Kelly King.

Recipes

SLIP AND GLAZE COMBO

by Birdie Boone

CRACKLE SLIP FOR BISQUE
Cone 6

Borax	4 %
Custer Feldspar	19
Calcined Kaolin (Glomax)	19
Grolleg Kaolin	17
OM 4 Ball Clay	17
Silica	19
Zircopax	5
	100 %

To avoid lumps, dissolve the borax in boiling water before adding to the batch. Recipe derived from the Penland School of Craft.

20 × 5
Cone 6

Dolomite	20 %
Spodumene (Australian)	20
Ferro Frit 3134	20
OM 4 Ball Clay	20
Silica	20
	100 %

Glossy with great color response. Use very small amounts of oxides, including rare earth oxides (neodymium, erbium, and praesodymium which are now, unfortunately, quite expensive if they are even available), and the occasional Mason stain. I don't use more than 6% of anything in a line blend, which means that there's never more than 3% of any oxide or stain in a given glaze. I use very small amounts of copper (0.3% or less) and micro amounts of cobalt (0.05% or less).

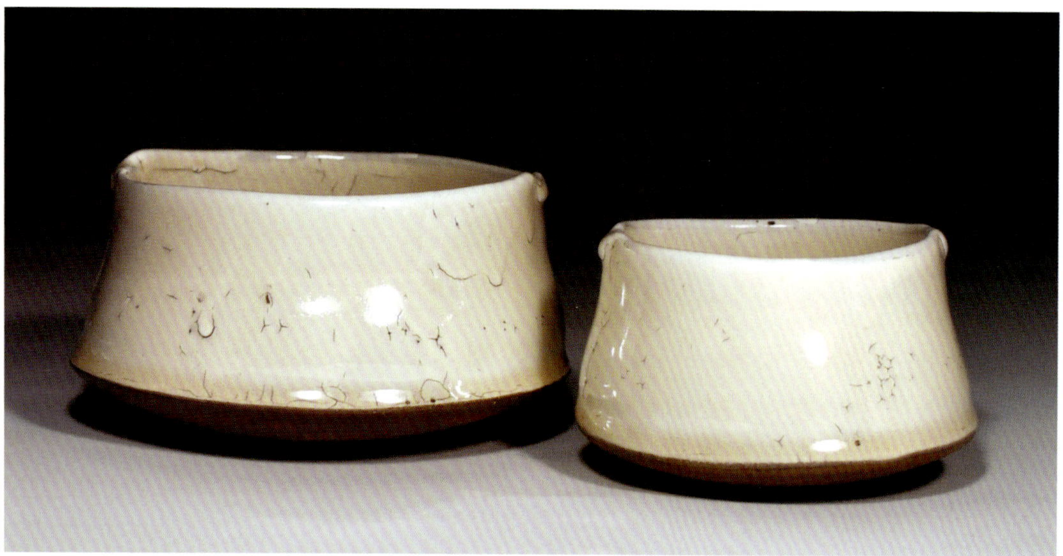

Belly bottomed bowls, up to 4½ in. (12 cm) in diameter, mid-range red clay, bisque slip, 20 x 5 glaze with 2% erbium oxide and 1% manganese carbonate (not dioxide), fired to cone 6.

CONE 6 BRONZE

by A. Blair Clemo

This tarnished-looking metallic glaze works well with deep patterns and texture built into the surface of a pot. It breaks over edges and pools in low spots to enhance the sense of wear and use.

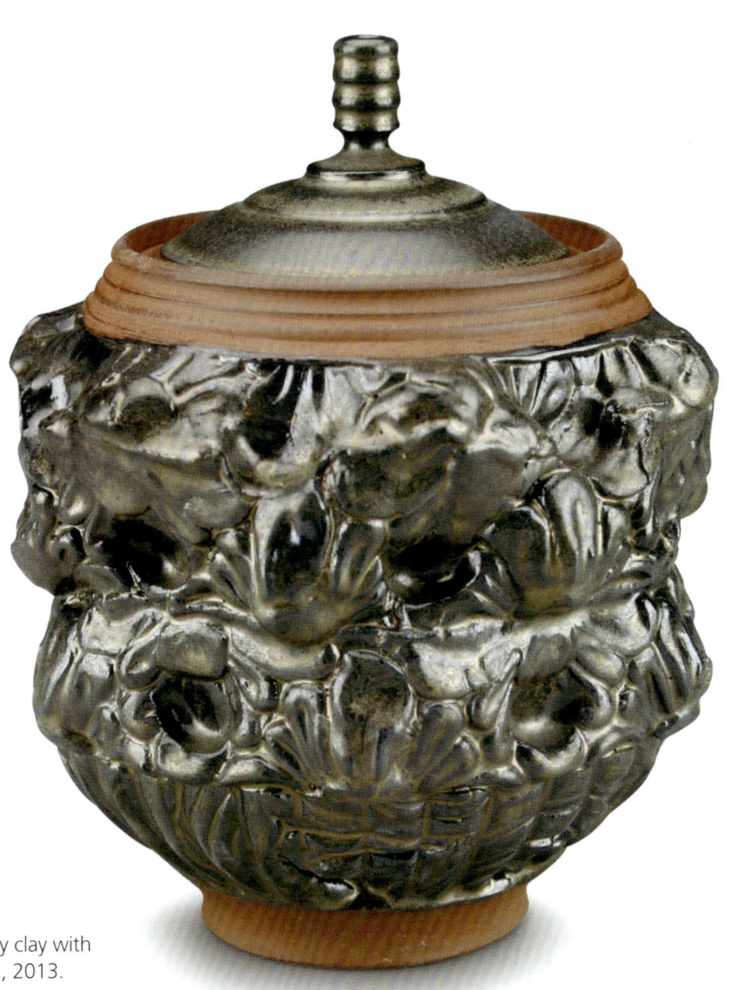

Jar, 8½ in. (22 cm) in height, Blair's Brown Body clay with Basic Bronze glaze, fired to cone 6 in oxidation, 2013.

BLAIR'S BROWN BODY
Cone 6 Oxidation

Ingredient	%
Red Art	60 %
Gold Art	15
OM4 Ball Clay	15
Silica	10
	100 %

This clay body is made without sand or grog, allowing it to be worked in the same way as a smooth porcelain body.

BASIC BRONZE
Cone 6 Oxidation

Ingredient	%
Red Art	60 %
Gerstley Borate	30
OM4 Ball Clay	5
Silica	5
	100 %
Add: Manganese Dioxide	45 %
Copper Carbonate	5 %

Note: This glaze is not food safe. When firing manganese dioxide, take extra precaution to avoid breathing kiln fumes, as they will be toxic.

Resources

Suppliers

A.R.T. Studio Clay Co. Inc.
9320 Michigan Ave.
Sturtevant, WI 53177-2425
www.artclay.com

Aardvark Clay & Supplies
1400 E. Pomona St.
Santa Ana, CA 92705-4812
www.aardvarkclay.com

Aardvark Clay & Supplies
6230 Kimberly, Ste. A
Las Vegas, NV 89122
www.aardvarkclay.com

Aftosa
1776 Wright Ave.
Richmond, CA 94804
www.aftosa.com

Alligator Clay Company
2721 W. Perdue
Baton Rouge, LA 70814
www.alligatorclay.com

Alpha Fired Arts
4675 Aldona Ln.
Sacramento, CA 95841
www.alphaceramics.com

American Ceramic Supply Co.
2442 Ludelle St.
Ft. Worth, TX 76105-1060
www.AmericanCeramics.com

Amherst Potters Supply
47 East St.
Hadley, MA 01035
www.amherstpotters.com

Archie Bray Foundation
2915 Country Club Ave.
Helena, MT 59602-9240
www.archiebray.org

Armadillo Clay & Supplies
3307 E. Fourth St.
Austin, TX 78702
www.armadilloclay.com

Atlanta Clay
3131 Presidential Dr.
Atlanta, GA 30340
www.atlantaclay.com

Atlantic Pottery Supply Inc.
725-21 Atlantic Blvd.
Atlantic Beach, FL 32233
www.atlanticpotterysupply.com

Axner Pottery Supply
490 Kane Ct.
Oviedo, FL 32765
www.axner.com

Bailey Pottery Equipment
PO Box 1577
Kingston, NY 12402
www.baileypottery.com

Bennett Pottery Supply
431 Enterprise St.
Ocoee, FL 34761
www.bennettpottery.com

BigCeramicStore.com
543 Vista Blvd.
Sparks, NV 89434
www.bigceramicstore.com

Brickyard Ceramics & Crafts
6060 Guion Rd.
Indianapolis, IN 46254
www.brickyardceramics.com

Buckeye Ceramic Supply
4077 Weaver Ct. S.
Hilliard, OH 43026
www.buckeyeceramicsupply.com

Campbell's Ceramic Supply Inc.
4231 C,arolina Ave.
Richmond, VA 23222
www.claysupply.com

Capital Ceramics, Inc.
2174 S. Main St.
Salt Lake City, UT 84115
www.capitalceramics.com

Carolina Clay Connection
2132 Hawkins St.
Charlotte, NC 28203
www.carolinaclay.com

Cattle Barn Clay Co.
4786 W. County Rd. 900 N.
Royal Center, IN 46978
www.cattlebarnclay.com

Ceramic Arts & Crafts Supply
3103 Mainway Dr.
Burlington, ON L7M 1A1 Canada
www.ceramicarts.com

The Ceramic Shop
3245 Amber St.
Philadelphia, PA 19134
www.theceramicshop.com

Ceramic Store of Houston, LLC
1002 W. 11 St.
Houston, TX 77008
www.ceramicstoreinc.com

Ceramic Supply Chicago
942 Pitner Ave.
Evanston, IL 60202
www.ceramicsupplychicago.com

Ceramic Supply, Inc.
7 Rt. 46 W.
Lodi, NJ 07644
www.eceramicsupply.com

Clay Art Center
2636 Pioneer Way E.
Tacoma, WA 98404
www.clayartcenter.net

Clay Planet
1775 Russell Ave.
Santa Clara, CA 95054
www.clay-planet.com

Clayscapes Pottery, Inc.
1003 W. Fayette St.
Syracuse, NY 13204
www.clayscapespottery.com

Clayworks Supplies, Inc.
4625 Falls Rd.
Baltimore, MD 21209
www.clayworkssupplies.com

Clayworld, Inc.
1200 E. Houston St.
San Antonio, TX 78205
www.clayworld.com

Columbus Clay
1080 Chambers Rd.
Columbus, OH 43212
www.columbusclay.com

Continental Clay Co.
1101 Stinson Blvd. NE
Minneapolis, MN 55413
5303 E. 47th Ave.
Denver, CO 80216
www.continentalclay.com

Cornell Studio Supply
8290 N. Dixie Dr.
Dayton, OH 45414
www.cornellstudiosupply.com

Davens Ceramic Center
5076 Peachtree Rd.
Atlanta, GA 30341
www.davensceramiccenter.com

Evans Ceramic Supply
1518 S. Washington
Wichita, KS 67211-0654
www.evansceramics.com

Florida Clay Art Co.
1645 Hangar Rd.
Sanford, FL 32773
www.flclay.com

Free Freight Pottery Supply LLC
5107 Edith Blvd. NE
Albuquerque, NM 87107
www.freefreightclay.com

Freeform Clay & Supply
1912 Cleveland Ave
National City, CA 91950
www.freeformclay.com

Funke Fired Arts
3130 Wasson Rd.
Cincinnati, OH 45209
www.funkefiredarts.com

Georgies Ceramic & Clay Co. Inc.
1471 Railroad Blvd. #9
Eugene, OR 97402
756 N.E. Lombard
Portland, OR 97211
www.georgies.com

Glaze Mixer
2156 Cambridge Ave.
Cardiff, CA 92007
www.glazemixer.com

Great Lakes Clay & Supply
927 N. State St.
Elgin, IL 60123
www.greatclay.com

Greenbarn Potters Supply, Ltd.
9548 192nd St.
Surrey, BC V4N 3R9 Canada
www.greenbarn.com

Highwater Clays of Florida
420 22nd St. S.
St. Petersburg, FL 33712
www.highwaterclays.com

Highwater Clays, Inc.
600 Riverside Dr.
Asheville, NC 28801-2140
www.highwaterclays.com

Kentucky Mudworks, LLC
825 National Ave.
Lexington, KY 40502
www.kentuckymudworks.com

Krueger Pottery Supply
8153 Big Bend Blvd.
St. Louis, MO 63119
www.kruegerpottery.com

Laguna Clay Co.
14400 Lomitas Ave.
City of Industry, CA 91746
www.lagunaclay.com

Laguna Clay Co.
61020 Leyshon Dr.
Byesville, OH 43723
www.lagunaclay.com

Leslie Ceramic Supply Co.
1212 San Pablo Ave.
Berkeley, CA 94706
www.leslieceramics.com

Marjon Ceramics, Inc.
3434 W. Earll Dr.
Phoenix, AZ 85017-5284
426 W. Alturas
Tucson, AZ 85705
www.marjonceramics.com

Mid-South Ceramic Supply Co.
1416 Lebanon Pike, Ste. C
Nashville, TN 37210
www.midsouthceramics.com

Midlantic Clay
900A Creek Rd.
Bellmawr, NJ 08031
www.midlanticclay.com

Minnesota Clay Co. USA
2960 Niagara Ln.
Plymouth, MN 55447
www.mnclay.com

New Mexico Clay, Inc.
3300 Girard N.E.
Albuquerque, NM 87107
www.nmclay.com

Northeast Ceramic Supply
621 River St.
Troy, NY 12180
www.northeastceramicsupply.com

Plainsman Clay, Ltd.
702 Wood St. S.E.
Medicine Hat, AB T1A 1E9 Canada
www.plainsmanclays.com

Portland Pottery Supply
118 Washington Ave.
Portland, ME 04101
www.portlandpottery.com

Portland Pottery Supply South
87 Messina Dr.
Braintree, MA 02184
www.portlandpottery.com

Rochester Ceramics, Inc.
102 Commercial St.
Webster, NY 14580
www.rochesterceramics.com

Rovin Ceramics
253 Dino Dr., Ste. A
Ann Arbor, MI 48103
www.rovinceramics.com

Runyan Pottery Supply, Inc.
Clio Industrial Park
820 Tacoma Ct.
Clio, MI 48420
www.runyanpotterysupply.com

Santa Fe Clay
545 Camino de la Familia
Santa Fe, NM 87501
www.santafeclay.com

Seattle Pottery Supply
35 S. Hanford St.
Seattle, WA 98134-1807
www.seattlepotterysupply.com

Sheffield Pottery, Inc.
U.S. Rt. 7
Sheffield, MA 01257-0399
www.sheffield-pottery.com

Standard Ceramic Supply Co.
PO Box 16240
Pittsburgh, PA 15242-0240
www.standardceramic.com

Trinity Ceramic Supply, Inc.
9016 Diplomacy Row
Dallas, TX 75247-5304
www.trinityceramic.com

Tucker's Pottery Supplies, Inc.
15 W. Pearce St.
Richmond Hill, ON L4B 1H6
Canada
www.tuckerspottery.com

U.S. Pigment Corp.
815 Schneider Dr.
S. Elgin, IL 60177
www.uspigment.com

Material Mfg.

Ferro Corporation
www.ferro.com

Hammill & Gillespie, Inc.
www.hamgil.com

Industrial Minerals Co.
www.clayimco.com

Mason Color Works, Inc.
www.masoncolor.com

Old Hickory Clay Co.
www.oldhickoryclay.com

R.T. Vanderbilt Co., Inc.
www.rtvanderbilt.com

Resco Products, Inc.
www.rescoproducts.com

Glaze Software

Glazemaster
PO Box 88
Pocopson, PA 19366
www.masteringglazes.com

GlazeSimulator
www.GlazeSimulator.com

HyperGlaze
6354 Lorca Dr.
San Diego, CA 92115-5509
www.hyperglaze.com

INSIGHT
1595 Southview Dr. SE, Ste. 407
Medicine Hat, AB T1B 0A1 Canada
digitalfire.com/insight

Books

The Ceramic Spectrum
Robin Hopper
The American Ceramic Society
ceramicartsdaily.org/bookstore

Developing Glazes
Greg Daly
The American Ceramic Society
AC Black, London
ceramicartsdaily.org/bookstore

Colour in Glazes
Linda Bloomfield
The American Ceramic Society
AC Black, London
ceramicartsdaily.org/bookstore

Glazes Cone 6: 1240°C/2264°F
Michael Bailey
University of Pennsylvania Press
AC Black, London

Glaze Projects
Richard Behrens
The American Ceramic Society
ceramicartsdaily.org/bookstore

Glazes & Glazing: Finishing Techniques
Anderson Turner, Editor
The American Ceramic Society
ceramicartsdaily.org/bookstore

Glazes: Materials, Recipes and Techniques
Anderson Turner, Editor
The American Ceramic Society
ceramicartsdaily.org/bookstore

Mastering Cone 6 Glazes
John Hesselberth and Ron Roy
www.masteringglazes.com

Videos

Understanding Glazes: How to Test, Tweak, & Perfect Your Glazes
with John Britt
The American Ceramic Society
ceramicartsdaily.org/bookstore

Glossary

Alberta Slip
Slip clay highly fluxed with iron. Substitute for Albany Slip

Albite
Pure sodium feldspar with the chemical formula $Na_2O{\cdot}Al_2O_3{\cdot}6SiO_2$. Very rare in nature.

Alkalis
The group of chemical elements that includes lithium, sodium, and potassium. These are the most powerful ceramic fluxes and work at the lowest temperatures. They also tend to lend brighter colors to glazes.

Alkaline Earths
The group of flux elements that includes magnesium, calcium, strontium, and barium. While suitable for all temperatures, these fluxes are used in larger amounts at higher temperatures. They also tend to produce more muted glaze colors.

Aluminum Oxide (Al_2O_3)
Also referred to as Alumina. Not a typical glaze material by itself, but is a refractory component in clays. Adds stiffness to glazes.

Amphoteric
A material capable of acting as an acid (glass-former) or a base (alkaline flux) in a glaze. Acts as a bridge between the two depending on the situation (see Aluminum Oxide and Boron).

Ball Clay
Ball clays are pretty much interchangeable in a glaze recipe. If using 15–20%, no other suspension agents needed. Common types: C&C Ball Clay, Kentucky OM 4 Ball Clay, Tennessee Ball Clay.

Barium Carbonate ($BaCO_3$)
Used to develop crystalline matte glazes. Toxic. Substitute Strontium Carbonate at 75% and test for color development.

Barnard Clay
Used for iron slip glazes. Substitute SG758 from Laguna. Also known as Blackbird Slip or Blackbird Clay.

Bentontite
A specific clay mineral which has high specific surface area (SSA), swells when wetted, and consequently has high drying shrinkage. Used to make wet clay bodies more plastic and to reduce settling of coarse ingredients in glazes. 1–2% added to glaze as suspension agent.

Bone Ash
Opacifier and used to promote opalesence.

Borax
Small amounts increase fluidity, large amounts lower firing temperature.

Boron (B_2O_3)
A low-temperature glass former and flux (see Amphoteric).

Cedar Heights Redart
Iron bearing earthenware clay.

Chrome Oxide (Cr_20_3)
An amphoteric/refractory that melts at 4109°F, and volatilizes at 2192°F. It is a green powder used by potters that doesn't dissolve well in a glaze melt, resulting in opaque, mainly green colors. Red, pink, gray, brown, and orange colors are also possible.

Cobalt (Co)
An extremely powerful colorant that almost always produces an intense blue, but it doesn't have to be that way all the time. This oxide is actually quite versatile and can make glazes that run the gamut from green to purple, pink to blue violet, blues mottled with red, pink, and even an intense black. There are four major factors that can affect a glaze's color: the clay and slip beneath it, kiln atmosphere,

fired temperature, and the glaze composition, including the colorants.

Colemanite
Source of boron. Substitute Gerstley Borate or Gillespie Borate.

Coloring oxides
Black Copper Oxide: greens to black
Black Iron Oxide: see Red Iron Oxide
Chrome Oxide: green
Cobalt Carbonate: blues and purples
Cobalt Oxide: blues
Copper Carbonate: greens
Copper Oxide: see Black Copper Oxide
Iron Oxide: see Red Iron Oxide
Light Rutile: Calcined Rutile
Manganese Carbonate: purples
Manganese Dioxide: Browns and purples (in combination with cobalt).
Nickel Oxide: Grey or brown
Red Iron Oxide: Tan to dark brown
Rutile: Creams, tans, and browns in oxidation, oranges and blues in reduction.
Spanish Red Iron Oxide: Fine grained Red Iron Oxide, acts as flux.

Devitrification
The crystallization of a glaze as it cools.

Dolomite
Flux containing Calcium Carbonate and Magnesium Carbonate.

Feldspar
Any of a group of natural crystalline aluminum silicate minerals containing sodium, potassium, calcium or barium. Alkali feldspars (those containing sodium and potassium) are used most in ceramics.

Feldspar (Potash)
Cornwall Stone (also called Cornish Stone), Custer Feldspar

Feldspar (Soda)
Kona F-4 Feldspar: Use Minspar 200
F-4 Feldspar: Use Minspar 200

Flux
The material in a glaze that lowers the melting temperature of the glass formers. Also called a modifier as it modifies the melting temperature of a glaze. Fluxes come in two forms: the alkalis (lithium, sodium, and potassium) and the alkaline earths (magnesium, calcium, strontium, barium, and zinc). Atoms of a powerful flux, say sodium, flow into a particle of silica to dissolve it. Heat provides the energy for this flow to occur. The extent of silica dissolution by fluxes is a function of peak firing temperature.

Frit
A synthetic source of glaze flux and frequently of alumina and silica, manufactured by melting the ingredients together, cooling the resulting glass, and grinding it to a fine powder. Used as a major ingredient in glazes, a frit encapsulates otherwise water-soluble flux elements and in some cases, also boron.

Frit Substitutes
Ferro 3110: Fusion F-75
Ferro 3124: Pemco P-311
Ferro 3134: Pemco P-54
Ferro 3269: Pemco P-25

Gerstley Borate
Source of boron, similiar to Gillspie Borate and Colemanite

Gillespie Borate
Source of boron, similiar to Gerstley Borate

Glass Former
Material in a glaze that makes up the physical body, the glass network, of the glaze. This is predominately silica, but usually also includes alumina and may include boron in increasing amounts as firing temperature is lowered.

Intermediate
Materials that perform similarly to the major group of glass formers and modifiers but also contain properties of other groups. For example, iron functions predominately as a colorant, but in heavy concentrations can play the role of a flux.

Kaolins
EPK Kaolin
Grolleg Kaolin
Calcined Kaolin (Glomax): Used to control raw glaze shrinkage and cracking.

Iron Chromate (Fe_20_3 Cr_20_3 or $FeCr0_3$)
An iron–chromium ore commonly used to produce grays. It gives opacity and can be used with cobalt, iron, and manganese oxides to produce blacks. With tin in oxidation, it can develop a pinkish gray.

Lithium Carbonate
Glaze flux that extends firing range and promotes brilliant colors.

Magnesium Carbonate
Produces matt surfaces, increases glaze viscosity.

Nepheline Syenite
Feldspar substitute.

Potassium Dichromate ($K_2Cr_2O_7$)
A bright orange crystalline material that is generally used at low-temperatures to create bright reds with lead frits in oxidation. It is toxic and soluble.

PV Clay
High potassium feldspathic clay similar to Cornwall Stone.

Silica (SiO_2)
Available in 200, 325 and 400 meshes. Use 325 mesh for glazes.

Silicon Carbide (SiC)
Used for special effects and local reduction in an oxidizing atmosphere.

Specific Surface Area (SSA)
The amount of surface area of a material per unit weight of the material.

Spinel
Mineral with alkaline oxide and amphoteric oxide. RO/R_2O_3. Gemstones are an example of natural spinels while in ceramics, these spinels are used to produce commercial colorants because they are chemically stable in molten glass. A purple can be created by combining cobalt and alumina oxide, $CoAl_2O_3$, into a cobalt aluminate stain.

Spodumene (Australian)
Lithium feldspar. Australian Spodumene is whitest available. Test other Spodumenes as substitutes.

Stains
1. Coloring oxides suspended in water (a.k.a. an oxide wash). May also contain frit and/or kaolin (usually EPK). *2.* Commercial ceramic colored powders that are used in glazes, clay bodies, and slips/engobes. Prepared coloring oxides that are fritted, reground, and colored with organic dyes to simulate fired color.

Strontium Carbonate
Popular substitute for Barium Carbonate. Use 75% when substituting.

Talc
Source of Magnesium and Silica that reduces thermal expansion in glazes and acts as an opacifier.

Tin Oxide (SnO_2)
Most powerful opacifier.

Titanium Dioxide (TiO_2)
Used as opacifier and promote matte surfaces.

Whiting
Calcium carbonate used as a flux.

Wollastonite
Source of calcium and silica, powerful flux.

Zinc Oxide (ZnO)
Lends opacity and encourages crystal growth when used in large amounts. A common constituent of matt glazes, affects colorants, promoting brilliance with copper and dulling iron and chrome.

Zircopax Plus
Zirconium silicate used as an opacifier in glazes.